IDENTITY POLITICS AND TRIBALISM

THE NEW CULTURE WARS

Nikos Sotirakopoulos

SOCIETAS
essays in political
& cultural criticism

imprint-academic.com

Published in the UK by
Imprint Academic Ltd., PO Box 200, Exeter EX5 5YX, UK

Distributed in the USA by
Ingram Book Company,
One Ingram Blvd., La Vergne, TN 37086, USA

ISBN 9781788360623 paperback

A CIP catalogue record for this book is available from the
British Library and US Library of Congress

Contents

Acknowledgements

I owe a huge 'thank you' to:

- The Prometheus Foundation: for its generous support, and for funding the production of this book.
- The publishing house, Imprint Academic: they gave the book a chance, despite its potentially controversial nature. This is not a given in today's intellectual climate, as I learned the hard way.
- Gregory Salmieri: this book would not have some of its best intellectual insights without our discussions and his mentorship. Obviously, we do not share the same view on many topics, so any issues with the book are on me.
- Joanna Williams: her support during the various adventures that this book has been through has been tremendous.
- Costas Spanos: besides being a great friend, he also proved to be a great proofreader.
- Tal Tsfany, the Ayn Rand Institute, and the Objectivist Academic Center: for all they have done for my intellectual and professional development.
- Claire Fox, Frank Furedi, and the team around the Battle of Ideas: for all the food for thought they have given me throughout all these years.
- My colleagues at York St John University: for providing a supportive professional environment, despite any philosophical disagreements.
- My family: besides everything else they have offered me, they inspired in me the passion for knowledge and ideas.
- You, the reader: for picking up this book. I hope you will get value out of it.

Introduction

People who know me consider it weird that I wrote this book. 'You're critiquing political passions getting out of hand, and people being overwhelmed by tribal emotions? You're guilty of both!' On one level, they are right.

Until around a decade ago, I was dreaming of barricades, general strikes, and a cataclysmic revolution that would overthrow capitalism. Actually, I was not only dreaming about it, but I tried to make it happen, which is why I joined the Youth of the Communist Party of Greece in my early adulthood. Fast-forward to the second decade of the 21st century, in my 30s I find myself at an opposite pole of the political spectrum: being an (at least in the eyes of colleagues and friends) 'extremist' for individual rights, freedom, and a *laissez-faire* economy, joining groups that support such causes, giving talks, arguing on Twitter, and writing articles and books.

Nor am I immune to the strong emotions of what someone might understand as tribalism. Quite the contrary; my other big passion in life besides politics has been sports, where I get quite 'tribal'. On paper, I have been critical of the phenomenon that Michael Billig (1995) has described as 'banal nationalism', with rituals around the flag, the parades, the national mythology, and all the folklores. Yet, I have caught myself getting goosebumps when our national team's players are lined up while the Greek anthem is playing before important games. I have felt a lump in my throat when Greek athletes win a gold medal at the Olympic Games and stand on the podium holding our blue-white flag. Watching these events away from home as a Greek ex-pat only adds to the emotion of the occasion. Thus, this book is not written from a detached standpoint of someone who cannot understand why people get passionately caught up in politics and why they are overwhelmed by strong feelings of belonging. I can get all that; yet, I see something uglier happening around me, in my social circles and generally in the public sphere.

Actually, a lot of people have sensed that something has changed in recent years. 2016 is seen as a turning point, with the Brexit vote in the UK and the victory of Donald Trump in the US election. The summer and autumn of 2020, with the pandemic, the lockdowns, the murder of George Floyd and the following weeks of protests and rioting, and the Presidential elections in the US have been the culmination (up to this point) of this process. 'What is happening to the world?', many are asking.

What is more, these political and cultural tensions more and more infiltrate our personal lives. 'Did you hear the news about Carla and Mike?', a friend messaged me one afternoon in late 2018. 'They're breaking up. It all started in a dinner conversation with some colleagues. They were bashing Jordan Peterson, but Mike defended him and revealed he actually liked some of his online lectures. Carla was shocked, they had a fight, and told him she doesn't even recognize him anymore. It all went downhill from there...' Names and minor details are altered, but the story is real. Also, it is not an isolated incident.

How we perceive and react to public figures, political events, and the latest news cycle is becoming more and more a defining characteristic of who we are. According to one piece of research, 16% of participants had stopped talking to a friend or a relative because of the 2016 US election (Whitesides, 2017). Divorce lawyers in the USA have reported couples wanting to end their decades-long marriage due to one of the spouses voting for Trump (Langmuir, 2018). Meanwhile, in the UK, the Brexit vote of 2016 on the EU-membership referendum exacted a heavy toll on many romantic couples and friendships (Mangan, 2016; Frostrup, 2016; Chakelian, 2018). Anyone who has spent even 5 minutes on any dating app will have come across statements such as 'If you are a Tory/Brexiteer, swipe left' (this means a rejection on Tinder). But it is not only central and polarizing political events, such as the US elections and Brexit, that are creating such divergences. At least three people I know have confided in me that they are struggling to find a new quality razor for their shaving, but they'd never go back to Gillette. The reason is the company's infamous advert portraying traditional masculinity in negative colours, as violent and passé (McCluskey, 2019). Apparently, some skin irritation from an inferior razor is a price worth paying for making a statement in today's culture wars.

Not unpredictably, political passions have often escalated to violence. From assaults in American universities against speakers and attendees in public lectures to the bloody events in Charlottesville in 2017, to terrorist attacks by white supremacists and religious fundamentalists, to the murder of Labour MP Jo Cox by a perpetrator of Nazi convictions in the UK in 2016, to the weeks of rioting, violence, intimidation, and vigilantism in the American streets in the summer of 2020, to the storming of the US Capitol in January 2021, we have more and more indications that the problem of an ever more toxic public sphere is real.

This book aims to examine where this toxicity is coming from, and what is its distinctive characteristic. Of course, there have been many good works in the last few years trying to navigate the topic of the recent social, cultural, and political tensions. Many of them had very interesting insights that have been an influence in my work. Yet, I think there are some important parameters missing from the debate, which is why this book is joining it.

There are many possible explanations as to the root of the problem of our current struggles. Lukianoff and Haidt (2018) did a thorough job portraying elements in the education system and the socialization process that have led young people today towards personality traits such as self-righteousness and intolerance that are related to many episodes in the culture wars, especially in universities. Campbell and Manning (2018) elaborated on how elevating victimhood as a sought-after status contributes to such self-righteousness and adds fuel to group conflicts about who oppresses whom. Other writers have focused on specific battlefields of the culture wars, such as free speech (Fox, 2016; Hume, 2015) and gender (Williams, 2017). There have also been good works about the left and its role in today's culture wars (Cobley, 2018; Murray, 2019), but also about the contribution of the populist and far right (Nagle, 2017; Sedgwick, 2019). Others have highlighted the impact of what can be loosely referred to as postmodern ideology and critical theory in eroding society's grasp on the concepts of objectivity, individuality, and universalism (Pluckrose and Lindsay, 2019).

For Douglas Murray (2019), we find ourselves in a world where the grand narratives of the past, from religion to revolutionary political movements, have collapsed, and thus there is a void in existential meaning. He described a recent rise of 'liberal intolerance', which is part of the quest by some activists and institutions to impose on the public sphere progressive values such as 'social justice', diversity, and intersectionality (despite the fact that, in his view, we live in perhaps the most tolerant and protective of individual rights society in history). Yet, the objective conditions matter less, as for Murray this struggle is indicative of a desperate soul-searching. 'In an era without purpose, and in a universe without clear meaning, this call to politicize everything and then fight for it has an undoubted attraction. It fills life with meaning, of a kind' (Murray, 2019, p. 255). Such a framework is shared by other intellectuals, such as Jordan Peterson. For him, our current predicament is a continuation of the totalitarian mindset that created the horrors of the 20th century, such as Stalinism and fascism, which in their turn were also an attempt to fill in an existential void since we had, in Nietzschean terms, killed god (Peterson, 2018).

Influenced by the insightful points in these readings, I will attempt to go a step further, and also challenge some of their assumptions. To understand the situation, it is key not to isolate the problem solely on one side of the political spectrum. It is not fanatical postmodernist neomarxists and feminists, or some racist far-rightists, that merely need to be exposed and defeated for the problem to go away. Nor do I believe that in the absence of grand narratives or religion we are doomed to existential uncertainty that needs to find an avenue in nihilism and hatred. I am also challenging the view that we can get over today's bitter divisions in the public sphere by compromising 'somewhere in the middle'. It is ideas that move history, and thus testing them through a robust debate is a healthy process that can push a society forward. Some ideas are good, and we would be better off if they were to prevail; others are bad and they should be defeated. Thus, my aim in writing this book is a different one from merely claiming that we should not get too passionate with politics, or that we should point the finger to one side of the culture wars in the battle against the other.

The topic of the book is the social, political, and cultural conflicts of today, viewed not as separate incidents, but as being linked by a thread. This work is not an exhaustive account of the turbulent events of 2016 or of 2020. Its aim is to set the context and offer a historical perspective on where this turbulence has come from. I will explain today's toxic public sphere by providing a frame that explains the way many people experience the world, each other, ideas, and politics. A flawed worldview creates constant conflicts, bitterness, and often violence, without allowing a healthy confrontation of ideas. The flaw that can explain the nature and expression of these conflicts is a tribalist worldview that overwhelms people's thinking. It makes them see themselves and others not as individuals, but as primarily members of groups with opposing interests, often based on unchosen characteristics, such as gender and race. I will also try to show where this worldview comes from, and what kind of ideas and philosophical developments made its appeal possible. At the end, I will suggest what the alternative to the tribalist worldview is, and why we would be better off by adopting it.

Regarding the structure of the book, I will begin by examining what exactly tribalism is, and I will then define and explain the other key terms of the title, i.e. the culture wars and identity politics. This will be the necessary framework to understand the incidents and the events examined later in the book as phenomena having common roots and characteristics. Further on, to understand the intellectual atmosphere in which we find ourselves today, I will provide an overview of the strands of the left and the right that are most relevant to recent cultural and political conflicts. It is important to observe how similar ways of thinking and of viewing the world have a history that has led to bitter divisions and violence in the not-so-distant past. Mentioning some dark moments of the 20th century does not constitute a claim that tribalism will necessarily lead us to new bloodshed or civil wars. However, it is a reminder of how things can go terribly wrong, and how bad ideas, when followed to their logical conclusion, can have disastrous effects. Before dark periods, the signs were usually there, but people failed to read them or react to them in time. As the famous quote by historian F.W. Maitland goes, 'what now lies in the past once lay in the future'.

Then, I will proceed to examine three case studies: free speech, racial thinking, and the 'gender wars'. The main reason I am using these cases studies is that free speech, race, and gender are fields that nowadays generate high tensions in the culture wars. There are more areas that could have been analysed, such us immigration or religion, but in the three case studies I have chosen the lines of the battle are relatively easier to decipher, and offer an interesting insight: both sides make claims that in some ways mirror each other. Thus, the idea behind the structure of each chapter is to examine both sides of the argument, and to show how they are underpinned by a similar mindset and worldview.

Even the most well-intentioned reader might have two objections at this point:

(a) 'How can you put together, let alone analyse, in the same breath movements such as feminism and the manosphere, or anti-racists with the alt-right? You are giving moral sanction to some very bad people and you are putting them in the same category with those fighting a good fight for a more just society.'

(b) 'You are examining some movements that are quite fringe. Who cares what some intersectional feminists, or critical race theorists, or some obscure identitarian traditionalists are saying? Surely you cannot claim that they are setting the intellectual tempo of our society?'

Indeed, I realize it might sound strange and provocative to claim that there are some similarities between overt racists and people who view themselves as anti-racists, or between conservatives who passionately believe they fight for free speech and leftists who want to impose speech codes or deplatform speakers. But what needs to be remembered is that the premise of this book is that there is a common denominator in today's popular ideas *across* the political spectrum, which can shed light on worldviews and practices that are, on the surface, quite different. Pointing out this common denominator does not constitute an equal moral evaluation of the two sides. Similarly, examining some fringe movements is not a claim that they are representative of people who identify as being with the left or the right. Yet, it is a claim that quite often these radical movements are the logical conclusion and the materialization of some quite mainstream ideas. They are a glimpse from the future, if these ideas remain uncontested or taken uncritically at face value. In addition, in turbulent times fringe ideas can find themselves quickly in the mainstream. In the summer of 2020, for example, following the tensions in the aftermath of George Floyd's killing by a police officer, critical race theory was seen by one side as a long overdue insight into the institutional racism of American society. For the other side, this theory was seen as a Trojan horse aiming to undermine the cohesion of society, and even the then President of the USA Donald Trump took a position on the matter, characterizing critical race theory as 'divisive, anti-American propaganda' and ordering the removal of any material relating to its teachings form Federal agencies (Cineas, 2020). Thus, I am convinced that these movements need to be examined and comprehended, because they can be useful in understanding some of the ideas that shape our current world.

Before we start our journey with this book, one more thing: I invite you, dear reader, to bear with me when I say something that could be considered as alienating towards the side you politically affiliate with. I truly hope that you will not assume I have bad intentions when we disagree. In many ways, you and I are probably similar. We are passionate about ideas, we take them seriously, and we want to find the truth. We surely want to do good and make the world a better place. So let's embark on this pursuit of trying to understand what is happening out there; for unless we understand the world, any attempt to change it might result in actually making things worse.

The tribalist mind

In Rwanda, within 100 days during the spring and summer of 1994, approximately 500,000 to 800,000 Tutsis were massacred, usually with machetes, by the rival group of Hutus. The reasons for the massacre are related to political and class divisions that go back some time. Yet, the killing zeal that overtook the Hutus is difficult to understand or explain.

Many readers may regard the Rwandan tragedy as something that happened far away, to isolated people living under the premises of parochial traditions, but this is far from the truth. It only happened three decades ago, and in a society where English and French are among the official languages (Hetzfeld, 2008). The majority of Rwandans are Christian Catholics, and some of the most zealous organizers of the pogroms were middle-class teachers, small shop owners, and even clergymen. The Hutus and the Tutsis are people who used to work together, play together, and often get married to each other. As an imprisoned killer recalled, 'you kill the Tutsi woman you used to listen to the radio with, or the kind lady who put medical plants in your wounds, or your sister who was married to a Tutsi. Or even, for some unlucky devils, your own Tutsi wife and your children, by general demand' (idem, p. 103). An interesting element of the evil that took place in Rwanda is that there was no racial, religious, lingual, or any other obvious difference between the Hutus and the Tutsis. So how would the killing mobs know who to go after? 'The answer is simple. The killers did not have to pick out their victims: they knew them personally. Everyone knows everything in a village' (idem, p. 60).

The horror in Rwanda is the most obvious and naked exhibition of *tribalism*: of the worldview where people see and evaluate themselves and others not primarily as individuals, but as members of groups with antithetical interests. Often, these groups are unchosen. There was nothing a Tutsi could do to deny the 'membership' of that tribe. One can see this in how the Hutu killers viewed their victims: 'Our Tutsi neighbours, we knew they were guilty of no misdoing, but we thought all Tutsis at fault for our constant troubles. We no longer looked at them one by one; we no longer stopped to recognize them as they had been, not even as colleagues' (idem, p. 113).

Most people acknowledge the destructive nature of the tribalist worldview that divided the Tutsis and the Hutus. However, this book will show that various less visible or dramatic forms of tribal thinking exist in contemporary European and American societies. And these tribal mindsets are growing stronger: they have often become the predominant prism through which many people view the world and their fellow human beings. I will argue that this worldview needs to be recognized and opposed in all its expressions and on every occasion. But to recognize and fight tribalism, we first need to understand it as a phenomenon, and this is the subject of the present chapter.

Wired for tribalism?

In the last years, many interesting books have been written about tribalism, examining it mostly from the point of view of psychology. Although I do not agree with everything in these books, or with the approach some of them take on the issue, there is a lot of value in them for someone examining tribalism. Thus, I will begin by reviewing some of these authors' claims, and then I will elaborate on how my position is related to them.

Greene offered the widest possible definition of tribalism: 'the (often unapologetic) favouring of in-group members over out-group members' (2015, p. 69). The size of the group could change from kids in a school to a small village to a nation and to a whole race, but the feelings of belonging and bonding to 'our people' have similar characteristics. Lukianoff and Haidt saw tribalism as 'our evolutionary endowment for banding together to prepare for intergroup conflict' (2018, p. 58). This is related to a view seen time and again in the literature, according to which strong tribal bonds offered an advantage to small communities that faced constant threats, be it from nature, or from external intruders.

The fact that human beings are animals that can survive and flourish in social settings and, thus, tend to form groups is seen by many as the basis for tribalism. But I will claim that the leap from forming unions to tribalism is a large one, and one that can be avoided. So let me make this clear from an early point: forming groups, societies, and bonds of solidarity is perfectly fine, and is not necessarily synonymous to tribalism. We benefit from strong relationships with other good people, and under the proper conditions they can make our life immeasurably better. But forming groups is not necessarily tribalism. The way I will use the term 'tribalism' refers to something more than bonding in communities and having strong emotions towards our comrades. But more on that later.

For Chua (2018), tribalism is an instinct of belonging and identification; yet, this also makes it a strong instinct towards excluding and dehumanizing. Lukianoff and Haidt agreed with this last point: tribalism is a strong feeling that 'binds', but also 'blinds' (2018, p. 58; see also Haidt, 2013). There are even researchers who claimed that feelings of solidarity and belonging are impossible if some form of an external 'other' or threat is not present (Greene, 2015, p. 69). This identification, having as a point of reference an outsider or an 'other', makes sense. Explaining to children the concept of sweetness becomes easier when we provide them with a milk chocolate and then with a grapefruit juice in order to also present its opposite, which is bitterness. Yet, the fact that it makes sense does not mean that hetero-determination, i.e. constructing one's identity by contrasting it to something else, cannot lead to problems. When one sees oneself not only as different from someone else, but also one elevates this difference to an existential prism charged with an ethical meaning, then the other can become someone with opposite interests and, potentially, an enemy.

Many works introduce tribalism by presenting various kinds of psychological experiments that claim that there is something inherent in the way our brain works that favours in-group members to outsiders. An example could be the experiments by Polish psychologist Henri Tajifel, who would distribute strangers in two groups by flipping a coin or based on how accurately they estimated something as mundane as the number of dots on a piece of paper. Then, participants were asked to distribute money to others, and the best indicator of their preference was favouring people in their ad-hoc group and at the detriment of 'outsiders' (Lukianoff and Haidt, 2018). For Greene (2015), such tendencies for a preferential treatment to insiders are innate within us, and also universal. Tribalism is seen more as a biological reality, rather than a learned social construct. Chua (2018) put it in different words: tribalism is an instinct. She brought up the well-known phenomenon of 'schadenfreude', i.e. the guilty pleasure in the failure of people we categorize as 'the other'. An example of schadenfreude could be the satisfaction we experience when a rival football team loses a game, even if they did not play against our team, nor our team had anything to benefit from such a defeat. For Chua, schadenfreude has a neurological basis, thus adding up to the school of thought that sees tribalism as almost a biological reality (2018, p. 41).

Greene (2015, p. 99) provided some interesting psychological tendencies and features of tribalism, including:

– strong views about what are the most important values, and how they should shape not only our lives, but also the lives of others. Thus, tribalism is expected to also play an important role in politics and the way people negotiate their relationships in a society. Yet, not all ideological views emphasize as strongly the will to impose one's views on others, nor do they descend into tribalism. For example, researchers on the issue have claimed that classical liberals and libertarians are the least willing to impose their views on others, whereas some conservatives and parts of the left tend to be more 'imperialistic' in their view of the world (Greene, 2015).

– a commitment to a sense of justice and fairness, which is, however, biased in favour of those in the group and skewed towards outsiders. This in practice means that tribalism leads to double standards. When a member of our group is doing something objectionable, the default urge is to question whether things have actually happened this way, or to view the incident in a lenient way, acknowledge various excuses, etc. Yet, when a similar act is done by someone belonging to a hostile group, then the urge is to immediately rush to a harsh judgment, without giving much benefit of the doubt.

– an underestimation or an indifference towards the way tribal behaviour can harm others. Dehumanizing an individual as an 'other' can mean a lessening of our ability to empathize. To paraphrase a famous quote of the theoretical physicist Steven Weinberg about religion, normally good people do good things and bad people do bad things; but under the tribalist mindset, good people can do bad things. Quite often, I would add, without realizing how bad these things are.

Psychologist and linguist Steven Pinker (2012) claimed that political affiliations can be shaped by events and the struggles of smaller groups that had taken place centuries ago, and that factors such as geography can play a role on how one's values were originally formed. He gave the example of the Scots and Irish herders who settled in the American south and west. Their profession and the harshness of life at the frontier required them to develop a code of honour based on the knowledge that they would not be pushed over, that they would redress any animal theft, and that overall they were capable of defending themselves in a predominantly anarchic environment. On the other side, settlers on the east coast, due to the proximity of the majority of the population to city centres where the law was applied by the authorities, developed a 'softer' culture, where one's masculine reputation was less important as a survival trait. For Pinker (2012), these broad characteristics can, at least partially, explain why the American South still today predominantly votes for gun rights-advocating, morally strict, tradition-valuing Republicans, whereas the North and the coastal metropolitan centres vote more for Democrats who are happy to expand the role of the government.[1]

In this section, we saw how scholars approaching tribalism as an inherent psychological phenomenon claim that:

(a) human beings have a strong proclivity towards tribalism, which is a feeling of bonding towards members of their group, and of exclusion towards outsiders;

(b) tribalism can contribute towards forming values and ideas that are difficult to change, and can even pass from one generation to another.

Lukianoff and Haidt summed up their position, which Chua and others also share, as follows: our mind is 'prepared for tribalism' (2018, p. 58). Does this then mean that we are wired for tribalism? Is tribalism a fate we cannot escape?

Tribalism as an epistemological choice

One way I differ from the majority of the literature on the topic is that I refer to tribalism more as a particular way of viewing the world and as a specific mode of thinking, which is ultimately *chosen* and which is *not* universal, nor does it characterize all human beings at all times. If tribalism was a fate that we cannot escape, then its utility as a prism through which one could under-stand modern phenomena such as the culture wars would be

---

[1]   Though, as we will see later in this book, the idea that Republicans and more traditionalist conservatives want to limit the role of the state is open to many objections.

limited. It would be like trying to explain an airplane crash by blaming gravity. Gravity is always there; yet, a crash is a rare incident requiring further explanations. However, tribalism is not always there, and even when it dominates the thinking of people, there is always an alternative and a way out of it.

To illustrate the above points, let me return to the example of Rwanda. In the months and years leading to the 1994 massacre, a critical mass of the population operated under a very particular way of thinking and behaving, according to which their group allegiance and the hatred for the other group was dominating their life. Yet, less than three decades after the orgy of terror and anomie in 1994, Rwanda is above the regional and world average in the Freedom Index, measuring a country's record in rule of law, judicial efficiency, etc. (Heritage.org, 2019). Clearly something has changed in the way many of its people go through life.

One of the main premises of this book is that each one of us has control over how to operate his or her mind. If tribalism was indeed an inescapable instinct beyond our control, then it would not be subject to moral evaluation. Then, the Hutu murderer in Rwanda would be acting out *in extremis* an otherwise normal mental mode of operation. Taking all the above into consideration, among my aims in this book is to understand why people sometimes act under such a 'tribal mode', to show the negative results of it, and to see how we can avoid enacting the same mistakes in the future.

Crucial in understanding the optional and non-deterministic character of the tribalist worldview is appreciating the operation of *free will*. Every day, we face myriad decisions where, in order to address them, we have to switch our mind on. As philosopher Ayn Rand posited, human consciousness is *volitional*, i.e. to put our mind into operation is an act of choice (Rand, 1964). Free will is not so much about the processes of the brain when it comes to taking a mundane decision such as to press a red or a green button, or to order a steak or chicken, as experiments in psychology often focus on (Binswanger, 2014). For Rand, free will is actually operating on a more fundamental level, and it is the choice to switch on our mind, take the effort to make sense of the world, and come into contact with reality. Thus, free will gives us a choice about the mode through which our mental processes operate (idem, p. 322). This could be under a rational mode, where the arbiter is objective reality. Under this mode, a person judges others based on the merits of their character, their actions, etc., rather than as representatives of their chosen or unchosen group. Of course, free will means that one can give up this responsibility to think rationally and instead proceed in operating under a different mode. People can drift in a dazed state of having switched off mental alertness, or even use mental bandwidth to suppress what is seen in front of them and, thus, evade reality. The example would be the Hutu killer we met earlier (Hetzfeld, 2008, p. 113) who declared that he knew very well that the Tutsi in front of him who was about to be massacred had done nothing wrong; yet, in order to perform his tribal duty he needed to suppress his judgment and persuade himself that all Tutsis deserve death.

Free will is a factor of major importance in understanding the role of tribalism, because it indicates that the latter is not a default. As Binswanger put it, 'the power to initiate a rational process makes man an autonomous, self-regulating being, not a robot programmed by outside forces' (2014, p. 322). Instead of a determinism that would leave human beings at the mercy of impulses, instincts, and of an uncontrollable 'wiring', understanding free will leads to the conclusion that human beings can self-determine how they think and approach reality (Ghate, 2016, p. 107). This is why Rand considered humans as a being of 'self-made soul' (2007, p. 1020). In the same way an artist makes a sculpture or someone works out to build a beautiful body, human beings can 'shape' their mind and build their character according to their values (Ghate, 2016, pp. 106–107). One's character is the result of myriad decisions that add up in time. These decisions can be taken rationally, having in mind a long-range process of what is objectively good, according to a clear purpose that will enrich one's life, or they can be taken following a whim and a spur-of-the-moment pleasure that might contradict one's future goals (if one has any to begin with).

An objection here could be the following: if there is such a thing as free will, why do we see so many people engaging in groupthink? Also, why can one observe patterns of behaviour met disproportionately in specific social environments? Going back to Pinker's claim (2012), is it not true that often people from common backgrounds sharing the same traditions tend to have similar worldviews? Yes, empirically such observations might be correct, but they do not prove that tribalism is an inherent necessity, nor an inescapable fate. They merely point to the fact that groupthink and conformity are easy options when one fails, or does not bother with, the task of independent thought and judgment. Binswanger explained: 'When one fails to think for oneself, one still has to know what ideas to accept, what values to pursue, and how to act. The easiest and most common "solution" is to conform to the beliefs and values of those around one' (2014, p. 359). Put simply, we are not necessarily wired for tribalism; it is just that often we are too lazy to think for ourselves, and *then* tribalism comes in handy.

Ayn Rand went a bit deeper on the mindset of tribalism and linked it with what she described as an 'anti-conceptual mentality' (1984, p. 51). This means the tendency to not question things beyond the level of the immediately given; instead of complex concepts, one prefers to stay at the level of easily perceivable concretes. The example would be the Hutu who would consider a Tutsi as the enemy just because they belong to different tribes, or the white supremacist who hates an African American for the colour of the latter's skin. Higher abstractions such as individual rights, justice, and merit require mental bandwidth that one operating under the anti-conceptual mentality refuses to spare. Yet, this leaves the individual with a quite limited view of the world, as only a fraction of one's mental capacity is put to work.

One way to get the illusion of overcoming such a limitation is to join forces with other people who view the world in the same anti-conceptual way and look for the safety of the group. For Rand, tribalism is the name that describes the phenomenon when this shallow and lazy view of the world is adopted by the members of a group (idem, p. 59). Put simply, tribalism is a symptom of the giving up of responsibility by an individual, or a group of individuals, to use their mind and reason to make sense of the world, and rather trust the group to do so. For many, delegating the responsibility of thought and judgment to others is a seemingly convenient and easy way to go through life, and this can also explain tribalism's popularity as a mode of thinking throughout the ages.

Taking all the above into consideration, tribalism can be understood as a chosen epistemological orientation, i.e. as something influencing the way one chooses to perceive and interpret the world. The element of choice is of importance here: despite a temptation that we might feel towards our thought being influenced by feelings, the social environment, or group loyalty, there is always the opportunity to recalibrate our consciousness towards a more objective and impartial judgment. Thus, tribalism is not an instinct: it is a way of thinking, a mindset, and the prism through which the world can be viewed, once one has failed to use his or her own reason and individual judgment.

I described tribalism as a way of viewing oneself, others, and the world, where the main point of reference is the group. It is now time to elaborate on this definition.[2]

- Under the tribalist mindset, people are not seen first and foremost as individuals, but as members of groups. They are seen as avatars of their group identity; in other words, as repre-

---

[2]   Many thanks to Greg Salmieri for helping me to expand the definition of tribalism, and on his various insightful comments on this chapter and on this book in general.

sentatives of the alleged characteristics of their group. When an anti-Semite sees a Jew, the judgment is not based on the latter's individual merits or shortcomings. The anti-Semite sees that person as carrying the whole package that he, the perceiver, has in his mind about what constitutes a Jew. Such a mindset is also at the basis of the worldview of racism. This is to be expected, as all collectivistic worldviews share the epistemological prism of tribalism. As philosopher Leonard Peikoff mentioned when describing collectivistic ideologies, in all of them the group is 'the unit of reality and the standard of value' (1983, p. 17).

- Not only are people viewed as avatars of their group identity, but these groups are seen as having antagonistic relationships to each other. Be it class, race, nation, religion, gender, or one's sports team, there is a win-lose competition where the gains of one group are the losses of another.

- Usually, belonging to such a group is based on unchosen characteristics (such as race and gender). We can see here tribalism's convenience: it does not require specific effort, as the categorization of people in groups often happens based on characteristics that are easily detected at the perceptual level. It takes a lot of effort to pass an objective judgment on a person; it takes less effort to figure out that this person is of a particular race and then project on him or her the positive or negative connotations one might have for that race.

- The group based on which someone builds a tribalist worldview can also be a chosen one, as one's political affiliation, or, in the case of hooligans, the team they support. The crucial defining factor here is that once they see themselves as part of that group, loyalty to the group overshadows their independent judgment. Incidentally, within a particular context there might be very good reasons to stay loyal to a group (as for example agreement in fundamental values), but a rational evaluation is not the way the tribalist thinks.

To clarify, there is no contradiction in people joining a group based on ideas and values, and focusing on a common goal, but also retaining their individual judgment. A group of revolutionaries coming together to overthrow a tyranny is an example of that. Yet, if then this group betrays its principles and becomes tyrannical itself, but its members evade their rational judgment and conform anyway, this could be considered an elevation of group loyalty above ideas. As we will see in the next section, such an expression of political tribalism can explain why the left and the right today are seen more as groups of people opposed to each other, rather than bound together by an ideology. Their ideas can change and fluctuate; their identification with their side, and their opposition to the other side, does not.

The example of Martin Latsis, a high-ranking officer in Cheka (the secret communist police in post-1917 revolutionary Russia — the predecessor of GPU and NKVD), sums up quite well the mindset of tribalism examined in this chapter: 'We are not fighting against single individuals. We are exterminating the bourgeoisie as a class. It is not necessary during the interrogation to look for evidence proving that the accused opposed the Soviets by word or action. The first question you should ask him is what class does he belong to, what is his origin, his education and his profession. These are the questions that will determine the fate of the accused' (cited in Solzenitshyn, 2003, p. 21). This is brutal and naked epistemological tribalism: what matters is not objective reality and the facts of each case; what should determine one's judgment is the group affiliation of the judge and the accused. What we have here is the group being elevated above reality as the ultimate horizon of one's consciousness. This is the reason I am describing tribalism as a worldview.

Culture wars and identity politics

So far, we have seen the definition of tribalism and its characteristics. Now it is time to turn to the other two terms that appear in this book's title: the culture wars and identity politics. Identity politics have been one of the main vehicles of tribalism, and the conflict between the different tribes has mostly been prevalent at the level of culture. Thus, both terms are important and require clarification.

'Culture wars' is a term historically associated mostly with the USA. Hartman described a schism that took place within American culture around the early 1960s. On the one side there was what he called 'normative America' (Hartman, 2015, p. 5): hard-working, believing in individual responsibility and meritocracy, and embracing the 'bourgeois' values of consumerism and capitalism. At the same time, though, a counter-culture was emerging challenging the post-WW2 consensus through the way people dressed, the music they listened to, the substances they consumed, and the view of society they had. The beatniks and the hippies were prominent personifications of that culture. In retrospect, it can be argued that the counter-culture changed the face of large parts of America significantly.

A great portrayal of the conflicting values, aesthetics, and worldviews of the emerging culture wars can be seen in an episode of the TV series Mad Men, a period drama depicting the advertising industry in the 1960s, with the background being the changing face of the American society. In season 1, episode 8 ('The Hobo Code'), the protagonist, the successful advertiser Don Draper, visits one of his mistresses. In her house, there is also a small gathering of intoxicated beatniks. The following dialogue takes place, as Don, visibly annoyed by a discussion with the counter-cultural outsiders, prepares to leave:

Beatnik 1: I wipe my ass with the Wall Street Journal!
Don (rolling eyes): Stop talking... make something of yourself.

Beatnik 2: Like you?… (pause of silence)… You make the lie.
You invent want. You're for them, not us.
Don (putting on his expensive suit jacket): Well, I hate to break
it to you, but there is no big lie. There is no system. The uni-
verse is indifferent.
Beatnik 1: Man… why do you have to say that?
(Don moves towards the door. There seem to be some police
sirens and lights nearby in the neighbourhood.)
Beatnik 2: The cops… you can't go out there.
Don: *You* can't.

In this 1.5-minute scene, we see a great dramatization of the 'two
Americas' developing in the 1960s. On the one side, we see the
beatniks, who despise Don and whatever he represents: from the
newspaper he is reading to the society of consumption he is
facilitating. They are not sure what they want to become, but it
cannot be something like Don. Yet, their rejection of instrumental
reason and conventional morality, and the way they fight 'the
system' (the use of illegal substances, for example), leads them to
view the world through a prism of fear: 'You can't go out there.'
Don, on the other hand, appears composed, reality oriented ('The
universe is indifferent'), unconvinced that there is something
wrong with the system—or that there is a system at all—and
confident that he can face the world: he *can* go 'out there'; the
beatnik can't.

In the following decades, the culture wars would spread and
include a variety of issues, such as education, abortion, and
marriage. Chua described them as 'a fight for the right to define
our national identity' (2018, p. 173). I will define culture wars as
controversies that are related to values, ideas, and lifestyle
choices, but which are also often elevated to the political sphere.
Thus, they can also indicate an ideological alliance with political
implications. For example, many Republicans are calling for
stricter measures on abortion and many around the left are calling

for regulations against discrimination that is currently allowed on grounds of religious freedom.

The culture wars today are more vibrant than ever, and not just in the USA. The motto proclaiming that 'the personal is political' has been even more prominent today than in the late 1960s, when it firstly became popular among the Women's Liberation movement. Thus, a variety of issues that in the past would fall under the sphere of the 'personal', such as our consumption choices or our interpersonal relationships, advertising, or the film and sports industries, become more and more politicized. But this relationship works both ways: politics are often less about radically different visions for the future and a clear division between left and right, and more about occupying specific positions in the trenches of the new culture wars.

Which begs the question: what do we mean by 'the left' and 'the right'? Do they even make sense as terms, beyond being the heritage of the geographical division of different political groups on the seats of the French parliament after the Revolution of 1789?

Let me use an extreme example: how can one put under the umbrella of 'the right' Ayn Rand *and* Edmund Burke *and* Donald Trump? Rand was an ardent individualist, a champion of reason and the Enlightenment, who considered one's life as his or her highest value and the measure of all things. Burke was an advocate of traditional values, sceptical of the developments of the Enlightenment and of the primacy of reason, and considered public duty as among a person's highest calls. And Trump is someone without clear principles, who is against free trade, who wants to control big corporations, but vows that 'America will never be a socialist country'. Incidentally, one could claim that the same problem applies to the left: what do Chairman Mao, Michele Foucault, and Black Lives Matter (BLM) have in common? Yet, in the eyes of many conservatives, they are all 'on the left'.

Here is another classification: we are told that the left is the 'movement of progress' and the right 'the movement of order'. But this does not tell us much. Nowadays someone on the right has more chance of being in favour of 'disruptive' technologies and platforms like Uber or 3D-printing, whereas the left seems to be more about halting the destabilizing effects of capitalism than suggesting a radical alternative. Yet, I will still use the terms right and left as they are mostly used in public discourse, as they do make sense in a helpful way. They might not indicate clearly defined philosophies, but they do indicate political groups and alliances. Once we know that someone is 'on the left', we can predict that they are for some specific causes (for example, less income inequality), but also that they tend to see others within the milieu as morally virtuous, whereas those on the other end of the political spectrum could be regarded with suspicion. Conversely, the same logic can be found on the right. Also, people tend to be influenced on topics they don't have a strong opinion about, based on the group's line on that particular issue. For example, a religious person on the right might become more sceptical of state intervention in the economy, because such a position is attributed to the left, i.e. the other tribe.

The fact that left and right more and more signify alliances, rather than ideologies, also explains why we can see them significantly changing their ideas on specific issues across the decades. For example, in Chapter 5 we will see how the left is more and more turning itself against free speech. Under the view of the left as a group of people, rather than as an ideology, such a switch should not surprise us.[3]

Moving to identity politics, most scholars have linked the term with the rise of the New Social Movements in the 1960s, such as the feminist movement (Snow et al., 2007). They were about addressing issues beyond politics and the economy, such as the recognition and integration of formerly marginalized groups. However, identity politics go beyond expressions such as the LGBT+ or the feminist movement. Melucci offered a good

---

[3]   I owe this insight to my personal communication with Dr Greg Salmieri.

definition, describing them as 'forms of collective action based on the affirmation and defence of one's identity' (1996, p. 186). So the central characteristic of identity politics is the elevation of identity as the main element of political affiliation. West elaborated: 'a social identity becomes political when it is recognized as the basis for political allegiances and action on behalf of the group in question' (2013, p. 79). Thus, one can see reactionary movements such as white nationalism *and* progressive emancipatory movements under the same analytical umbrella of identity politics. Obviously, this does not imply that they should be granted the same moral sanction.

Lukianoff and Haidt made a distinction between two kinds of identity politics (2018, pp. 60–62). The first is what they called 'common humanity identity politics': mobilizations organized for the rights of a group that is discriminated against based on its members being part of that group. An example is the civil rights movement in the USA during the 1950s and the 1960s. Here, the group is fighting for rights that are unjustly denied to its members. Black Americans of the South wanted to be part of the universalist notion of individual rights, following the values and principles of the Enlightenment that were behind the American Revolution and the Declaration of Independence. As philosopher Andrew Bernstein put it, the campaign could be better understood as the 'individual rights for black Americans movement'.[4] In addition, as Lukianoff and Haidt mentioned, Dr Martin Luther King's message was one that did not exclude non-blacks; it appealed to everyone's common core, which is our humanity and the rights that we need in order to live as human beings (2018, p. 60).

Next, however, Lukianoff and Haidt referred to a second category of identity politics, which they called 'common enemy identity politics' (2018, p. 62). In this case, what brings together the

---

[4]   Based on personal communication with Dr Bernstein.

group is the bond of identifying another group as the enemy. This is the opposite of Dr King's message: we cannot get along with the others, because there are no common characteristics uniting us, only an unbridgeable gap dividing us. An obvious example is the pathological hatred and the dehumanization of the Jews by the Nazis in the Third Reich; yet, at a lower level, many expressions of modern tribalism have a similar 'us vs. them' ethos. Later in their book, Lukianoff and Haidt related this divisive attitude to a tendency they called 'negative partisanship'. They provided as an example how 'Americans are now motivated to leave their couches to take part in political action not by love for their party's candidate but by hatred of the other party's candidate' (idem, p. 132). Pakulski (1991) called this attitude 'negative value consensus': as rigid political ideologies and universal categories lose their appeal, and as subjectivism and personal morality become core factors of political mobilizations, more and more people engaged in campaigns and movements are bonded not by what they stand for but what they stand *against*. In the tribal atmosphere that is engulfing western societies, it will be shown that identity politics more and more tend to resemble the second type in Lukianoff's and Haidt's paradigm, i.e. 'negative partisanship–common enemy' campaigns.

*

To sum up, in this chapter the theoretical framework on which I will base my examination of tribalism has been established, and some key terms have been defined. What we saw is that many claim that tribalism is a universal inherent tendency met throughout history and in different societies. Yet, there is a better way to view the phenomenon: although people have the tendency to form groups and bonds of loyalty and solidarity, this understandable need can go wrong. Often, reason and the responsibility of individual judgment are abandoned and the group becomes the ultimate horizon of one's worldview. Yet, it does not have to be this way. The volitional nature of consciousness means that one can choose not to be a tribalist; actually, being a rational being with free will and having to exercise individual judgment is what makes human nature special in the first place (Locke, 2017).

The way the majority of people choose to think and the way they view the world can have a huge impact on a society's success or failure. A question that arises is what elements in a society's culture and dominant philosophical trends influence whether it will be characterized by a mainly tribalist outlook or not. Such an intellectual endeavour would require a depth of work that goes way beyond the scope of this book (though it has been attempted by others; see Peikoff, 2012). Yet, taking into account the subject of this book, which is the understanding of today's culture wars, a different kind of historical overview can be attempted. The current sociopolitical climate has, to a large extent, been influenced by intellectual developments around what we can loosely describe as the left and the right in recent decades. I will now turn towards describing what made the left and the right what they are today. By doing so, I will also highlight the tribalist elements that are present in their thought and identity. After doing so, we will be in a better position to properly understand the three case studies that dominate today's culture wars.

The left...

Unite and divide

'Proletarians of the World Unite!' I still remember the first day I ever saw that captivating motto: Tuesday 17 November 1998. It was a national holiday for schools in Greece, commemorating the revolt of the students against the military junta in 1973. The revolt culminated in bloodshed, with the intervention of the army, and a tank breaking the gate and invading the polytechnic school, which was the centre of mobilizations in Athens. Both my parents participated in the revolt, and my mother was actually only metres away from the tank. I connected some dots in my head, telling me that since the military junta was by reactionary ultra-conservatives, and since it had the sanction of the USA, then the revolt must have had a left-wing character. Thus, on 17 November 1998, I decided to buy the newspaper of the Greek Communist Party, *The Radical*. There it was on the first page: the sickle and hammer, accompanied by Marx's famous ending line of the *Communist Manifesto*, encouraging the proletarians of the world to unite in brotherhood. That day was the beginning of a 15-year period where I identified myself as a Marxist. During these years, I became a member of the Communist Party's Youth, I joined picket lines shoulder to shoulder with bulky construction workers, I participated in my first proper fight (nothing personal — we were fighting the right-wing student union to kick them out of an assembly), I inhaled the tear gases of the Greek riot police, I read (three times) Volume 1 of Marx's *Das Capital*, and I had relationships, romances, and flings that began by discussing anything from Lenin to the 20th Congress of the Communist Party of the USSR and from the Cuban Missile Crisis to Slovenian philosopher Slavoj Zizek.

To some readers, my captivation by the hammer and sickle, the symbol of regimes that have led to the deaths of approximately 50 to 110 million people in the 20th century, and my decision to join a party that considered a tragic turning point in the history of the USSR the abandonment of a proper Marxist-Leninist line by the successors of Stalin, might sound morally appalling. The reason I mention it is not as a form of internal catharsis or of facing the mistakes of my youth. It is to emphasize the power that ideas, unquestioned philosophical premises, and personal background can have in forming one's political identity. I still believe that individuals have free will and volition to make their own way in life. After some point, being an apologist for Stalinism was my responsibility and only mine. Yet, understanding the appeal of communism to someone like myself, who now considers himself an advocate of freedom and individualism, is interesting as an insight into how ideas can be formed and established in one's mind.

Greece was a country where conservative and violent elements of the political right had a tight grip in culture and society for decades. After the German occupation ended in 1944, a civil war followed, with the royalists and the bourgeois political elites on one side, backed by the UK and later by the US, and the communists on the other. The war ended in 1949 with the total defeat of the communists. Henceforth, the left properly and freely participated in political life only after the downfall of the seven-year ultra-conservative military junta in 1974. The communists were portrayed, and often actually were, martyrs who had endured persecutions, executions, torture, and exile for staying loyal to their principles. These stories run deep in my family. I had an uncle who was living in exile in the Czechoslovak Socialist Republic, whereas my mother was part of the illegal Communist Youth during the 1967–1974 junta and of the thereafter legalized Communist Party of Greece (KKE) until the collapse of the Soviet Union. I grew up with the heroic poems and music of communist artists such as Yiannis Ritsos and Miki Theodorakis that were integral in the Greek cultural tradition of the last decades. The left had won the battle of ideas. Thus, becoming a leftist was almost the natural thing to do for someone who liked the arts, had an aspiring sense of life, was an atheist, and did not appreciate the parochial conservatism of the right. And since everything pointed to the fact that the left was the moral choice, the logical conclusion was to join the most principled advocate of these ideas: the Communist Party.

In my 15 years on the left, and especially during my four years in the Communist Party Youth, I saw some of the most determined and devoted people I've met in my life. People waking up at 4am to join the picket line of the ship-workers' strike, in the freezing cold at dawn; people pulling two consecutive all-nighters around the student elections so that they can track down and persuade every last potential voter; people losing their job due to their trade-union activity; and people donating a large proportion of their small income to the Communist Party. Irrespective of our moral evaluation of a communist party and its philosophy, this devotion, which in the 20th century has led so many people to kill and sacrifice themselves, needs to be understood.

The first element that makes the left diachronically so powerful is the moral high ground it enjoys, and the lack of any serious philosophical challenge to it from the mainstream right. During the years I had considered myself a leftist, I did not doubt for a single second whether I was on the moral side. Even when I had heated discussions with conservatives or social democrats, they never attempted to question the left's moral righteousness. The argument was that my ideas were 'good in theory, but will not work in practice' (from the centre-left), or that the tactic is wrong (from the rest of the left), or that the same virtuous goals can be achieved in a better way by other means, without the violent downsides (from the centre-right). It was difficult to question the left's premises when even its opponents considered them as fundamentally correct.

The other element that is characteristic of building strong bonds within the left is the 'us vs. them' division. This is a double-edged sword: the 'them' could be those on the wrong side of morality and history, but also others in the left who belong to a different group. Actually, once I had established within myself that I was a communist, there was a hard choice I had to make: with whom of the various communists was I to affiliate? In Greece for decades there has been a Greek Communist Party (KKE), a Greek Marxist-Leninist Communist Party (M-Λ KKE), a Greek Communist Party (marxist-leninist) (KKE (μ-λ)), and a Revolutionary Greek Communist Movement (EKKE). Their difference and the reason for a split could be something as trivial as Albanian's communist leader Enver Hoxha's fallout with China around 1975, and what this signified for the international Marxist-Leninist movement. There were also countless other parties and groups that had ideological references to Marx and Lenin, all in fierce opposition to each other. This grouping does not even include those in the 'reformist' left, the 'autonomists', the anarchists, etc.

Quite telling about the sectarianism inherent in the left is the history of the Situationist International, the group of the artist and intellectual Guy Debord (famous for his work *The Society of the Spectacle*), which was quite influential in the May 1968 revolt in Paris. Through the various splits and excommunications, Situationist International ended up having literally two remaining members: Debord himself and Gianfranco Sanguinetti (Hecken and Grzenia, 2008). It would have been a situationist gesture *par excellence* for Debord to take the final step and actually expel his last remaining comrade, and then perhaps also excommunicate himself, but he actually preferred to dismantle the organization altogether.

One could claim that there is nothing special here: sectarianism is a central tenet of all ideologically demanding movements (Christianity is an example), and it is merely about people taking ideas too seriously, which is a good thing. But it goes beyond that:

such disagreements within the left did not stay at the level of civilized discussions. From the period of Great Terror in the USSR in the 1930s, to the liquidation of the anarchists and the Trotsky-ists by the Stalinists during their fight against the common enemy of fascism in the Spanish Civil War, the left was always torn by internal violent conflicts. An example illustrating the absurdity of the inner tensions within the left took place in Italy in the 1970s. Following the crackdown by the Italian authorities on the communist urban guerrillas, but also of the wider radical move-ment of *Autonomia*, the Marxist intellectual Toni Negri was arrested and imprisoned. He was considered the 'Cattivo Maestro', the evil theoretical influencer of the youth's radicaliza-tion. In a nearby cell, members of the terrorist group Red Brigades were also imprisoned. In the eyes of the state, Negri and the Red Brigades were loosely on the same side. But the *Brigadisti* had a different view. They held a 'martial court' among themselves in their cell, where they officially condemned Negri to death as a class enemy (Lotringer and Marazzi, 2008). Luckily for Negri, they never managed to reach his cell to enforce the penalty.

Therefore, there is a question arising: is there something inherently tribal in the leftist worldview? To answer this, we will now turn to an authoritative source: Marx himself.

Marx and the proletarian mind

To get deep into Marx and his philosophy, one needs to engage with the totality of his work, and especially with at least the first volume of *Das Capital* (Marx, 1990). Yet, we can get some of the main themes of Marx's philosophy popularized and condensed in an earlier version in the *Communist Manifesto* (Marx and Engels, 2007):

(a) Human history is characterized by conflict among groups: class struggle.

(b) Relations of production and the level of the productive forces (such as labour and technology) direct the character of each society, and play an important role on the consciousness of individuals.

(c) Although history is not predetermined, it seems to follow some laws and to be directed towards a succession of societies. Each one is more complex than the previous, leading ultimately to the communist society. Communism will be the highest stage in the realization of humans' potential, through the immersion of the individual with the social.

A question that arises is what, if any, role did Marx consider for the individual in shaping history. This is closely related to whether Marx is a determinist. It is very easy to spot countless passages from his work that clearly point towards a view of history that leaves little space for human agency. Yet, there is also the view that sees Marx in his theory of history as actually celebrating the transformative role of human agency. If history is open to change, and if according to one of Marx's most famous lines 'men make their own history, but they do not make it just as they please' (cited in McLellan, 2000, p. 329), then humans actually play a very active role in shaping their destiny (Furedi, 1990, p. xxi).

Yet, my claim is that even if one accepts the most liberal interpretation of Marx's thought as actually not prohibiting agency and human initiative, then still Marxism has a very strong leaning towards a collectivistic view that leaves the individual in the back seat. The reasons go beyond Marx's theory of history, and have also to do with his epistemology, which means his theory of how we gain knowledge and an understanding of the world. Many critics will point to Marx's famous line from his 'Preface' to *A Contribution to the Critique of Political Economy* stating that 'It is not the consciousness of men that determines their being, but, on the contrary, their social being that determines their consciousness' (cited in McLellan, 2000, p. 425), and will consider it a checkmate pointing towards Marx's determinism. Yet, as he usually did,

Marx made many other claims that contradicted the famous passage from the 'Preface'. Kolakowski (2008) pointed out how Marx never actually named his premises regarding epistemology; we can only approach them vaguely from the rest of his thought.

For Marx, knowledge has always had a social character. Knowledge responds to every particular era and should be judged taking this into accordance. As Kolakowski made clear (2008, p. 128), this is the key to understanding Marx's theory of false consciousness. Marx did not claim that there is a true pro-letarian consciousness that leads to truth and a false bourgeois consciousness that leads to alienation. Consciousness simply is, and relates to factors beyond the realm of individual knowledge, that can be found on the level of the social, such as one's relation to the means of production. This is why the ideological fog of false consciousness will only dissolve when the proletariat accom-plishes its historical role and then humans will live what Marx called a non-alienated species' life. Kolakowski named Marx's complicated and incomplete epistemological position as 'generic subjectivism' (2008, p. 145), which in simple terms means that knowledge is formed on a level beyond the individual; it is, thus, socially constructed.

Such a theory is anti-individualistic. It implies that an indi-vidual cannot make sense of the world *objectively* and *as it is*. Even worse though, this is not due to a mistake that can be corrected, but this is our predicament until the apocalyptic process of communism will lead to the passage from the pre-history to the real history of our species. Yet, this brings us to the conclusion that the mind, an individual's main tool of navigating this world, is far from trustworthy. But if reality makes little sense based on reason, then this world is actually a very scary place. Marx agreed with this and called this state that we find ourselves in a capitalist society 'alienation'; a concept that, although it is so central in his work, is not defined in a clear way. In various places it means alienation from humans' real nature (which is not clearly specified by Marx), from the product of our labour, from other human beings, or from nature (Meszaros, 2005).

The guidance that Marx provides on how humans can navigate this complex and often alien world is that any overcoming of this existentially dreadful situation can happen through the immersion of the individual into a wider, social consciousness: class consciousness. Thus, one can observe that Marx's epistemology has a collectivistic character in it: consciousness operates and is to be understood on the level of a society and is analysed based on how it affects groups.

My main argument is that the blueprint for the disastrous record of communism was already there in Marx's ideas, and has to do, among other things, with the elements I mentioned above related to his philosophy, but also with his epistemology, i.e. his theory of how human beings know and are in contact with reality. At the centre of Marx's analysis is the *group*, which is crucial to how people make sense of the world. Thus, it is not a coincidence that, in a political system built on Marx's blueprints, the life of the individual and his or her values is not the primary concern. And if we also take into account the strong 'us vs. them' element of the Marxian theory of exploitation, according to which society is the field of a class struggle, and the historically accumulated hatred or envy for the rich and privileged (real or imagined), then the dehumanizing of the 'class enemies' in communist countries was a predictable next step.

Having traced the strong presence of collectivism in the philosophy of Marx, or at least seeing how it has primacy over individualism, we can only expect this collectivism to also materialize at a political level. A concretization of collectivism, of the idea that the group is above the individual, was the chilling motto of the notorious S-21 prison in Cambodia, where the Khmer Rouge communists tortured and killed thousands of their victims during their rule between 1975 and 1979: 'to keep you is no gain, to destroy you is no loss' (Pran, 1999). The individual is merely an instrument, a representative of the group. If they are part of the wrong group, the life of the imagined 'class enemy' — which in Cambodia included even people with the slightest resemblance to a middle-class background — is expendable. For individuals to be ends in themselves, what would be required is a view of the world that is totally different from the one of Marx, where the navigating tool would be the individual mind, and the measure of all things the individual's life.

Many have drawn a straight line from the ideas of Marx to the actions of the NKVD thugs or of the Khmer Rouge torturers. This is a difficult debate that goes beyond the scope of this book. What I do claim, though, is that attributing philosophical priority to the collective, and considering the individuals as agents of groups (whether a class, a race, a nation, etc.) rather than ends in themselves, is not a good starting point as a blueprint for a society. I also pointed out a specific issue in the ideas of Marx, which is the existential and epistemological supremacy he gave to the group. Put in simple words, communism went wrong because at the core of its philosophy the world is made up of groups in opposition to each other, and reality makes sense through the prism of the group. The name I give to this worldview is *tribalism*.

The New Left

Large parts of the left, and most of its intellectuals, have since the 1960s disassociated themselves from the communist movement. This was mainly due to:

(a) The revealing by Stalin's successor, Nikita Khrushchev, at the 20th Congress of the Communist Party of the Soviet Union in 1956 of the crimes committed during Stalin's era;

(b) the international outcry at the bloody interventions of the Soviet Union and the Warsaw Pact against the pro-liberalization revolts in the socialist countries of Hungary in 1956 and Czechoslovakia in 1968;

(c) the publication and popularity of *Gulag Archipelago* by Soviet dissident Solzhenitsyn in the early 1970s, articulating the horrors of the labour camps in USSR;

(d) the progressively visible shortcomings of planned economies to provide prosperity for their citizens equal to that of the semi-free economies of the West.

Yet, to say that this breach between the Marxist intelligentsia and the communist regimes was decisive would be letting many of them off the hook. Even after 1956, Jean-Paul Sartre maintained an ambivalent relationship of tolerance towards various socialist dictatorships (Scruton, 2016). Louis Althusser (1966) wrote a pamphlet praising the period of terror, hysteria, and persecutions in China known as the Cultural Revolution—an event which Alain Badiou (2010) would still today consider one of the closest examples of a country reaching 'real' communism. Meanwhile, the amount of people endorsing the Cuban or the Vietnamese regimes as a breath of fresh air in socialism is too big to even try to mention names. Also, until well into the 1970s, Italy and France had massive communist parties which, besides their criticisms or reservations, had strong ties with the Communist Party of the Soviet Union (Revel, 2009). Still, it would be accurate to claim that since the mid-1960s, especially in the Anglo-Saxon world, but not only there, the face of the left and the ideas that appealed to young radicals have changed. Pivotal in this process has been the rise of a New Left.

For a deeper and more detailed analysis on the New Left, I refer the reader to my previous book, *The Rise of Lifestyle Activism: From New Left to Occupy* (Sotirakopoulos, 2016). Here, I will refer to the New Left in brief, and I will mostly highlight how it is different from the old left of the communist and labour movements, and how it has influenced the culture wars that we will examine in the next chapters. Klimke and Scharloth (2008) placed the New Left in what they referred to as 'the long 1960s', i.e. from 1956 until 1977. The starting point was 1956, when de-

Stalinization in the USSR and the invasion of the Warsaw Pact to suppress the Hungarian revolution created a turmoil in the communist milieu. This chain of events led to the 'official' birth of the New Left, with some of its prominent intellectuals leaving the British Communist Party and publishing a journal that would be named the *New Left Review*. 1977 is seen as the end of an era, as it was the year when some of the violent offsprings of the ideas and the movements of the New Left, the urban guerrillas of the *Rote Armee Fraktion* (RAF) in Germany and the Red Brigades in Italy, were defeated and further delegitimised. More generally, the New Left can be described as a set of ideas, a loose network of thinkers, and a series of social movements and campaigns that through the 1960s and for many years later left their mark on the intellectual and political life of the West.

The next thing to examine is what made many people (mostly young, middle class, and well-educated) join the ranks of the New Left. A typical view held by its critics is that the New Left was a movement of bored alienated youngsters, revolting against the world of their parents. There is some element of truth to that, as recognized by the activists themselves. The Port Huron statement, signalling the birth of the Students for a Democratic Society (SDS) in 1964, the most prominent offspring of the New Left in the USA, opened with the following words: 'We are people of this genera-tion, bred in at least modest comfort, housed now in universities, looking uncomfortably to the world we inherit' (Students for a Democratic Society, 1964). Yet, there were many reasons for some-one to be indignant in the 1960s. Racial discrimination in the United States against people of colour was still the law in parts of the country, and challenging it often met the violent response of the state machine. In addition, the Vietnam War was unfolding, in the midst of the Cold War. American soldiers, often drafted with-out their will, were losing their lives in jungles tens of thousands of kilometres away from home, and in the process they were obliterating villages of peasants who have never heard about communism in their life. Irrespective of one's evaluation of the

New Left, this was not a movement merely triggered by the boredom of spoiled kids.

Here is a quick presentation of the ideas of the New Left, compared to the old left, so that their differences will become evident:

Old left	New Left
Focus on the political level	Focus on the social level
Economy/political power	Culture/lifestyle
Political party, trade unions	Grassroots groups, social movements organizations
Marxism	Frankfurt School, post-structuralism, 2nd wave feminism, environmentalism
Values around discipline, sacrifice, austere working-class ethos	Experimentation with alternative values, counter-culture, subjectivist self-discovery
Universalism (at least in aspiration)	Particularism, identity politics
Communism/socialism	No particular political plan, 'autonomy', participation, social democracy
Mostly members from the working class	Predominantly middle class

I will briefly elaborate on some of the main characteristics of the New Left that have left a mark on later movements and mobilizations to the present day:

– Lack of ideological coherence. The mega-narratives of the past, such as Marxism-Leninism, were questioned. In place of strong ideas, the emphasis was on feelings and emotional connection. The 1960s were the 'Age of Aquarius', as the famous song declared; thus, at the centre of political mobilizations one could find loose networks mostly based on emotional attachment and common values, usually around an anti-establishment life-style (Sotirakopoulos, 2016).

– Links with an emerging counter-culture that appealed to young people. This is also related to who were the main partici-pants of the New Left: young middle-class people with a strong sense of alienation from the dominant values of the industrial capitalist society. The counter-culture of the 1960s was a pivotal moment for the culture wars that are still prevalent today.

According to Lerner, what is referred to by 'counter-culture' is
'norms and patterns of behaviour, emerging institutions (such as
rock festivals and communes), and beliefs and artistic traditions
that have coalesced to provide an opposing alternative to the
cultural templates of the main culture' (1971, p. 37). The symbolic
peak of the 1960s counter-culture was the Woodstock music
festival of 1969, attended by approximately 400,000 people and
resulting in a chaos of 'sex, drugs, and rock and roll' that remains
a point of reference of that era to this very day. For Roszak, the
young rebels of the counter-culture were 'searching for an outlet
for their frustration with everyday life, though still not necessarily
striving for overtly political revolt' (1995, p. 15). The borders
between lifestyle expression and politics were thin and not always
visible. Movements such as the Situationists in France and the
Provos in the Netherlands are good examples of this hybrid
between art and protest. Describing the intellectual atmosphere of
the early 1960s, Gitlin mentioned how 'in coffeehouses and
student unions scattered across the country, beat talk, pseudobeat
talk, avant-garde talk, political talk, sex talk, and literature and art
talk were buzzing and mingling, not always logically, at neigh-
bouring tables' (1993, p. 53).

– Emphasis on 'post-material' values. This has to do with the
timing of New Left's emergence: during the 1960s, when the post-
WW2 boom had discredited the Marxist predictions about the
immiseration of the working class. Thus, the focus of activists was
on issues around identity, discrimination against social groups
(such as people of colour, gays, and women), and the quality of
life in urban capitalist societies. There was a lot of criticism of a
loosely – if ever – defined 'alienation'. As one of the most famous
lines of the Situationist Raoul Vaneigem went: 'Who wants a
world in which the guarantee that we shall not die of starvation
entails the risk of dying of boredom?' (1983, p. 18).

– Campaigns focusing on direct action, rather than on institutionalized politics. The anti-Vietnam mobilizations, the free-
speech movement at the University of California in Berkeley, and

the anti-nuclear peace movement in the UK are prominent examples. An inspiration for direct action had been the successful civil rights movement in the late 1950s and early 1960s. It has to be noted that most of the movements that sprung up in the 1960s were lacking a long-range strategy; they were based more on single issues and the 'now'; 'action speaks louder than words' was a slogan that characterized many of these campaigns (Sotirakopoulos, 2016). The idea was: 'The world is in a mess, therefore something needs to be done. Theorizing has not produced much change, but action will.' This predictably bred some really bad outcomes. For Steigerwald, 'where reason is tossed aside and the instincts were unleashed, after sex and drugs, there was not much left but violence and destruction' (1995, p. 177). This was the case with some minoritarian parts of the New Left and some groups that split from the Students for a Democratic Society, such as the Weather Underground Group (also known as 'Weathermen') that deployed urban guerrilla terroristic activities, envisioning themselves as part of an anti-imperialist global struggle, where they 'brought the war home' in the name of the Vietkongs and the oppressed of the third world (Varon, 2004).

One can thus see how the ideological characteristics, the political orientation, and the cultural references of the New Left were radically different from those of the old left. Predictably, these movements would also differ in their philosophical worldview.

The New Left's existential uncertainty, and tribalism

A major difference between the old left and the New Left was the existential prism through which they viewed the world. The old left had the confidence that they could change the world and that they knew how to do it: organize in a party/trade union, take power, 'socialize' the means of production, build socialism/communism. The fact that, as shown above, on the individual level the capacity for reason was blurred and unclear in the Marxian universe did not hinder the belief that the working class, led by its political party, knew what had to be done. Perhaps this existential certainty about the potential of communism explains the eagerness of so many hundreds of thousands of workers and intellectuals to die for their ideas, from travelling to Spain with the International Brigades to fight the fascists and the oligarchs, to refusing to denounce their beliefs in the torture chambers in Greece or in Iran. Of course, their ideas were proven to have disastrous consequences, but this does not affect the argument I am making about the existential confidence that communism exhibited.

The New Left was the reversal of this tendency. The certainties of the past were collapsing. From thinkers like Herbert Marcuse and Cornelius Castoriadis to Guy Debord and Michel Foucault, what transcends their differences is their common rejection of the present state of things, paired with a scepticism as to what is to be done. Science, technology, and instrumental reason were not seen any longer as the guarantors of a bright future. The experience of the two world wars, the Holocaust, the nuclear threat and environmental instability raised questions about industrial society, irrespective of whether it is capitalist or socialist. 'Alienation', as a feeling of psychological detachment from one's self and society, was considered an existential bug of industrial civilization.

Erich Fromm took it a step further, viewing reason as the source of our misery, as it distinguishes humans from other animals that enjoy a 'harmony' with nature. Using religious language, Fromm saw a 'fall' of humans from our true self since we have proudly declared that nature is to be commanded and shaped for our needs. As he said, the human 'has transcended nature—although he never leaves it; he is part of it—and yet, once torn away from nature, he cannot return to it; once thrown out of paradise—a state of original oneness with nature—cherubim with flaming swords block his way, if he should try to return' (cited in Branden, 1967, p. 313).

Compare the existential pessimism—which is present throughout the narrative of the New Left and sees humanity as the Icarus who attempted to fly too close to the sun and is now paying the consequences—to the Prometheanism of the early Bolsheviks like Maxim Gorky, who stated that 'once the class struggle has been won, Soviet humankind will be free to engage its final enemy: nature' (Westerman and Garrett, 2011, p. 87). Nature and our 'prehistoric condition', i.e. the times before communism, were seen as a limit to be overcome, and nothing would be impossible once our potential would be realized in a society 'rationally planned' using reason (though a collective one) and science. Trotsky envisioned a proletariat fighting towards 'increasing the power of man over nature and to the abolition of the power of man over man' (Trotsky, 1938), whereas elsewhere he predicted that in communism 'the average human type will rise to the heights of an Aristotle, a Goethe, or a Marx. And above this ridge new peaks will rise' (Trotsky, 1924).

This confidence about the future was no longer there in the New Left. The pessimism of the counter-culture around the 1960s was concretized in popular music, used frequently as a soundtrack for that time's radical mobilizations.

Often, the songs of that period included visions of a dystopia of destruction, the cause of which is vague...

'I see a bad moon a-rising
I see trouble on the way
I see earthquakes and lightnin'
I see bad times today

Don't go 'round tonight
It's bound to take your life
There's a bad moon on the rise

I hear hurricanes a-blowing

I know the end is coming soon
I fear rivers overflowing
I hear the voice of rage and ruin.' (Creedence Clearwater
Revival, *Bad Moon Rising*)

...or related to the fears of the nuclear bomb...

'Don't you understand, what I'm trying to say?
And can't you feel the fears I'm feeling today?
If the button is pushed, there's no running away,
There'll be no one to save with the world in a grave,
Take a look around you, boy, it's bound to scare you, boy,
And you tell me over and over and over again my friend,
Ah, you don't believe we're on the eve of destruction.' (Barry
McGuire, *Eve of Destruction*)

...or to the interference of man with nature...

'Hey farmer farmer
Put away the DDT
I don't care about spots on my apples
Leave me the birds and the bees
Please!
Don't it always seem to go
That you don't know what you've got
Til it's gone

They paved paradise
And put up a parking lot
Hey, now they paved paradise
To put up a parking lot.' (Joni Mitchell, *Big Yellow Taxi*)

This cultural pessimism created the need for escape from a reality
that was scary and made no sense. This escape took various
forms, such as LSD trips, retreating to remote communes, and
discovering eastern spirituality. What lies behind all these was the

rejection of rationality and its emancipatory promises. The Frankfurt School was an embodiment of such a pessimism. For Adorno and Horkheimer, rationality has become a tool of destruction in the hands of malevolent forces, such as the NKVD thugs and the Nazi gauleiters, and there is no guarantee that science and technology will liberate us (Adorno and Horkheimer, 1997). Marcuse (2002) problematized economic growth and the triumph of the market in delivering the goods, as he saw in them the perpetuation of the workers' engulfment in the capitalist system. Thus, the message was: this world makes little sense, as we have overestimated the capacity of reason to guide us beyond existential uncertainty, while we have also unleashed forces that we cannot control and that may even be the cause of our demise, via nuclear war or environmental destruction.

Ayn Rand indicated that what would accommodate the existential agony created by the loss of confidence in reason was tribalism. 'If men accept the notion that reason is not valid, what is to guide them and how are they to live? Obviously, they will seek to join some group—any group—which claims the ability to lead them and to provide some sort of knowledge acquired by some sort of unspecified means' (Rand, 1990, p. 117). This is key to understanding the rise and prominence of identity politics after the 1960s. Clinging to a group can be a defence against existential fear. Also, the problematization of instrumental reason and of the big narratives of the past would consider notions such as working-class internationalism and global revolution as out of fashion. What was left? On one hand, coming together with other people who are similar to us on an obvious, perceptual level, such as our gender or race. Also, the fear of an unknowable and hostile world contributed to the rise of movements that attempted to mitigate this existential angst, such as environmentalism and various forms of New Age spirituality.

Obviously, the above analysis does not claim that anyone who joined these movements was an irrationalist or that they did not have valid claims. Around the 1960s and 1970s women were still facing limitations based on stereotypes and black people were still discriminated against in everyday life. In addition, pollution, the Three Mile Island nuclear accident, acid rain, and the 1973 oil crisis posed difficult questions about our ways of life. Yet, the way these questions were addressed was a sign of the times: the answer was not a confident universalist message of individual rights, of progress, and of the rational mind providing solutions. The answer was the politics of the group (as universalist narratives were falling out of fashion) and *less* progress, not more; steps back, rather than steps forward.

The New Left pushed a narrative that is still in effect today. First, it moved the goalposts, as now the evil of capitalism was not that it produced poverty, but that it produced a dehumanizing society of shallow affluence. Also, the New Left also changed the way one kept score, as now the emphasis was not on immiseration, but on vague evils such as 'alienation'. Thus, under such a narrative, capitalism is bad in an unfalsifiable way: it produces poverty, but also consumerism. It promotes 'formal equality' of individual rights, but also it marginalizes groups. The New Leftists were thus eager to find new revolutionary subjects, and various groups perceived as marginalized (many of them rightly so) were the obvious answer. Then, the intellectuals of the New Left projected on them their aspirations for political change. This is concretized in the famous closing of Marcuse's *One-Dimensional Man*, where he uses Walter Benjamin's line stating 'It is only for the sake of those without hope that hope is given to us' (Marcuse, 2002, p. 261).

Yet, in many ways the 1960s and the 1970s were actually a period of continuing progress. Humanity had conquered space, the revolution in agricultural methods was feeding millions of people who would otherwise starve, the poor were getting richer, the civil rights movement won the historic victory of equal rights for black people, and women were gaining ground in fighting the stereotypes of the past, rising even to positions of power, as was the case with Golda Meir being the Prime Minister of Israel. If someone saw individuals as capable achievers, who by the use of their mind are problem-solvers, then the world could be viewed with confidence. Yet, this was not the prominent intellectual fashion; thus, the world was seen as an out-of-control place at permanent risk, where clinging to some sort of group was a safety net against a threatening reality that was difficult to grasp.

These ideological characteristics of the New Left, with an emphasis on emotionalism, identity-building, and lived experience, were materialized and concretized in many of the movements and networks of the 1960s and 1970s. Some social movements' scholars, like Hetherington (1998) and Maffesoli (1995), directly referred to them as movements resembling tribes. Hetherington (1998) speaks of 'neo-tribes' of activists, and attributes to them the following characteristics, on which I will elaborate:

1. A search for authentic experiences and personal growth (Hetherington, 1998, p. 5). If the world out there makes little sense and reason has limited capacity for bringing us into contact with reality, maybe the truth can be found 'inside here', rather than 'outside there'. The prominent Berkeley activist of the 1960s, Jerry Rubin, described how he withdrew from trying to change the world to self-discovery: 'In five years, from 1971 to 1975, I directly experienced est, gestalt therapy, bioenergetics, rolfing, massage, jogging, health foods, tai chi, Esalen, hypnotism, modern dance, meditation, Silva Mind Control, Arica, acupuncture, sex therapy, Reichian therapy, and More House—a smorgasbord course in New Consciousness'. What was the point of all this? 'I... learned to love myself enough so that I do not need another to make me happy' (quoted in Lasch, 1979, p. 14).

2. Empathy and identification with the marginalized and oppressed groups (Hetherington, 1998, p. 5). The world is seen always through the prism of oppressed groups; the proletariat

is not a convenient example of this anymore, so the scope of what constitutes a victimized group had to expand.

3. Emphasis on the importance of establishing some distinct space for groups and networks of like-minded people (idem). Society out there is seen as an alienating place we cannot shape according to our values; thus, the solution is a retreat to voluntary marginalization in smaller communities. Isserman and Kazin estimated that in the early 1970s there were approximately 30,000 communes in the United States, accommodating almost 700,000 people, experimenting in various different lifestyles: from polyamory to New Age spirituality to organic farming and collective parenting (2008, p. 170).

4. Such spaces are operated by holding together groups linked by their emotional and moral solidarity (Hetherington, 1998, p. 5). The world is seen through the prism of emotions. One's strong emotions towards like-minded people, rather than a coherent ideology, became the glue holding together the neo-tribes.

5. Interest in knowledge that is rejected by instrumentalism of modern science, medicine, religion, and politics (idem). Such a tendency is predictable in a counter-culture that has rejected 'instrumental reason'. When people lose confidence in their main means of grasping the world and reality, then nothing in this world is taken for granted. This attitude could range from conspiracy theories to millenarian visions of an apocalyptic future, present in some communes that were off-shoots of the 1960s' counter-culture.

Maffesoli (1995) referred to a 'tribalization' of the population in the decades following the 1960s; he called that period, 'the time of the tribes'. Such a tendency was following the intellectual trends of the era. A lack of trust in reason as the universal capacity of the individual to make sense of the world means that each one of us is living in, metaphorically and epistemologically, different worlds.

Yet, this collapse of meaning creates an existential angst. Clinging together with other people based on superficial criteria, as Rand explained above, became a necessity and a pretence of security and meaning. Thus, hopefully, by now the link between a questioning of reason, metaphysical uncertainty, and tribalism has become clear.

One final remark needs to be made, before we leave behind the New Left. This section provided a criticism of its philosophy and of the way it viewed the world. This is not to dismiss, however, the steps forward achieved in the 1960s for many formerly marginalized groups in overcoming prejudices and negative stereotypes against them. As mentioned above, most of the grievances of the New Left were based on real injustices and problems, especially when it comes to women, LGBT+ people, and racial minorities (like black people in the USA). We will never know if and to what extent these steps forward were something already happening, and the degree to which the counter-culture and the movements of the 1960s accelerated that progress. But what is of the utmost importance for the purposes of this book is that the way the 1960s radicals viewed the world left a crucial mark on culture and heavily influenced the zeitgeist of the world we live in. Thus, two things could be true at the same time:

(a) The 1960s were a time of progress for many marginalized groups, and of interesting cultural and social experimentation, which gave us things like sexual liberation and the overcoming of many prejudices.

(b) The ideology and the counter-culture of the 1960s, with its questioning of reason, its focus on emotionalism, and its subsequent tribalism, left a seed that has only grown since and has today culminated in the ever-expanding culture wars and the prevalence of identity politics.

The 21st-century left: lived tribalism...

The presentation of the ideas of Marx, of the socialist/communist movement, and of the New Left plays a more important role than merely that of a historical overview. Their common denominators in their approach, which are the focus on groups and their unequal 'power', together with the diminishing of the importance of individual agency, can shed light on many phenomena of today, such as the current culture wars and their development around identity politics. In the last two sections, I will focus on some important trends in the left (mainly in the Anglo-Saxon world) in the last 20 years.

Activism in recent decades has a feature that links it with the characteristics of the New Left: protests that are less about some concrete proposals for change, and more about a gesture indicating moral disapproval, based often on a strong expression of emotions and on an alternative set of values. The recipients of these grievances are usually the perceived 'elites', the '1%', 'globalization', 'neoliberalism', 'patriarchy', and other signifiers that all point to the same notions: the capitalist system (or what is perceived as it), industrial society, free trade, and a culture of 'greed'. It is quite telling that often these protests, such as the Climate Camps in the UK and the Occupy Movement in the US and the UK, end up with activists setting up alternative micro-communities and engaging in a different style of living, apparently less 'alienating' and less infected by the 'cold logic of capitalism'. They are what I described elsewhere as 'protest camps' (Sotirakopoulos, 2016).

To understand this type of activism, it is important to mention something about the 1990s anti-roads campaigns in the UK, as they set the tempo for a model of protest that would become popular in the following years. The anti-roads movement was about setting up camps to stop the construction of new roads, fuelled by environmental and anti-capitalist concerns. In this movement, one can see evident the influence of the 1960s counter-culture. Mysticism and tribal identity-building were central in their romantic anti-industrialism and anti-modernity ethos. In the protest camp of Twyford Down, some of the key activists were some New Age travellers calling themselves the Dongas Tribe. Doherty described how they

> 'used dragon symbols, and drew boundary circles, invoking the power of magic to defend their site. It was argued by some in the group that rediscovering indigenous Celtic and earth-based spirituality would help to restore the balance of nature. Adopting a tribal identity, and in the case of Dongas, even a nomadic way of life, was also a means of situating themselves in the global struggles of indigenous peoples against ecological destruction.' (Doherty, 2000, p. 65)

Wall indicated how the irrationalism of the Dongas Tribe became a problem for the cohesion of the protest camp, as the New Age spiritualists were sceptical of other more 'urban' activists because the latter were, according to the Dongas, 'upsetting the karma of the place' (1999, p. 70).

Such characteristics were also present in the Climate Camps of the 2000s that drew inspiration from the anti-road movement (Sotirakopoulos, 2016). These protests were trying to raise awareness on the issue of climate change, and opposed particular projects that were considered environmentally destructive (such as the Kingsnorth Power Station outside Gillingham and Heathrow Airport's third runway). There, besides protesting climate change, participants were experiencing an alternative lifestyle on a communal basis. Soon, the baton was passed to a more urban movement: Occupy London.

The Occupy Movement of 2011 sprung up as a reaction to the 2009 financial crisis. The movement started in New York, but soon expanded to more cities and countries, including London, which will be my focus (source for all fieldwork notes and interview quotes: Sotirakopoulos, 2016). The activists claimed to speak for the 99%, and targeted the 1% of 'greedy capitalists and politicians', who were supposedly to blame for the financial crisis and the austerity measures that followed. Yet, the form and the message of the protest itself seemed to be more targeted against the 99% and their habits, values, and way of life. The actual target was, once more, some of the central tenets of an industrial market society: capitalist 'unsustainable' economic growth (raising questions about whether the protest was actually against austerity), consumerism, the food industry, aviation, and, as usual, 'alienation'. One could see posters, t-shirts, and stickers with messages such as 'your ignorance is their power', 'care for the planet means less consumption', and 'stop feeding your greed, go vegan'. Such an attitude was also present in some of the comments of activists I interviewed: 'Humankind is the craziest thing in nature and we have moved away from nature and animals, we are going to the supermarket and consuming whatever we want'; 'The idea of having fun because you have a lot of money needs to change. People need to stop being materialistic'; 'There is a spiritual apathy towards fellow men and women. This protest is a plea to people: we are in tents, we are freezing. Take courage from what we sacrifice and do something!'

Chua characterized the Occupy Movement as a tribe, focusing on how the activists would find status and identity in an otherwise alienating world by joining such a protest (2018, p. 142). Many of the campers told me that finding a community where they could contribute based on their talents (ranging from cooking, drawing, community organizing, to setting up solar panels) was as important as the political message they wanted to pass on. An activist in the US mentioned how the lived experience was key in what Occupy meant for her: 'It was, for hours, beautiful chaos. From that moment on until the end of our physical home some two months later, I heard the phrase "I've never felt so alive" repeated ad nauseam, largely because of how empowering it felt to constantly turn that chaos into our own makeshift self-creations, only to see them become chaotic again, and so begin the cycle afresh' (Milstein, 2012, p. 296).

As mentioned earlier, a characteristic of the New Left is a questioning of instrumental rationality. Occupy could not be an exception. There were workshops in spirituality where the 'guru' would declare that meditation had freed us from external reality, a tarot reading tent, posters with slogans such as 'the end is nigh', 'what would Jesus do?', homeopathy and alternative medicine workshops, a shamanic drumming circle, and a clowning session I participated in where people would go around dancing and mimicking animal sounds to let off steam. The questioning of instrumental reason was also present in the narrative of the activists I interviewed. One of them highlighted the primacy of emotions, which is a characteristic we also witnessed in the counter-culture of the 1960s: 'Humanity is detached from itself, no longer self-aware… instead of operating on a level of feelings, we get lost in a mindset of alienating structures, and the more we do that, the more psychopathic in nature we become.' Another activist rejected the idea of the Occupy campaign having goals, considering it a misunderstanding of what the protest was actually about: 'This is a spiritual movement. We are focusing on the now. Living in the moment is more important than making long-term plans.'

But if reason is alienating and feelings and emotions become a priority, how can a movement come up with a coherent agenda and construct an ideology? Well, in that case, ideology should take a back seat. One of the most constant themes among the activists I interviewed was their celebration of actually *not* having a particular ideology. 'That's the beauty of this protest, that you don't have a group of people with a certain agenda'; 'It is an inclusive movement, we don't ask people for qualifications or beliefs'; 'I am a socialist, but we don't want any of these old words'; 'Occupy is my ideology'; 'We are looking forward beyond separatist ideologies. This is the 21st century.'

The questioning of reason, the rejection of some of the core values of modern industrial capitalist society, and the will to form alternative small communities organized around bonding formed via emotions and moral grievances, is why I have characterized some forms of modern activism, and specifically protest camps, as 'lived tribalism'. Yet, there is another field of modern life where one can spot tendencies rooted in some of the ideas that were popular in the left of the 1960s and the 1970s. This time, though, the protagonists are not wearing sandals and colourful clothes, they don't live in tents, and they don't use compost toilets, like the activists in Occupy and the Climate Camps. They wear suits, and they can be found in air-conditioned offices in institutions such as universities and even in the business world, and they are related to what Cobley (2018) described as 'the diversity system'.

...and institutionalized tribalism

The importance that the left attributes to the pursuit of diversity, specifically when it comes to diversity in terms of gender, race, and sexual orientation, can be better understood in parallel to two other prevalent notions in today's public discourse: inter-sectionality and multiculturalism. By understanding these terms, their common denominator will become clear. What is meant by diversity is the ambition for an equitable representation of different groups. Multiculturalism is about the acceptance and also the granting of a moral sanction to different cultures, in order for their members to have more opportunities to fit into a diverse society and gain recognition and self-esteem. Intersectionality sees oppression as operating simultaneously in various axes of different identities (Chua, 2018, p. 183); an example would be a black lesbian woman, who is seen as more oppressed than a white heterosexual woman. Thus, intersectionality fits well within the system of diversity and multiculturalism, as it points towards which group has priority in getting a preferential treatment regarding its status.

It becomes clear what is common in diversity, multiculturalism, and intersectionality. It is not primarily about respecting every individual irrespective of race or gender and ensuring their rights are protected. The notion of 'colour-blindness' has not only fallen out of fashion within large parts of the left, but it is also considered by many an early sign of a racist mindset (see chapter 6). Diversity, multiculturalism, and intersectionality place at the centre of their analysis *the group*, and see individuals as merely avatars for the group identity they are carrying. This is a tribal mindset, which is why I will refer to the diversity system as institutionalized tribalism.

A good analysis of diversity as a system, where the premises of multiculturalism and intersectionality are embedded, comes from Ben Cobley in a book with the fitting name *The Tribe* (2018). There, he explained how diversity has become central not only in the narrative of the left in the UK, but also in its practice. Even more, he explained diversity as an institutionalized wide bureaucratic mechanism, which guarantees control and power to those involved in its administration. To use the language of Foucault, I will claim that diversity has become a 'discourse of power': a system of language and practices that has elevated itself to an unquestionable truth, has become institutionalized from the public sector to big businesses, and produces hierarchies and relations of control.

Cobley (2018) described the main steps through which this system of diversity has established itself:

- Group identity has become the most important determinant of how one's place in the world is viewed. This identity is static and thus risks stripping its subjects from agency.
- The various identities create hierarchies of groups that need to be 'recognized' and 'represented'.
- The static image of identity, together with the presumed vulnerability of the various groups, creates a need for those who will 'protect' but also administer this hierarchical system.

As Cobley explains, 'the progressive liberal left fits into the system of diversity by presiding over it, overseeing formal and informal favouritism towards the favoured fixed identity groups in the system' (2018, p. 48). The system creates the need for the production of its ideological administrators; the apparatchiks who guarantee its perpetuation, its smooth reproduction, and the disciplining of those who challenge it: diversity teams, equity and inclusion experts, academics doing research on relevant fields, HR officers, etc.

This system is convenient for our era, in which ideological affiliations and alternative political visions have been weakened. It might be difficult to come up with an alternative economic system or a different model of production, but it is much easier to determine oneself as the protector of 'vulnerable' or 'marginalized' groups. This can have as an effect the perpetual widening of the category of vulnerability. Thus, today we find ourselves in the peculiar position that the 'marginalized' are a vast majority of the population: women, non-heterosexual individuals, people of colour, religious people beyond the Judeo-Christian faith, working-class people, children and young adults, the older generation, people with disabilities, and people struggling with mental health issues. As it often happens with tribalism, these various groups are also considered to be viewing the world through their own prism. This explains the peculiar spectacle that Cobley notices of the Labour Party providing different manifestos for different groups, such as a women's manifesto, an LGBT manifesto, and a BAME (Black, Asian, and Minority Ethnic) manifesto (2018, p. 164).

The above remarks do not indicate that the majority of people who advocate diversity or intersectionality, or even the 'administrators' of the diversity system in universities and other sectors, are power-lusters who use vulnerable people (actual or imagined) to promote their ends. If one creates a mix with a tribalist view of the world and a 'victimhood culture' (Campbell and Manning, 2018) that sees individuals as unable to cope, then the rise of a system that needs to navigate and mitigate the vulnerability of the different groups is not only predictable, but also presents itself as a perceived necessity to those who understand society in such terms.

This is where this chapter comes full circle. I began by attempting to spot the premises in the Marxian system that can indicate some of its shortcomings. They include the belief that history is not shaped by individuals that are capable of rational thinking, but is subject to powers that are often beyond their reach. Related to this is the idea that if history is not shaped by individuals, then the starting point that explains the direction of the world is the struggle between different groups. The expected materialization of these premises is political collectivism, where the individual is subdued to the demands and the historic destiny of the group.

We also saw how in the 1960s the left went through a transformation. The certainty about the historical progression led by the universalist aspirations of Marxism experienced a setback. Since revolution and full-blown economic and political transformation was unrealistic for the foreseeable future, or perhaps even undesirable, the focus was on changes in the here and now, and often within one's personal life. Compared to the horrors of Stalinism and Maoism, this can be seen as a step forward. There is also a case to be made that the culture and the values around the New Left have created a more diverse and tolerant society. Yet, the philosophical shortcomings of the New Left would have consequences. The questioning of what its scholars called 'instrumental reason' has further undermined the belief in the capacity of individuals to deal with challenges, shape the world around them based on their values, and build a better future.

What has remained common in the old left's collectivism and the New Left's identity politics and its analysis of society as intersections of power is that both result in what I describe as 'epistemological tribalism': seeing the world through the prism of groups. In the case of the old left, there was a group with universalist aspirations (the working class), whereas post-1960s, the groups are multiple, with vague and fluctuating borders between them. Yet, in both cases the individual does not enjoy either existential or epistemological primacy.

Many will attribute the prevalence of this worldview to the dominance of the New Left in education and the 'culture industry'. While this might be true up to a point, there is another reason why tribalism is such a dominant worldview, and it's the fact that it is shared by large parts of the supposed rival of the left: the right.

...and the right

Despite leaving behind the left some years ago, I have never considered myself right-wing. Yet, in the weird times we are living in, it has often been easier for me to have intellectually interesting discussions with people closer to what one would consider 'the right' or the wider conservative, classical liberal, and libertarian milieu, rather than with people on the left. I expected that the majority of people supporting more individual autonomy, more freedom of speech, and more abundance for everyone would be on the left; yet, I found more of them on the right. Have the political poles been reversed? There might be an element of truth to that, but there is also a simpler explanation: the right is such a wide notion that it is difficult to utilize it as an umbrella term to understand one single movement with some discernible historical role.

Throughout its history, parts of the right were actually a movement *in reaction* to something. Early conservatives were against some of the ideas of the Enlightenment and of classical liberalism (though, mysteriously, classical liberals today are seen as being 'right-wing'), royalists were against the French revolution, early 20th-century fascism rose as a reaction mainly to communism, the American New Right rose as a reaction to the New Left, and so on. Thus, one could claim without having bad intentions that the adjective 'reactionary' is quite descriptive of the history of parts of the right. But also, within what most people understand as the right, one can find many good ideas that have pushed forward our understanding of the world and the battle for a rights-respecting society: from insightful, though today forgotten, sociologists, such as Robert Nisbet, to bright political philosophers like Robert Nozick, to great economists like Ludwig von Mises and Friedrich von Hayek, to inspiring novelists and philosophers like Ayn Rand. Interestingly, and I would say unfortunately, the influence of such figures on the political right and on mainstream conservatism has been, at best, marginal and at the level of lip-service, but mostly non-existent.

In this chapter, I will examine the 'genealogy' of some right-wing trends. This will not be a history of the right in general, but of the parts of it that shed some light to the phenomena within the scope of the book. Thus, I will do two things: (a) go back in time and see where some rightist ideas and values come from; (b) examine the post-WW2 history of the American right, in order to understand how we got to the modern culture wars and to Donald Trump's tenure in the White House.

A revolt against reason and the individual

A couple of centuries ago, the western world was experiencing two revolutions. On the one hand, the ideas of liberalism and the Enlightenment were shaking the intellectual consensus that stood for ages. Some radical thinkers like John Locke saw people as ends in themselves, capable of reason, and able to achieve virtue by 'non-heroic' means like trade and industriousness. At the same time, in France the masses of the many were appearing at the political forefront, and in that process the status quo in Europe was trembling. Thus, a starting point in our intellectual trip can be the royalists, and the representatives of the church and the aristocracy in the post-1789 Revolution national assembly in France. They used to sit towards the right part of the hall, and thus the term 'right' had its first ever use. Soon, throughout Europe there would be an intellectual and political movement opposing the new revolutionary ideas both in the intellectual realm and in politics.

An example is the philosopher and statesman Edmund Burke, who lived and wrote in the 18th century. He is considered one of the most prominent figures in the history of conservatism, and has influenced the 20th-century right in the US and the UK. Yet, one finds in Burke also elements of future reactionary right-wing movements: an uneasiness with rationality, and a reliance on the authority of tradition. After all, a society based on individual autonomy guided by reason means that elements such as custom, hierarchy, and identity need to take a back seat (McManus, 2017). Another philosopher of that time who was inspired by the same worries was Joseph de Maistre. He also saw a society where morality and values that are guided by dry and objective reason was unfulfilling, and called for a reappreciation of the traditional hierarchies of authority and religion (McManus, 2018). The dichotomies between tradition and progress, reason and faith, and the individual and the community would be troubling conservatives for centuries to come, and up to this day.

The answer to the retreat of traditional society was expressed in emotionalist terms and a longing for an idealized past, driven by a sense of loss and decay. An example here is the 19th-century Scottish writer and philosopher Thomas Carlyle. His view of life can be captured in his famous motto that 'the History of the world is but the biography of great men' (2015, p. 17). For Carlyle, with the advancement of the Enlightenment and of bourgeois society, the moral order of centuries was crumbling. The spontaneous order of the market, that his compatriots Adam Smith and Adam Ferguson were celebrating, made history uncontrollable and unpredictable. The great men of the sword were overshadowed by the merchant, the banker, and the man (or, God forbid, the woman) of letters. For Carlyle, these were troubling developments. 'In his view, some were meant to rule and others to follow. Society must be organized hierarchically lest his ideal of greatness would never again be realized' (Tucker, 2017 p. 142). Carlyle was also uncomfortable with the world of rationality and of the primacy of empirical reality. What he considered as the greatest privilege of the great men of history was their connection to the 'Unseen World', or the 'No-World', the transcendent universe of the Good and the eternal. In his eyes, too much preoccupation with the world of experience is less important, as it is merely an appearance, and not the real thing (Carlyle, 2015, p. 20).

At the same time, the Romantic movement gained ground in Germany. It wanted to mitigate the effects of modernity by putting forward the idea of the people — 'volk' — and of the land as a sacred point of reference. According to this worldview, culture is not related to the productivity and imagination of the individual mind, but to the spirit of *the people*. Furedi (2017) saw as the main characteristic of Romanticism and of other reactionary movements a distinct view of the world, based on the group, which he called 'epistemological separatism'. This tribal mindset was the counter-current to the celebration of the rational individual of the Enlightenment, and was the driving force of a growing nationalism. Thus, we can understand the focus of future conservative and traditionalist movements on identity: it is the one element that can remain stable and provide links to one's roots in an ever-changing and uncontrollable world.

The early 20th-century reactionary right and fascism

The urge for control and the revolt against the unpredictability of freedom that grew during the 19th century had its counterpart in an even nastier expression of collectivism: racism. At the beginning of the 20th century, racism was beyond ideologies and had acquired the status of science. Thus, it gave particular fuel to those obsessed with eugenics and the optimal biological 'central planning' aiming at a 'nobler' society. Eugenics played a role in public policy not only of totalitarian states, but also in the Progressive Era in the USA (Tucker, 2017). The scientific status that racial theories of supremacy enjoyed in the early 20th century also made easier the initial legitimization of fascism and Nazism in the eyes of many in polite society.

To understand the rise of Nazism and fascism, we also need to talk about the role that anti-communism played in their development. Though it could be argued that different forms of collectivism had similarities in their mindset, in politics they had many reasons to be lethal enemies. Communism was, in theory, about doing away with tradition, promoting universal suffrage, internationalism, militant secularism, and the withering away of the state. For traditionalists and the proponents of the old order, such a view was an existential threat. The fervent anti-communism of the fascist right is another reason why it enjoyed legitimacy in higher circles of many societies where tradition, the old aristocracy, and the church were powerful (Payne, 1995). The best example of this tension between the 'old' and the 'traditional' against the 'new' and the 'radical' was the bloody civil war in Spain from 1936 to 1939. On the one side were the democratic left, the anarchists, the Trotskyists, and the Stalinists (with their inner tensions and the eventual liquidation of most fractions by the Stalinists), against the royalists, the fascists, the old feudal elites, and the church (Beevor, 2006).

Trying to figure out what is at the centre of the Nazis' mindset, we fill find epistemological tribalism. The political theorist Carl Schmitt was an example of this tendency, and here is a character-istic example of it: 'An alien may be as critical as he wants to be... he may be intelligent in his endeavour, he may read books and write them, but he thinks and understands things differently because he belongs to a different kind, and he remains within the existential conditions of his own kind in every decisive thought' (quoted in Peikoff, 1993, pp. 64–65). Interestingly, this originally reactionary and conservative view, i.e. that people based on their identity view the world differently, would become a progressive creed some decades later, as I elaborate in different chapters of this book.

An intellectual who is an embodiment of the worldview around reactionary anti-modernist movements was the Italian Julius Evola (1898–1974). His influence on pre-WW2 reactionary thought, but also on the various later neofascist and neo-

reactionary movements in Europe, makes him particularly interesting for the scope of this work.

The first thing to notice about Evola is his rejection of the idea
that there is one objective material reality; a theme, as we have
seen, common among the opponents of modernity. Evola had
experimented with various forms of mysticism, from Buddhism,
Taoism, and other forms of eastern spirituality, to Dadaism and
alchemy. He used the term 'reality' in quotation marks, while he
considered the 'universal', which is the mystic and the divine
(1995, p. 25), as its opposite. Thus, there are two dimensions in the
world. How can common mortals reach the magic world of
universality? Agreeing with Carlyle, he saw this as the mission of
the great men, who operate as a bridge, as a path, between the
seen and the unseen. Building on the steps of other reactionaries,
Evola saw the bourgeois world as stripped of opportunities and
structures for these great men to thrive and guide the rest to glory
(Evola, 2003). Rationality and instrumental reason strip the world
of its magic. Thus, like most traditionalists, Evola was whole-
heartedly opposed to capitalism.

But his stronger vitriol was reserved for the ideas of individualism and humanism. The rational mind and the autonomous
individual render the mystical world of the unseen obsolete and
parochial. When reason becomes the mode of operation, according to Evola, the eternal and that which is really valuable is lost
(1995, p. 319). Evola was not an advocate of progress either, as he
saw it merely as a rationalization for liberals and progressive
humanists to celebrate the glorification of the bourgeois humankind (idem, p. 333).

Evola's epistemological subjectivism helped him escape the
issue of whether he was a Nazi-like racist. No, he would say, as he
did not take a merely biological take on racism; one's soul should
also be taken into consideration. Thus, someone belonging to an
'inferior race' could self-identify with a superior race, if his soul
was in tune with that superior race (idem, p. 167). In this way,
Evola prefigured many discussions of the 21st century about the

social construction of biological categories. Yet, his racism became overt when he talked about 'the decline of superior races' (idem). The biggest risk he saw was overpopulation, and the quantitative expansion of 'undesirable' people. In his own words: 'one can say that the superior Western races have been agonizing for centuries and that the increasing growth in world population has the same meaning as the swarming of worms on a decomposing organism or as the spreading of cancerous cells' (idem). Interestingly, such language that sees people as a plague on the planet is also used today by respectable commentators and environmentalists, like Sir David Attenborough (Gray, 2013); the difference is that today *all* of us are seen as a cancer on earth, and not only the 'inferior races'.

Post-World War II reactionary thought: identity vs. the modern world

After the Second World War, and with the crimes of Nazism casting a heavy shadow, Evola concentrated more on his socio-cultural critique. He tried to find how great men can live and flourish in a society stripped of opportunities to pursue glory, virtue, the sacred, and the eternal. It is interesting to notice that his work, and especially his book *Ride the Tiger: A Survival Manual for the Aristocrats of the Soul* (2003), reads like a reactionary *alter ego* of the Frankfurt School's criticism of modern capitalism. Evola was surprised to find that the sense of life of the marginal counter-cultural artistic movements with which he flirted in the pre-War era had now taken centre stage in the confused zeitgeist of the 1960s. He had read many of the thinkers of the New Left, and he sometimes quoted them when criticizing the same things they found problematic: alienation, the dry rationality of the technol-ogical world, the commodification of interpersonal and romantic relationships, and even music and jazz. This is neither to say that there is a proto-fascist element in New Left scholars like Marcuse, nor that Evola rediscovered himself as a leftist. It is to say, though, that the verdict of the reactionary right and of the New Left on who is to blame for our apparently unfulfilling lives is the same: capitalism, liberalism, and the bourgeois morality.

To describe the inner state of the great men in such non-heroic times, Evola quoted Herman Hesse's anti-hero from his novel *Steppenwolf:* 'I'd rather feel burned by a diabolic pain than to live in these sanely temperate surroundings. A wild desire flares up in me for intense emotions, sensations, a rage against the whole toneless, flat, normal, sterilized life, and a wish to destroy something—perhaps a warehouse, a cathedral, or myself—and to commit outrageous follies' (cited in Evola, 2003, p. 25). Apparently, this feeling still today hits a nerve among right- and left-wing anti-capitalists. One of the films that has left a cultural legacy in recent decades is *Fight Club,* based on the book by Chuck Palahniuk (2006); a point of reference among both the anti-consumerist radical left of the anti-globalization movement and later of the neo-reactionary right. The anti-hero of *Fight Club* is the mysterious Tyler Durden, leading a group of disillusioned and alienated men who rediscover themselves through violence and subversive terror. The famous monologue of Tyler Durden in the movie reflects Evola's despair for what he sees as the emptiness of the bourgeois world:

'God damn it, an entire generation pumping gas, waiting tables; slaves with white collars. Advertising has us chasing cars and clothes, working jobs we hate so we can buy shit we don't need. We're the middle children of history, men. No purpose or place. We have no Great War. No Great Depression. Our Great War is a spiritual war... our Great Depression is our lives. We've all been raised on television to believe that one day we'd all be millionaires, and movie gods, and rock stars. But we won't. And we're slowly learning that fact. And we're very, very pissed off.'

Taking a wider overview on the modern reactionary right, we see
that the delegitimization of Nazism and fascism after the Second
World War was of such scale that most of the parties and movements of the milieu in Europe and the USA have adopted a
different outlook, dropping the symbols of such a sinful past. It is
a reactionary ideology suited for the 21st century, as it mobilizes
on ideas that are quite prominent in popular culture: the centrality
of identity in human experience, that society is split into groups,
that consumerist capitalism is driving us towards cultural
homogenization, etc. (Sedgwick, 2019). This is where Evola comes
into play. His longing for a lost era of virtues and sacred values
provides a frame that fits many of the new far right, neo-
reactionary, traditionalist, and self-described identitarian movements, to which he has been a central influence. Understanding
these movements is crucial, as they provided the inspiration for
the rise of the so-called alt-right in the USA, which we will meet in
chapter 6.

A misunderstanding has to be avoided here. Many of the new
populist right-wing movements in Europe, such as UKIP in the
UK or Salvini's Lega Nord in Italy, have mostly focused on a
simple agenda, like an opposition to immigration and multiculturalism, or to the further integration of the European Union,
or to 'globalist' internationalism, and it is unclear whether they
have a precise ideological background. Thus, we need to
distinguish phenomena of populist 'revolts' like Brexit, which are
still within the parameters of liberal democracy, from the subversive radical ideas of the ideological non-mainstream right that
we will now examine.

A movement with a clear ideological agenda and under
Evola's influence is the *Nouvelle Droitte* (New Right) in France, one
of the first reactionary networks that tried to cut ties with the old-
style far right and create a new profile. *Nouvelle Droitte* never
acquired notable significance as a political movement within
France; yet, its ideas have influenced the international identitarian
movement in Europe and the USA. *Nouvelle Droitte*'s leader is

Alain de Benoist: an intellectual of an eclectic taste, influenced not only by figures such as Evola, but also by Antonio Gramsci, Guy Debord, and others of the New Left. As an identitarian, he emphasizes the importance of cultural ties related to one's group. He distances himself and his movement from racism though, and celebrates the idea of ethnopluralism, where different cultures coexist peacefully, though not close to each other. De Benoist is a fervent opponent of free market capitalism and globalization, and is attracted to mysticism and paganism (Camus, 2019).

It is interesting to observe the intellectual interaction between the New Left and the New Right. One of the strongest identitarian groups in Europe has been Generation Identity in France. Its manifesto is subtitled 'A Declaration of War Against the '68ers' (Willinger, 2013). French identitarians see today's culture in peril, and they blame this on the generation of their fathers who uncritically accepted the ideas of the 1960s' counter-culture and of the New Left. The opening lines of the manifesto of Generation Identity, written in prosaic form, bring in mind the opening lines of the Port Huron statement, with which the New Left introduced itself to the USA (see previous chapter):

> 'You want to know who we are? Where we come from? What moves us?
> We'll tell you.
> We are the changing times; we are the rising wind; the new generation. We are the answer to you, for we are your children.
> You've thrown us into this world, uprooted and disoriented, without telling us where to go, or where our path lies. You've destroyed every means for us to orient ourselves.
> [...]
> You've questioned and criticized everything, so we now believe in nothing and no one.' (idem, p. 16)

Often, when someone's goal in life is *not* to become their fathers, they end up resembling them in more ways than they would want to admit. Like their fathers, identitarians feel alienated in a world that makes little sense. Their cry is more an emotionalist outburst, rather than a coherent political plan. Like their fathers, they are sceptical of modernity, and they are uncomfortable with our domination over nature. As most in the reactionary right, they are anti-capitalists, and environmentalism gives them just another stick with which to beat the free market: 'we'll free our planet from the deathly grip of capitalism and create a society in which the economy serves culture, and not the reverse' (idem, p. 96). Like their fathers, and like the relativism present in the intellectual mainstream of recent decades, they proudly declare that 'we go through life without being certain of anything, because we don't want to be certain of anything' (idem, p. 22).

There are more movements on the continent influenced by the New Right and identitarianism, such as in the Scandinavian countries and Eastern Europe. A prominent anti-liberal voice is Russian nationalist Alexander Dugin, who envisions a geo-political domination of traditionalist ideas through the project of 'Eurasianism', with Russia at its leadership, opposing Anglo-Saxon liberalism (Laruelle, 2019). Interestingly, Dugin has strong links with white nationalists and identitarians in the USA.

The reader might be surprised to see movements on the right openly calling themselves identitarians. After all, a central theme of the culture wars today is people on the right revolting against the identity politics of the left. But for the collectivistic reactionary right, it could not be any other way. It is the *group* that gives someone identity and orientation in the world. National Socialism is an example of such a worldview. For the Nazi intellectual Alfred Rosenberg, 'right is that which Aryan people find right; wrong is what they reject' (quoted in Peikoff, 1983, p. 88). It is not for a Jew, a Slav, or someone from a different group to judge the decisions of an Aryan, as the world is not perceived by the individual mind, but by the collective spirit of the group. Thus, identitarianism and epistemological and political tribalism are closely interlinked.

At the end of this section, I will sum up the main themes that are present in the narrative of the identitarian and reactionary right today:

- Modernity and industrial society have taken away the sense of community and tradition. Instrumental reason focuses on the ephemeral and the mundane, at the expense of the sacred.
- Unrestrained capitalism is alienating and corrosive for the character of an individual and of a nation.
- We are estranged from the environment and from a nature that we are exploiting for materialistic ends.
- Globalization and transnational institutions are just means towards the spread of neoliberal capitalism.
- Individual rights is a limiting notion, as it does not take into account the rights of groups.
- Social cohesion is built around identity.

It is interesting that, by changing only a few words, this could also be seen as the worldview of many on the left. This does not mean that the right and the left are the same. It means, though, that they are reactions to similar phenomena: the change brought about by the ideas of the Enlightenment, the appearance of the individual as a bearer of rights to the forefront of history, political liberalism, capitalism, and the Industrial Revolution and the world it created. At the same time, though, the right and the left continue to develop as reactions to each other. Understanding this can shed some light to our next case study: the post-WW2 American right.

The American right from the 1940s to Buckley

The USA is a peculiar case for someone interested in the tradition of the right, as historically American conservatism has had some different characteristics from the European right. It is built more on the tradition of individual rights and freedom, rather than on a collectivist identification to a group. Irrespective of what were the actual motives of Abraham Lincoln, the historical fact is that slaves were liberated by a Republican president. Also, for decades in the 20th century, racism and groups like the KKK were successfully infiltrating the progressive Democratic Party (McVeigh, 2001). Thus, the historical division between left and right is of limited help in understanding reactionary conservatism in the US. But since this book is mostly about examining the context of the culture wars and the identity politics of today, I will avoid a long historical overview; I will instead begin my analysis of the American right from the aftermath of World War II.

After WW2, the Republican Party (also known as GOP — the Grand Old Party) found itself in a complex situation. Despite the rhetoric about a worldwide clash between capitalism and communism, expressed at home with McCarthy's campaign and abroad with the war in Korea, the USA was no longer a predominantly *laissez faire* country. After the Progressive Era in the early 20th century and the New Deal in the 1930s, the state played a very active role in managing the direction of the economy. This was accepted by large sections of the Republican establishment. For example, the Republican administration of Eisenhower (1953–1961) not only did not challenge New Deal programmes, but actually expanded them in some areas such as social security (Harris, 1997). Yet, within the wider milieu of the American right there was already from the 1930s a strong intellectual pole that was uncompromisingly opposed to the New Deal, expressed by thinkers such as Ayn Rand, Henry Hazlitt, and Leonard Reed (Doherty, 2007). This dichotomy between the free market and the expansion of state power would be a constant dilemma from which Republicans have never really escaped.

In an essay with the telling title 'Conservatism: An Obituary', Ayn Rand (1967) presented the intellectual conundrum in which conservatives found themselves: a consistent defence of capitalism would drive them towards an ethical territory in which they'd feel quite uncomfortable. A championing of individualism and of the pursuit of wealth in this life can be proven to be incompatible with the ethics of Christianity. Thus, according to Rand, conservatives had to avoid such a strong moral defence of capitalism. Instead, they adopted a middle-of-the-road approach, which celebrated not so much capitalism, but the 'American way of life'; a notion quite vague and open to various interpretations.

Yet, this meant that conservativism became a political movement whose strongest 'selling point' would be social and cultural issues. This is a key moment for the thesis of this book. It provides an insight into why later the culture wars would become the privileged terrain where the American right would establish its own identity and entrench its troops. As was also the case with the left, a focus on the field of culture and lifestyle is often a sign that the fields of ideology and of a clear political programme are exhausted. Thus, the culture wars are a necessary feature, rather than a bug, in today's politics. Their roots can be found in both the left and the right becoming less confident about their philosophical and political principles, and thus finding existential conformity in smaller issues, that gained the significance of symbolic battles.

Coming back to the history of the American right, in 1964 the presidential candidate for the Republican Party was Barry Goldwater. He ended up losing to Lyndon Johnson by a landslide, but his campaign is still noteworthy. For a change, it was a Republican campaign that was highly ideological, economically liberal, promising to attack the New Deal consensus, and highly aggressive against communism on grounds of ideas and values. Berlet and Lyons (2000) characterize this campaign as a high point of what they call the old right. At the same time, however, it was its twilight. Post-Goldwater, the American right would change. The process was already underway. The architect of a new kind of conservatism was not a career politician, but a talented, witty, and frustrating—mostly, but not exclusively, for those on the other side—journalist: William F. Buckley, the editor of the flagship conservative publication *National Review* and host of the public affairs show *Firing Line*.

Buckley adjusted Burke's conservatism to the reality of the 1960s (Horwitz, 2013, pp. 36–37). There would be adherence to *some* ideas, to *some* degree, but on a flexible level. Ideas and values such as individual liberty and the free market had to be balanced with American tradition, religious sensitivities, and the needs of the United States' expansive role in the world and the crusade against communism. It is not a coincidence that one of the first people that Buckley tried to intellectually isolate from this new brand of conservatism was Ayn Rand, the atheist and uncompromising advocate of individualism and *laissez faire* capitalism. Rand was seen as an 'ideologue', and ideologues were not included in Buckley's vision of a pragmatic conservatism (Biddle, 2018). Buckley also distinguished his brand of conservatism from what today we'd call right-wing populism. In the 1960s, the main expression of such populism was the John Birch Society, a group with a conspiratorial anti-elitist outlook, that expressed, though, a tradition of American isolationism (Berlet and Lyons, 2000, pp. 177–181). Another fringe element of the wider right-wing milieu that was excommunicated by Buckley was the free market libertarians (some of them would later become known as 'anarcho-capitalists'), a network having at its centre the writer and scholar of the Austrian School of Economics Murray Rothbard (Malice, 2019). Essentially, the Birchians, Rothbard, and Rand had very little, if anything, in common. But, in the eyes of Buckley, they were all 'extremists'. Thus, by denouncing them all indiscriminately, he made a statement about the type of pragmatic and ideologically flexible movement he wanted. However, let us keep the right-wing populists and the libertarians in mind: after some decades they would seek their revenge from Buckley's brand of conservatism, as we will see later in this chapter.

The New Right and religion

A major characteristic of this new brand of conservatism that Buckley was building, and which contributed to the rise of what became known as the New Right (not to be confused with the French New Right), would be its strong religious character. A prominent role in the New Right would be played by Christian Evangelicals: a brand of Protestants with a strong belief in the idea of personal revival through the message of the Bible—which is why so many of them refer to themselves as 'born again' Christians (Schäfer, 2011).

In December 1969, *Time* magazine ran a piece called 'The Next Decade: A Search for Goals' (cited in Rand, 1999, p. 164), where it attempted to provide an overview of what had happened in the 1960s and, most importantly, how it would affect the upcoming 1970s. At one point, it said: 'The most significant trend of the '70s may well be a religious revival... In reaction against the trend towards secularization, there may well be a sweeping revival of fundamentalism, particularly in its fervent, Pentecostal [brand of Protestantism] variety.'

This prediction was spot on. The relaxation of the austere ethics around hard work, delayed gratification, self-control, family values, etc. that was promoted by the counter-culture created a backlash from more conservative Christians, who saw religion as the counterweight to a bourgeoning decadence.

Yet, as Schäfer (2011) showed, the relationship between the counter-culture and the rise of the new Evangelicalism as a political force is more complicated. Actually, many religious activists were influenced by the forms of mobilization and the values of the counter-culture. The 1960s were about self-discovery, and this narrative is not far from the idea of being 'born again' through the message of the Bible. Actually, many people went straight from the counter-culture of the 1960s to a grassroots church in the 1970s; ergo the then-popular slogan 'getting high on Jesus' (idem, p. 11). But there is another way that the 1960s gave rise to the Christian right. As mentioned in the previous chapter, the counter-culture coincided with an intellectual atmosphere of pessimism and doom. In such an atmosphere, the Christian message of salvation and of a happy end, though maybe in an afterlife, was appealing (idem, p. 97).

By the 1970s there was a new critical mass of Evangelical Christian voters who would offer loyal support to the Republican Party. There were also many voters from the South who already from the 1960s were abandoning the Democratic Party, uncomfortable with the new inter-racial reality it supported following the civil rights campaign. During the 1970s, there was an attempt within the American right to adapt the Christian message with support (or toleration) for the free market—to the limited and nominal extent to which the GOP itself supported it. The story was that the free enterprise system encourages virtuous behaviour, such as hard work and delayed gratification, whereas a growing welfare state encourages anti-Christian attitudes, such as single-parent families. Various Christian groups that were campaigning on single issues, such as abortion or prayer at schools, were coming under the umbrella of bigger networks that were orbiting around the GOP (Horwitz, 2013, pp. 95–96). Thus, Republicans tried to build the narrative of a 'moral majority' that was silent, as opposed to the loud progressive secular New Left, but which represented 'real' hard-working Americans. Adding to the mix strong anti-communism, enhanced with the religious tone of a crusade against evil, one can see how around the 1970s Evangelicals and Republicans were becoming a good fit.

It has to be mentioned, though, that not everything happening during the 1970s in the American right revolved around the religious revival. From Nixon's victory in 1968 and throughout the 1970s, politically the American right had achieved some victories, such as a relative rolling-back of some regulations (though usually accompanied with the introduction of others). Even the administration of a Democrat like Carter in 1976 followed a relatively pro-market policy (Anderson, 2000). Some *laissez faire* economists who had been around for decades were now becoming more prominent, such as Friedrich von Hayek and Milton Friedman. A number of free market people, some of them related via loose networks such as the Mont Pelerin Society, tried to promote their ideas in academia or through think tanks, and hopefully influence policy-making (Turner, 2011). Yet, as Friedman would often mention in his interviews, he wished he had the influence that his opponents thought he had.

Another network of people that became an influence towards the construction of a new brand of conservatism during the 1970s were the so-called neo-conservatives (also known as 'neo-cons'). Their story and ideological journey towards the GOP is quite different from the Evangelicals (Horwitz, 2013). The first guard of neo-cons were mostly upper middle class white-collar liberal (in the way the term is understood in the US) New York Jews. They were fervent anti-communists, as some of them were Trotskyists (and, thus, anti-Stalinists and anti-Soviet Union) in their youth, and many were children of immigrants from communist countries. Yet, they were worried that the assault by the New Left on the values and institutions of the USA were weakening it in its war against the Soviet bloc. Thus, these disillusioned liberals started looking for a new message and a new ideological home. They started gravitating towards ideas that would bridge freedom, individual responsibility, and a strong community, as expressed by intellectuals that were pivotal in American Republicanism, such as Alexis de Tocqueville (idem, p. 116). Yet, compared to other conservatives, neo-cons were more supportive of the welfare state, and not strong believers in *laissez faire* capitalism. Eventually, they would feel comfortable joining forces with the Christian right, as they respected the latter's commitment to personal responsibility and traditional American values. Their biggest influence in the New Right would be their militant approach to foreign policy and of the special role that the US had to play in global affairs.

From Reagan to the Tea Party

There were various factors that during the 1970s led to the rise of a New Right that was ready to fight back not only against the political and socio-cultural influence of progressivism and of the New Left, but also against a sense of decadence and corruption in the country. The main ones were (Schaffer, 2011; Horwitz, 2013):

- The threat to the American way of life and traditional values posed by the New Left, the counter-culture, and sexual liberation.
- The *Row vs. Wade* landmark decision of the US Supreme Court in 1973, which declared the banning of abortion unconstitutional.
- The humiliating defeat in Vietnam, together with other foreign policy embarrassments such as the hostage situation of 52 American diplomats in Homeini's Iran for more than a year in 1979, which injured the image of the superpower.
- The Watergate scandal, which led to the resignation of President Nixon in 1974.
- The economic hardships triggered mostly by the 1973 oil crisis, and the idea that the Keynesian consensus of the post-World War II period was reaching an end.

The candidacy of a Republican like Ronald Reagan in 1979 seemed to ride the momentum of a whole decade in the conservative milieu, which gave him an easy victory in the 1980 elections. He spoke the language of individual freedom and rhetorically attacked the idea of big government. He was supported by a large grassroots network of Evangelical Christians who saw him as the guy who would finally fight back in the culture wars. He was tough on foreign policy, he called the Soviet Union an 'evil empire', and put forward a policy of arms race that would eventually exhaust the already stagnant Soviet economy. William Buckley could finally smile. His vision about a vibrant and yet pragmatist conservatism would materialize. Reagan also won the

1984 elections, and in the mind of most conservatives is considered the best modern US president (Kilgore, 2018).

During the same time, the UK had a Prime Minister with similar ideas and rhetoric: Margaret Thatcher. The fact that she and Reagan constituted such a dynamic political power-couple makes the 1980s an era of a 'conservative revolution' in the eyes of many people. Yet, Reagan was not really the firebrand that many expected him to be before his election. His administration did not focus much on social policy issues, and did not challenge the legalization of abortion, nor did he push for what the Christian right would consider small symbolic victories, such as the reinstitution of school prayer (Berlet and Lyons, 2000, pp. 242–243). Nor was Reagan an uncompromising defender of *laissez faire* capitalism. He lowered taxes and his Oval Office looked favourably upon ideas of free market economists like the monetarists of the Chicago School and Milton Friedman, but Reagan actually increased federal expenditure, including in areas such as education and health; predictably, there was also a rise in national debt and in the budget deficit (Carlton, 2018).

After the end of the Cold War, and lacking a leader with the charm of Reagan, the right in the US was in search of a new narrative. George H.W. Bush won the elections in 1988, and he witnessed the collapse of the Eastern Bloc and of the USSR. He was a pragmatist, but not as charismatic as his predecessor. Thus, in 1992, he found himself challenged in the GOP primaries by a figure unlike the party insiders: the paleoconservative Pat Buchanan. We discussed earlier how Buckley had already 'expelled' right-wing populists from the GOP since the 1960s. Buchanan, for whom the term populist would not be an insult, came with a quite different agenda from the neo-conservatives and the pragmatists: economic nationalism, isolationism, and emphasis on traditional values are at the core of paleoconservatism (Malice, 2019). Buchanan will be remembered for officially launching the conservative counter-attack in the culture wars at the most official of occasions: during the 1992 Republican Convention in Houston.

In what is now remembered as 'the culture war speech', and with an eye on the upcoming elections against the Democrats' duo of Bill Clinton and Al Gore, Buchanan used a language and a narrative that was an all-out assault against progressive America. He characterized the Democratic Convention as the 'greatest single exhibition of cross-dressing in American political history', where '20,000 radicals and liberals came dressed up as moderates and centrists'. He quoted an LGBT activist saying that Clinton and Al Gore are 'the most pro-lesbian and pro-gay ticket in history' (which apparently for Buchanan was not something to be celebrated for a potential US President), and he accused Hillary Clinton of 'radical feminism'. In the most famous line of his speech, he said: 'This election is about much more than who gets what. It is about who we are. It is about what we believe. It is about what we stand for as Americans... It is a cultural war, as critical to the kind of nation we will one day be as was the Cold War itself' (Buchanan, 1992).

Buchanan failed to win the Republican nomination in 1992 or in 1996, and since then has never been at the political forefront. Yet, at the turn of the century he wrote a book that, according to the historiographer of the movement Michael Malice, would provide the worldview for the new anti-establishment right of the 21st century (2019, loc. 2564). The book had the telling title *The Death of the West: How Dying Populations and Immigrant Invasions Imperil Our Culture and Civilization* (Buchanan, 2002). There, Buchanan made an argument that since then has become a rallying cry for many in the periphery of the Trumpian right and among white nationalists: that *a nation lives and dies by its demographics*. By importing large amounts of immigrants, the argument says, the US will lose its unique character. And, as if this is not bad enough, its ability to resist will be lowered by the impact that the cultural dominance of the New Left has had on young people. In retrospect, many of the predictions of the book can be seen as exaggerated. Yet, Buchanan's ideas are no longer a fringe part of American conservatism. In 2015, conservative commentator (and one of the early and most fervent supporters of Trump's candidacy in the GOP primaries) Ann Coulter wrote a book along similar lines, with the equally telling title *¡Adios, America!: The Left's Plan to Turn Our Country Into a Third World Hellhole* (2015). Immigration is seen by Coulter as a weapon in the hands of the left to alter the character of the US and to win prospective voters. The argument was similar to the one by Buchanan; the main difference is that Coulter's narrative was now shared by a future US President: Donald Trump.

Returning to the early 2000s, if one axis of Buchanan's paleo-conservative narrative was his traditional values and his belief that they were mostly compatible with a predominantly white and Christian America, his other big message had to do with the claim that the US had over-expanded on the world scene and had to follow a more isolationist policy. This view was also shared by many libertarians, especially so-called 'paleolibertarians', of the network around the Mises Institute that preached the late Murray Rothbard's anarcho-capitalist message. Despite their disagreement on economics, paleoconservatives and paleolibertarians shared the populist anti-elitist sentiment and a disdain for the neo-conservative establishment (Malice, 2019). This disdain only grew bigger due to the foreign policy followed by George W. Bush, and especially after the invasion of Iraq in 2003.

Towards the end of the second Bush administration, the clouds of the financial crisis were looming. For paleolibertarians, this proved the destructive role of central banking and of the state's intervention in the economy, whereas paleoconservatives pointed at the corrupting effect of metropolitan elites. Thus, the ground was fertile for a revolt against mainstream conservatism, which was seen by many at the grassroots level as anaemic and boring, constantly capitulating to the cultural influence of the left, engaging in destructive wars, and mismanaging the economy. This zeitgeist of uneasiness with the mainstream gatekeepers of the GOP was expressed by the campaign of Congressman Ron Paul for the nomination of the party in 2008 (Doherty, 2012).

Paul, who was close to paleolibertarianism, had been an outsider of American conservatism for years, with a long congressional career and a presidential campaign with the Libertarian Party in 1988. The incident that really put him in the spotlight was his altercation in a Republican Presidential debate with the then front-runner, former New York mayor Rudi Giuliani on 15 May 2007. For Ron Paul fans, it is referred to as 'the Giuliani moment'. Paul mentioned how foreign over-expansion was antithetical to the Constitution, the spirit of the Founding Fathers, and traditional conservative values. He also mentioned his 'blowback theory', according to which the 9/11 attacks were a reaction to US intervention in the Middle East. Giuliani called him back to order and asked him to withdraw his comments. But Paul did nothing of the kind and only doubled down on his message (idem). Irrespective of one's evaluation of Paul's blowback theory, this moment signified something important: that the window of allowable opinion within American conservatism was expanding. The rest of Paul's campaign only verified this, as it inspired an unprecedented grassroots enthusiasm from different walks of life: libertarians, paleoconservatives, young people with no prior engagement in politics, counter-cultural nerds with a talent for creating internet content that attempted to outweigh the other candidates' presence in mainstream media, and various people with a tendency for conspiratorial, anti-elitist, and populist ideas (Paul himself would appear at various times on Alex Jones' popular but conspiratorial programme).

The perceived weakness of Ron Paul's Revolution, as his campaign became known, was his lack of credentials from the gatekeepers of mainstream Republicanism, the media, and big donors. Yet, this weakness became his strength, by the wide mobilizations of his grassroots networks of supporters, using social media, road signs, leaflets, and impressive fundraising achievements (idem, p. 107). Paul did not win the nomination, but that was not his major goal. There was now a vibrant and enthusiastic network of people around the Republican Party who were outside the allowable frame of conservatism, as they were:

- opposed to the Party's establishment;
- sceptical of the central government;
- advocating decentralization (some even supporting the rights of the states to secede);
- more counter-cultural (predictably, Paul's libertarian supporters were in favour of drugs legalization);
- sceptical of established knowledge and narratives.

One of the most prominent slogans by Paul, who is an advocate of the Austrian School of Economics, was ending the Federal Reserve and highlighting the negative impact of central banks on the economy. Thus, when both the Republicans and the Democrats—both Bush and his successor in the presidency Barack Obama—bailed out the banks after the financial meltdown of 2007 and threw billions of dollars of 'helicopter money' to the economy, Paul's message was resonating even more (Woods, 2009). This time, he was not alone. A network of various conservative, paleoconservative, and libertarian groups, individuals, politicians, and media figures gave rise to the Tea Party campaign, using the symbolism of the anti-tax revolt in Boston in 1773. The movement singled out what was loosely viewed as the Washington consensus: President Obama, his bailouts, his proposals for a statist health care reform, high taxation, and excessive regulations (Horwitz, 2013). The Tea Party also managed to put pressure on mainstream conservatives in the midterm elections of 2010, electing some political outsiders, and gave momentum to Ron Paul for another vibrant and noisy (though again eventually unsuccessful) campaign for the Republican nomination in 2012.

Meanwhile, conservatives were focusing even more on the culture wars. Journalist and writer Andrew Breitbart pointed out who the real pillar of the liberal establishment was: the culture industry (Breitbart, 2012). Breitbart's most famous motto was 'politics is downstream from culture', and he was probably right. Although he died unexpectedly in 2012, a new generation of conservatives was getting the message. The battle for the soul of America was not to be won in Washington, but in lecture theatres, on social media, and on the airwaves, and it would be a long endeavour.

In retrospect, in 2007, when a quiet looking 71-year-old congressman from Texas entered the GOP primaries, there were not many signs that within a decade the face of the American right would be so different. Ron Paul was not a culture warrior, as he mostly saw himself as an educator on the impacts of big government and of the over-expansion of US's foreign policy (Doherty, 2012). But Paul had shown that there was space for outsiders in the US political scene, and there was a vast base of people not being represented by any of the two major political parties. Moving towards the 2016 elections, many people were wondering who would be the next Ron Paul to rock the boat of the GOP primaries. There were ambitious candidates with a strong ideological agenda and with credentials in the Tea Party movement, such as Rand Paul (Ron's son) and Ted Cruz. But no one foresaw the hurricane that would blast everything and everyone: Donald J. Trump.

The Trump phenomenon

It is difficult to understand such historical shifts as they happen, but Trump's election in 2016 was a politically monumental occasion for at least two reasons:

(a) As Malice is right to mention, Trump did not simply move the Overton window of allowable opinion to the right; this would take way more time, and would also require a lot of intellectual capital. Trump actually created his own Overton window (2019, loc. 1468). There were different rules applying to everyone else, and different rules applying to him. At some point during his 2016 campaign, Trump mentioned how he could shoot someone in the middle of the road and get away with it. He was right—he probably could. The more the mainstream media attacked him, the more his narrative as the outsider who would 'drain the swamp' was reinforced. Nagle characterized 2016 as the year when the mainstream media lost their hold over formal politics (2017, p. 3). Trump won while having the vast majority of media outlets against him, including parts of the Fox network, and *National Review*. This was something that was not supposed to happen.

(b) On a deeper and more long-range level, Trump's victory signifies a major break of American conservatism from the tradition that supposedly gave birth to the ideals of the movement: liberalism, *laissez faire* capitalism, and the vision of the Founding Fathers for a small state that is the servant of the individual. One could argue that mainstream Republicans were only paying lip-service to such values, and would usually compromise for a mixture of pragmatism with some traditional conservative values. But Trump won precisely by openly going against all these tenets of conservatism. He promised a protectionist anti-free trade economic policy, tariffs, and sounded like a wannabe central planner, deciding which big corporations are good and which need to be put in their place and strong-armed into doing the 'right' thing, such as moving their production back to the US.

Yet, Trump can be seen more as a symptom of his times, rather than a cause. A symptom of decades of politics devoid of clear ideological principles, and a symptom of a public sphere overwhelmed by emotionalism. More importantly, he is the symptom of a culture war that has been on a slow burn for decades. Chua (2018, p. 5) asked an interesting question: how is it possible that so many working-class Americans, men and women, saw a billionaire mogul who flies on private jets, has towers bearing his name, and lives in a mansion decorated in 24k gold, as one of them and as their man? The answer she gave is that, in a sense, he *is* one of them and he *is* their man, in a way that matters more and more in politics: *culture-wise*. He talks like them, eats fast food, is not particularly interested in things that they aren't particularly interested in (like his carbon footprint or recycling), and he doesn't constantly patronize them for being racists, bigots, politically-incorrect, etc. Most importantly, for people who see the political establishment as alien and detached, 'his enemies, they feel, is their enemies' (idem). A popular meme among his supporters is the one depicting him as 'God Emperor Trump'. And Trump indeed won a major battle, but it was not only a political one. In 2016 he was victorious in the field that seems to matter more today: the culture war. Yet, he was not alone. Even a God Emperor needs good generals, lieutenants, and feet on the ground.

The 'deplorables': right-wing counter-cultural rebels

Around 2016, when commentators talked about the irregular army of journalists, bloggers, youtubers, and trolls that mobilized around Trump's nomination, using a transgressive narrative including jokes, memes, provocative statements, and even outright overt racism, the term used was 'alt-right' (alternative right). I find this term not really helpful, as the alt-right is only one part of that wider network, and it has some particular characteristics, such as its racial worldview and the open promotion of white nationalism, which are not shared by the wider network around Trump (we will talk more about the alt-right in the chapter about new racism). Hillary Clinton, during the 2016 campaign, referred to the core of Trump's milieu as 'deplorables' (Reilly, 2016), which backfired and was used by Trump's supporters as a badge of honour.

I will call the network that supported Trump—more because of what he stood against, rather than for any loyalty to him or the GOP—in 2016 (and, to a lesser extent, 2020) as the counter-cultural right. This is due to the importance this milieu put on the culture wars and their significance to politics. The talk of the town among the 'deplorables' is about issues like the impact of feminism, free speech, censorious SJWs (acronym for social justice warriors, as the activists with leftist ideas are called by their opponents), the effects of the immigration of people from other cultures on American society, etc.

Quite often within the narrative of the counter-cultural right, and especially among neo-reactionaries, one comes across the notion of the 'Cathedral', which sheds light on how parts of the right understand the culture war. According to the godfather of the term, Curtis Yarvin (also known among that movement as Mencius Moldbug, an eccentric neo-reactionary antiegalitarian who envisions a post-democratic society based on a combination of personal liberty and sovereign authoritarianism), 'the left is the party of the educational organs, at whose head is the press and the universities. This is our 20th-century version of the established church... we sometimes call it the *Cathedral*—although it is essential to note that, unlike an ordinary organization, it has no central administrator. No, this will not make it easier to deal with' (Moldbug, 2009). Thus, for the movement the message is clear and simple: bring down the Cathedral, i.e. the progressive leftist domination in culture.

Another characteristic of the counter-cultural right is their transgressive character, and their will to provoke and shock the established norms, reminding us of the hippies and the counter-culture of the 1960s. Theirs was a revolt against the established conservative bourgeois values of America. Today, the counter-cultural right is revolting against progressive liberal values. It is a battle focused on culture and meaning, rather than on institutional policies; it is what the New Right in Europe labels 'metapolitics' (Francois, 2019). Yet, not all conservatives who engage in the culture wars are part of the right-wing counter-culture. An example is the conservative pundit Ben Shapiro, who is vocal on issues around Judeo-Christian values, abortion, and free speech, but was against Trump's nomination (though he supported him in 2020) and who tries to avoid being provocative or intentionally 'edgy'.

Angela Nagle elaborated on the ethos of provocation by the cultural warriors of the right: 'its ability to assume the aesthetics of counter-culture, transgression and noncomformity tells us many things about the nature of its appeal and about the liberal establishment it defines itself against. It has more in common with the 1968 left's slogan "It is forbidden to forbid!" than it does with anything most recognize as part of any traditionalist right' (2017, p. 28). The trolls and the provocateurs took this transgressive ethos to an extreme, where nothing is taboo anymore: from Nazi symbols and racist memes, to 'doxing' people (revealing their personal details) and making fun of the Holocaust. Malice (2019) claimed that most of these people have little interest in racial or patriarchal superiority: it just happens to be that race or feminism are the sacred cows of today's western culture, and thus they are the legitimate targets to be attacked for any ambitious transgressive outsider. Right-wing provocateur Milo Yiannopoulos explained why he saw it as OK for them to make racist jokes: it is not an actual claim of racial supremacy, but a 'performative' racism (cited in Malice, 2019, loc. 3054). Another interesting (and growing) part of the counter-cultural right is the one mixing politics, aesthetics, masculine vigour, and western supremacy. The quasi-satirical, quasi-political, quasi-heroic and self-motivating, quasi-racist book *Bronze Age Mindset*, with an author with the *nom de guerre* Bronze Age Pervert (nd), which became a sensation in right-wing counter-cultural circles around 2019, is an example of this tendency.

Most of the activists of the counter-cultural right met on online forums such as Reddit and, when they got kicked out of there, at 4chan and 8chan. A key moment for the creation of this transgressive movement was the controversy that became known as Gamergate, which was about the backlash by online gamers against criticisms of game-culture by feminist writers (for a detailed and balanced story of Gamergate, see Nagle, 2017, pp. 19–24). Beyond the details, the fact is that 'Gamergate brought gamers, rightist chan culture, anti-feminism and the online far right closer to a mainstream discussion and it also politicized a broad group of young people, mostly boys, who organized tactics around the idea of fighting back against the culture war being waged by the cultural left' (idem, p. 24). Malice elaborated on why transgressive online activists were an important asset for the Trumpian right on the culture wars: they are young, hidden behind anonymity, they don't care about the rules, they have a lot of spare time, and they are tech-savvy and clever (2019, loc. 1338). The result was ugly: online harassment of opponents, threats, revealing of personal details, and lack of concern for any 'rules of engagement'.

But all the racism, the Pepe the frog memes, the cultural references to films such as *Fight Club* and *The Matrix* (the counter-cultural rebels refer to the process of one being 'red-pilled', i.e. seeing the truth and escaping the false world of the Cathedral), the lingo about 'cuck-servatives' (a derogatory term for main-stream conservatives, who are supposedly giving up western civilization to the left and immigrants, like cuckolds), the bom-bastic performances of Milo Yiannopoulos posing on Instagram with various male lovers… how are they even remotely related to the right as we knew it? They are not, Nagle claimed; actually, they are evidence of the defeat of old-style conservatism, and of its irrelevance (2017, p. 57). Right-wing counter-culture is a con-scious revolt against what it sees as a constantly compromising and defeatist mainstream right. Reactionary writer Vox Day, referring to the wider phenomenon of the anti-establishment right using the term alt-right, sums up its identity and historical trajectory: 'When the Alt-Right comes to power, one of its first acts should be to dig up the corpse of William F. Buckley and burn it. He was, without question, a significant part of the problem; he was no true soldier of the right, but rather, the treacherous captain of the left's Cuckservative Guard' (Day, 2017).

But such a 'sacrilege' had its equivalent in the sphere of mainstream politics. In July 2015, the then candidate for the GOP nomination Donald Trump said the unthinkable: that the former senator, presidential candidate, and POW in Vietnam John McCain was *not* a war hero. 'I like people that weren't captured', he added, to the audience's shock (CBS News, 2015). No need for any respect to the legacy of the past, no need to pay tribute to the sacred cows of the conservative movement. This is how Trump was 'one of them' in the new counter-culture: he played by his own rules, and he could get away with it. But if Trump was the 'God Emperor', figures like Milo were the lieutenants, and the meme-generating anonymous trolls at 4chan were the ground troops, who was the general? That title goes to Steve Bannon.

Bannon, and the international of nationalists

If there is one character I researched for this book that has all the ingredients of a great Hollywood villain, it is Steve Bannon. I even have the suspicion that his eccentric dress code (a shirt over a shirt over another shirt, and often a coat) is intentional to highlight the whole persona Bannon has chosen for himself. Irrespective of our moral evaluation of him, Bannon takes politics seriously, and one can easily imagine him staying late at night wracking his brain over how best to push forward his envisioned global nationalist-populist revolution.

Having spent many years not only in the business world, but also in Hollywood and journalism, Bannon knows and understands the 'Cathedral' from within. When Andrew Breitbart died unexpectedly from a heart attack in 2012, Bannon took over the Breitbart News network and slowly moved its direction from a conservative to a more nationalist and populist outlook. The prominent conservative pundit Ben Shapiro left Breitbart, protesting how under Bannon it had turned into 'Trump Pravda' and how it 'openly embraced the white supremacist alt-right', thus betraying the legacy of Andrew Breitbart who would not sanction such a turn, had he been around (Shapiro, 2016). In August 2016, Bannon was appointed as the person to run Trump's campaign. Defying all opinion polls and predictions, Trump won the elections and became President. Bannon was then appointed as a chief strategist, only to depart in August 2017, a few days after the violence in Charlottesville. Many claim he still remained in contact with Trump, but Bannon had also expanded his endeavours, allegedly offering (often off the record) advice to other populist politicians around the world, such as Salvini in Italy, Le Pen in France, and Bolsonaro in Brazil (Zerofsky, 2019). In 2020, he faced charges for fraud, orchestrating a project to fundraise the building of part of the infamous wall with Mexico that never materialized (Berman, 2020).

Bannon has not produced a manifesto or a publication where one can find his views gathered together in one place. His worldview can be deciphered through a number of speeches and debates of his that are available online. The most surprising thing for someone with his influence and his grandiose vision for change on an international level is how unoriginal his main ideas are. They have actually been present in conservative anti-liberal thought over the last two centuries, and we have examined them previously in this chapter. Summed up, here is Bannon's worldview:

– Economic nationalism. Bannon can tolerate capitalism only in so far as it serves what he understands as the interest of 'the people' and of 'the little guy' of a nation. He distinguishes between two kinds of capitalism. On the one hand there is a capitalism that supports the Judeo-Christian morality and the values of hard-working blue-collar people (cited in Buzzfeed, 2016). As we saw earlier, this is also the extent to which the Evangelicals of the New Right would accept the free market system, as promoting moral responsibility. Bannon is also acknowledging in capitalism the fact that it takes power away from what he calls the 'administrative state', which is the bureaucracy that he sees being controlled by progressives or corrupt politicians. Yet, Bannon claims there is a second kind of capitalism, which he calls 'the Ayn Rand or the Objectivist school of libertarian capitalism'. Bannon does not define it, but he is not happy with it, as it puts the individual's pursuit of self-interest above the group. For him, limits on how much wealth can be accumulated and a plan for how it should be distributed 'should be at the heart of every Christian that is a capitalist' (idem). Singing the same tune, Allum Bokhari and Milo Yiannopoulos, in an article that is among the most well-read and discussed in the history of Breitbart, provided a lengthy introduction to the emerging alternative right. There, they elaborated on its anti-free market worldview, which is shared also by Bannon:

'An establishment Republican, with their overriding belief in the glory of the free market, might be moved to tear down a cathedral and replace it with a strip mall if it made economic sense. Such an act would horrify a natural conservative. Immigration policy follows a similar pattern: by the numbers, cheap foreign workers on H1B visas make perfect economic sense. But natural conservatives have other concerns: chiefly, the preservation of their own tribe and its culture... For natural conservatives, culture, not economic efficiency, is the paramount value.' (Bokhari and Yiannopoulos, 2016)

- For Bannon, there is one big enemy, and it is the 'Davos Party' —the name is taken from the meetings held by the World Economic Forum in Davos, a mountain resort in Switzerland. Davos Party refers to the international financial and business elites, the intellectuals, and the media that support them (Clinch, 2017). Bannon and other populists also refer to them as the 'globalists', as they see them aspiring to create international institutions that will strengthen the grip of this technocratic elite on the nation states. For Bannon, the poster-

boy for the 'Davos Party' is the President of France Emmanuel
Macron (Maher, 2019).

–   The way to oppose the 'Davos Party' is an 'international' of
    political leaders that will still cooperate, but will put their
    nation states and their economies first. Bannon seems to be
    aware of the intellectual tradition from Evola to modern
    identitarians, and seems to be endorsing what we earlier
    referred to as 'traditionalism' and 'ethnopluralism': national-
    isms coexisting peacefully, each one preserving the (preferably
    Judeo-Christian) values of their nations, without aspirations
    for imperialistic expansion (Haynes, 2019, p. 146). Thus, he is a
    strong proponent of what he calls an 'America first' foreign
    policy, that would severely limit the intervention of the US in
    global affairs. At the same time, he is very anxious about the
    growing impact of China, which he considers a fascist
    mercantilist state. His advocacy for a protectionist economic
    policy has to do with an effort to contain the rise of China
    (Carden, 2019). He is less worried about authoritarian leaders
    such as Putin, as they might be corrupt and illiberal, but at
    least they promote the right conservative values. Thus, they
    could be part of the noble 'international' of nationalists.

Economic nationalism, populism, preservation of traditional
Judeo-Christian values, demolition of the 'administrative state', of
the 'Cathedral', and of the Davos Party, and 'America first'
foreign policy are thus at the centre of Bannon's worldview. His
ideas are not far from Buchanan's, from the John Birch Society, or
from other anti-liberal conservatives that we examined earlier in
this chapter. Whether his vision will succeed remains to be seen.
Trump's victory in 2016, his against-the-odds good performance
in the 2020 elections, and the Brexit vote have definitely shown
that anti-establishment movements have momentum and popular
backing. Bannon has made an interesting prediction: the future
will be populist; the only question is whether it will be right-wing
or left-wing populism that will rise victorious from this struggle

(Abramson and Shuster, 2018). There is a way this statement can be reworded: it will be a battle between right-wing and left-wing tribalism.

*

Up to this point, we have seen the historical, political, and philosophical background for the themes in this book. We have seen how a view of the world focusing on the disenfranchised status of various groups has been central for the narrative of the left, leading to identity politics being so prevalent in recent years. Then, we saw how the right has been mobilized by a sense of loss of the values and the lifestyles of a past that is under constant threat from different powers: modernity, liberalism, multiculturalism, and the ideological dominance of the left. This has led to the culture wars being a privileged field for the right to differentiate itself, in times when its actual differences with the left in terms of a political or economic vision are shrinking. This tango featuring the right and the left will become even more complex, as we will observe how the culture wars and identity politics will be the main focus for both of them, in a zero-sum game where one's victory is the other's defeat.

Free speech:
drawing the lines of battle

In the winter of 2019, I was invited to speak at the Ayn Rand Conference Europe in Prague, a two-day event the themes of which were individual freedom and tribalism. My speech was in the morning of the first day, and my enthusiasm for sharing a stage with intellectuals I've admired for years overwhelmed me to the effect that I never really paid attention to the schedule of the second day.

After the first day was over, there was a speakers' dinner in a small restaurant booked for the occasion. There, I sensed something odd taking place. There were a handful of people who didn't look like your average conference speaker. They looked as huge and intimidating as a blend of Viking fighters and Spartan soldiers of King Leonidas. There was also a woman among them who looked like the warrior princess Xena. I was too tired and excited from all the day's festivities to ponder any further who these people were. During the dinner, a well-kept gentleman in his early sixties came to our table to say hi to some people he knew. The person seated next to me introduced us: 'Flemming, this is Nikos…' Then it all made sense… this was Flemming Rose! He is the Danish journalist who published the cartoons depicting Muhammad in 2005, which triggered outrage and riots all over the world that cost the lives of around 200 people, and one of the top targets on Al-Qaeda's and other Islamic terrorists' hit lists. I had forgotten he was scheduled to be a speaker during Day 2 of the conference. Those people looking like ancient gods of war were his bodyguards, assigned by the Danish government to protect him always and everywhere.

Next day, and with the benefit of a good night's sleep, I could process the whole situation a bit better. His bodyguards were at various places in the building, preparing his arrival for his speech. He entered from a different entrance, unknown to the rest of us, and the only time he was 'alone' was on the panel. The bodyguards were dispersed everywhere in the room, beside him, behind him, opposite him, and diagonally, connected with an intercom system of headphones. Inside their jackets, some objects were bulging, leaving little to the imagination. Without exaggeration, it was one of the most memorable experiences of my life. In a way, I've never felt safer. There was a certain aura of expertise and competence that his security team was exuding.

The most thought-provoking thing for me was trying to get into Flemming Rose's shoes. He goes to bed every night and wakes up every day knowing that some of the worst people in the world want him dead. He knows they are not kidding. The list of victims of Islamist terrorists who were marked for taking a stand in favour of free speech is long:

- the Japanese translator of the 'blasphemous' book *Satanic Verses* in 1991, two years after Chomeini's fatwa against its author Salman Rushdie.
- the Dutch producer Theo van Gogh, assassinated in Amsterdam in 2004 for directing a documentary about the treatment of women in Islam.
- van Gogh's murderer also promised to kill the producer's collaborator, the 'apostate' Ayaan Hirsi Ali, who has been living under protection, even in high security army bases in the Netherlands, and who eventually migrated to the US.
- the 2015 massacre of the Charlie Hebdo cartoonists, and the list could go on.

Despite knowing that he is at the top of the hit list of such ruthless killers, Rose looks like a guy with a benevolent tranquillity. There were two questions that kept occurring to me: (a) How would I feel in his place? What would my life be like if I needed the protection of many people to go to the gym, do my grocery shopping, go out with a girl, and lecture at a class? (b) Is the trouble he is going through worth the stand he took in 2005, when he decided to publish the Muhammad cartoons in order to make a statement about the importance of the right to free expression without the fear of repercussions? There is no way to answer the first question; to answer the second question, though, we would have to discuss the issue of freedom of speech, which will be the theme of this chapter.

It is not only at the forefront of Islamist terrorism that questions around freedom of speech arise. In recent years, it looks like different controversies and battles of the culture wars have at their epicentre incidents that in one way or another have been labelled as free speech issues. Jordan Peterson had been a prominent scholar with numerous publications, teaching in prestigious universities; yet, he became a public intellectual with an audience of millions (and *persona non grata* for many on the left) when he got involved in the controversy over Bill C16 in Canada. The Bill is about offering further protection to individuals facing discrimination on various grounds; yet, due to its provisions that regard 'gender identity or expression' as protected characteristics, Peterson considered it a threat against freedom of speech, as it could potentially label the use of non-preferred pronouns for transgender people as hate speech—an argument the validity of which remains to be seen.

There are similar stories for other people within the so-called 'Intellectual Dark Web', the loose network of public figures taking a stance against the climate that suffocates free expression of ideas, like Sam Harris, Ben Shapiro, Dave Rubin, or Brett Weinstein. While they had meritorious careers, they entered the lives of most of us when they got caught up in controversies around free speech (usually in the form of being the targets of protests, intimidation, and 'no-platforming' at universities), or when they supported others who experienced it. These people disagree on many things; for example, Shapiro is conservative and very religious, whereas most people in the Intellectual Dark Web are liberal atheists. Yet, they all agree on the importance of free speech and the detrimental effects of the so-called 'cancel culture' of intimidation against people who fall outside the narrowing box of what constitutes 'allowable opinion'. At the same time, many on the left claim that the whole fuss about free speech is a pretence for the re-establishment of the cultural hegemony of the privileged, who have had their voice challenged for the first time, or an excuse for the right to spread hateful propaganda.

My aim here is not to present an overview of the numerous controversies around free speech that have taken place in recent years. Most people interested in the themes of this book probably already know the famous cases, such as the trouble that Nicholas and Erika Christakis found themselves in when they mildly challenged the view that Halloween costumes need to be the subject of university regulations so as to avoid racist stereotypes, or how the protests and intimidation by students forced Brett Weinstein out of his job at Evergreen College, when he objected to calls for white students and members of staff to stay home for one particular day, so that minority students could have a space to express their identity. They have also probably heard about the public shaming campaign against Nobel laureate Tim Hunt for an out-of-context joke that was considered sexist, the banning of some right-wing commentators from social media, or the various people who lost their jobs in the summer of 2020 for criticizing the Black Lives Matter movement. There are books that deal with these and other cases in detail, providing a very good analysis, such as Claire Fox's *I Find That Offensive* (2016), and Greg Lukianoff's and Jonathan Haidt's *The Coddling of the American Mind* (2018), or networks highlighting the cases and supporting the victims of 'cancel culture', such as the Free Speech Union (2020).

In this chapter, I will claim that most of these controversies around free speech are *not*, strictly speaking, free speech issues.

Yet, these controversies are related to free speech and are indeed very important to understand, because they provide an insight into some of the cultural and philosophical tendencies of our times that also fuel other socio-political tensions. This is why I claim that free speech controversies are where the battle lines of modern culture wars are drawn more clearly. The reason why the 'free speech wars' awake such passions is because they engulf so many crucial questions, such as what is an individual right, how do we view ourselves and the world, and what constitutes our agency. Usually, these questions are lost somewhere in the noise over the latest no-platforming controversy or the latest twitter-hunt; thus, we need to examine them further.

The fight for free speech: the mind vs. force

I started this chapter with Flemming Rose, because in his story one can see the naked essence of what is at stake: Flemming's mind, values, convictions, and worldview, vs. the Islamists' guns and death threats. He claims he has a right to express his beliefs. The other side claims there is no such right when it involves offending the Prophet, and the proper punishment is death. The punishment can either be delivered in a law-sanctioned manner (as in many Islamic theocracies), or by agents of divine justice, such as the Al-Qaeda gunmen.

Others take a milder stance: there is no right to offend the sensitivities of some people or of a group, but the punishment should not be death; after all, we should not go to extremes. The punishment could be a fine, as was the case in Scotland with the comedian Mark Meechan, known as Count Dankula, who uploaded a video in 2016 that was deemed offensive. He wanted to prank his girlfriend and prove to her that even a sweet pug can do bad things; thus, he taught it to give 'Nazi salutes' when hearing Nazi slogans. The court did not find the video that funny and fined Meechan £800 (Dearden, 2018). The punishment is different, yet the premise remains the same in these cases: free speech should have limits, and there are other values in society, such as the feelings of the offended, that are more important.

The advocates for free speech throughout the ages have provided some very good reasons as to why it should be celebrated and defended. Such claims include (Hume, 2015):

- Free speech is essential for a vibrant public sphere.
- Free speech can keep political power in check and prevent it from becoming unaccountable and despotic; thus, it is a critical ingredient of democracy.
- Free speech helps us better understand our beliefs, opens our horizons to new ideas, and helps us become independent thinkers, instead of merely uncritical reproducers of dogmas.
- Free speech is, and has always been, a tool for the less powerful to fight the powers that be and gain emancipation.

All these points are valid, and can be useful tools in the struggle for free speech. Yet, they are not enough, nor are they the primary reason why free speech is essential and a *right*. A good analysis on the issue comes from Ayn Rand and other scholars of her philosophy of Objectivism. For Rand (1964), the freedom to think and to speak becomes evident if one grasps the existential necessities of a human being. As all living organisms, humans have a specific nature; a specific identity; a specific way they survive and operate. As Rand put it, an individual's 'senses will not tell him automatically what is good for him or evil, what will benefit his life or endanger it... His own consciousness has to discover the answers to all these questions — but his consciousness will not function *automatically*... Man's particular distinction from all other living species is the fact that *his* consciousness is *volitional*' (Rand, 1964, p. 21). As opposed to animals, our survival and flourishing is not based on instincts. We have to use our mind and our rational faculty to grasp the world, to pursue what is true and what is good. From setting a fire to warm a cave to going to the moon, and from deciding what to do on a weekend to choosing whom to marry, human beings need to make choices that will be compatible with the requirements of reality and will put forward what is good for their life, not only for the now, but for the long term. At the same time, they need to think what is bad for them, and to denounce it. These complex processes require each and every individual to think and make decisions that are in their best interests; they can help and advise each other, but no one can do the thinking for someone else. This is why, for Rand, the freedom to think (to examine reality, to draw conclusions, and to doubt the false), and its material equivalent (the freedom to communicate one's thoughts, i.e. the freedom of speech), are *existential necessities.*

This existential necessity of free thought and speech can be denied in only one way: by the use of force and coercion. Galileo's observations led him to the conclusion that the earth revolves around the sun, but the threat of the Holy Inquisition's tools of torture demanded of him to defy reality and put someone else's creed above it. Thus, the initiation of force is wrong, as it undercuts 'the methodological integrity – the objectivity – of human cognition' (Wright, 2019a, p. 41). Reality requires a person to take X action, but then someone else intervenes by initiating force and is thus denying that person the means to lead his or her life. Let us concretize these principles further with a historical example.

From the 1930s until the 1950s, the official dogma in biology and agronomics in the Soviet Union was the theories of Trofim Lysenko. Due to his links to the Kremlin and the support he enjoyed from Stalin himself, Lysenko became the unquestioned authority, even though his ideas on agriculture and genetic inheritance of plants – which became known as Lysenkoism – were even then of questionable status (and for today's consensus, completely unscientific). Thousands of 'heretic' scientists who followed their individual mind and saw evidence of Lysenkoism's mistakes lost their jobs, whereas many ended up in prison, or in labour camps, and some of them paid speaking the truth with their life, such as the botanist Nikolai Vavilov (Birstein, 2001). Among Lysenko's victims, we do not even count the millions who died from famine due to failed crops in USSR or in China, where his pseudo-theories were adopted (Kean, 2017).

The tragedy/farce of Lysenkoism provides important lessons about the proper function of the mind in understanding the world and enriching human life. Lysenko's mistake was that instead of trying to grasp the nature of reality in terms of how plants breed, he attempted to fit reality into his scheme. His aim was to apply Marxism-Leninism to plant breeding, and basically make the plants develop a 'consciousness' of their own, where if they were 'taught' properly, they could flourish in different environments. As Kolakowski explained, the communist leaders wanted to believe that the new type of Soviet man could literally transform nature in a god-like manner (2005, p. 869). If reality did not bend itself to fit Lysenko's fantasies, too bad for reality. But this is not how things work. In the immortal words of Francis Bacon, 'reality to be commanded, must be obeyed'. Lysenko not only failed to obey reality, but he committed another hubris: he demanded that those who followed their mind and reason, and thus did not view the world through his irrational lenses, should be forced to do so. And if they declined to put Lysenko's fantasies above the judgment of their mind, they should perish in labour camps, never to be heard from again.

Since free thought and free speech are of such importance, it is essential that they are translated into political principles, in order for a society to support the flourishing of individuals. The scholar of legal philosophy Tara Smith made the case for the right of freedom of speech in an interesting way, by claiming that, although it is morally significant, the best way to understand and defend it legally is just by treating it as any other right. To explain this, she presented an outline of what a right is. A right is a right to something... to what? To freedom. Of what? Of action. Free from what? From others initiating force (Smith and Simpson, 2019). Thus, I have the right to speak, as I have the right to pursue hobbies, to fall in love, and to put pineapple on my pizza. Also, since it is a right, it is absolute, and there are no exceptions or limitations. It is not subject to modifications, opinion polls, reconsideration 'in the spirit of the times' or taking into account people's feelings, or anything else.

But, someone might ask, even a free speech absolutist would concede that threatening someone, or a mafia boss ordering a car to be blown up, or giving an enraged mob my address and asking them to burn my house are exceptions to free speech, right? Smith (2017) clarified that this is inaccurate. For sure, these actions are criminal. But they fall outside the scope of free speech to begin with. Thus, free speech is indeed absolute, and has no exceptions. But this does not mean it is not within a domain. Smith explained this principle with the example of King Louis XV, one of the most powerful rulers in history:

> 'Despite his tremendous power, Louis was the king of France; he was not the king of Britain, Westphalia, Ethiopia, or the Andes. His power was absolute, yet limited; it was held within a bounded domain. Does this mean that we misdescribe his power when we refer to it as absolute? No. In France, Louis' authority was subject to no other, second to none. The point is, the strength of one's authority is distinct from its scope, from the range of issues over which it is valid.' (2017, p. 64)

Thus, directly inciting violence or notifying someone that you'll blow up their car unless they break up with your ex-girlfriend are not 'exceptions' to free speech; they are criminal acts that fall outside the domain of free speech to begin with.

Another objection one might have is the following: if a punch or a direct threat are criminal acts that fall outside the scope of freedom of speech, why not also criminalize the publication of *Mein Kampf*, or a cartoon depicting the Prophet? Here, we need to understand the distinction between thought and force. I can read *Mein Kampf* or get offended that my faith is defied by others, and still go my own way. An offensive opinion, no matter how annoying it is, leaves me the option to shrug it off. As Wright put it, 'your ability to meet the requirements of your survival remains unhampered' (2019a, p. 42). That is not the case when I meet someone's fist, or when someone gives me an ultimatum at gun point. The gun now substitutes my free rational judgment.

Do rights such as the freedom of thought and speech create conflicts? What if I want to propagate Marxism-Leninism at the Republican Party Conference? If I am thrown out, is this not a violation of my right to free speech? The institution that guarantees that such dilemmas do not come up is property rights. Property rights are a direct outcome of our basic right, the right to life. To live, I need to think, and produce. Thus, my right to life means the right to keep the products of my labour and to dispose of them as I wish. Property rights help us clarify other rights, such as the right of freedom of speech. As Wright clarified, rights 'delineate zones of individual freedom, suitable for enabling each person in a society to take independent action in support of her own life and wellbeing' (2019b, p. 91). Thus, there are no contradictions in the right to free speech. I have no rights in other people's property; thus, I cannot demand a microphone or an audience from someone who does not wish to provide them to me.

It is now time to clarify what constitutes 'censorship', what is violation of the right to free speech, and what is not. Smith's work is very helpful here. She defined censorship as 'the government's forceful obstruction of a person's right to speak' (2017, p. 74). The Party's control of literature, cultural productions, and of the press in East Germany was censorship. The ten years in prison and the 1,000 lashes that the writer and blogger Raif Badawi received in Saudi Arabia for praising secularism is censorship. The different pieces of legislation in the UK that criminalize 'grossly offensive' language, chants in football grounds, the 'glorification' of terrorism, or the 'stirring up' of religious hatred are censorship (Hume, 2015, pp. 58–59). Despite the moral condemnation that Holocaust

deniers deserve, the criminalization of their views, and all the
laws on 'thought crimes', is censorship. The fine to Count
Dankula is censorship. The religious fatwa by Khomeini against
Salman Rushdie, the threats against Flemming Rose, and the
bullets of the Islamist terrorists against the Charlie Hebdo
cartoonists are not technically censorship, but they are violations
of the right to life, and a direct assault on free speech.

Censorship in various forms, overt (as in Saudi Arabia) or
covert (as in the UK), has been, and still is, the norm throughout
history. Yet, it is interesting to note that even dictatorships, of all
political persuasions, usually pay lip-service to freedom of speech;
although it is usually followed by a 'but...'. The anti-communist
leader of the military junta that would rule Greece for seven years,
Colonel Georgios Papadopoulos, in his first press conference in
1967, wanted to pass the message that his regime (that had
arrested and imprisoned numerous political opponents) was not
really illiberal: 'Each person can believe in whatever political
system they want; but the Greeks *cannot* believe in communism'
(cited in thecaller.gr, 2019). So there should be freedom for ideas,
just not for *all* ideas. But if Papadopoulos was known for his
incoherent rants that made little sense, around the same time one
of the most celebrated intellectuals of the last 50 years, Herbert
Marcuse, would deliver a similar message. This time, however,
the prohibited idea would not be communism, but the ideas that
he despised.

In 1965, Marcuse wrote an essay with the telling title 'Repressive Tolerance'. There, reminding us of today's concern about 'fake
news' and the alleged inability of the masses to tell right from
wrong, he observed that 'in endlessly dragging debates over the
media, the stupid opinion is treated with the same respect as the
intelligent one, the misinformed may talk as long as the informed,
and propaganda rides along with education, truth with falsehood'
(Marcuse, 1965). This verifies my characterization of the Frankfurt
School in a previous chapter as an intellectual movement wary of
the masses of ordinary people who are not to be trusted as

capable of properly exercising reason. Marcuse went on to claim that 'tolerance cannot be indiscriminate and equal with respect to the contents of expression, neither in word nor in deed; it cannot protect false words and wrong deeds which demonstrate that they contradict and counteract the possibilities of liberation' (idem). What are these 'false words' that should not be tolerated? Marcuse is surprisingly open: the ideas of the right. He came up with the Orwellian-sounding notion of 'liberating tolerance', that would mean 'intolerance against movements from the right and toleration of movements from the left' (idem). In practice, this would mean 'the withdrawal of toleration of speech and assembly from groups and movements which promote aggressive policies, armament, chauvinism, discrimination on the grounds of race and religion, or which oppose the extension of public services, social security, medical care, etc.' (idem). Marcuse's ideas have found proponents in today's no-platforming campaigns at universities, which is predictable, considering the high status that he and the Frankfurt School enjoy in the humanities and social sciences. Still, it is quite notable that one of the most outright and direct calls for censorship comes from a milieu that wants to present itself as a champion of tolerance and of a more open society.

Grey, and not so grey, areas

Luckily, we live in times when both the Inquisition and the system behind Lysenkoism are seen as horrors of a distant past. Humanist ideals have denounced torture, executions, and labour camps. Yet, our understanding of free thought and free speech still do not go deep enough. In December 2018 Dr Noah Carl, who had recently been awarded with a fellowship at the University of Cambridge, found himself in the middle of what in the era of culture wars we call an 'online mob': a group of academics, including some well-known radical intellectuals like the late David Graeber, were collecting signatures to have Carl removed from his position due to his research being 'ethically suspect' and 'methodologically flawed' (Adams, 2018).

Carl at the time was 28 years old and had an academic record that would be impressive even for someone in his late 40s. His 'flaw' was that he conducted research on the 'problematic' area, among others, of IQ and the factors that influence it. Due to the fact that a pseudo-science around race, biology, and IQ was used by late 19th- and early 20th-century racists to support their claims of racial superiority, the whole field since then has been treated with suspicion. Carl was accused of either contributing to or sanctioning the resurgence of such a pseudo-science. There is one hole in that narrative though: his accusers could not point to anything that he actually said or wrote that linked race and IQ in any way, nor could they specifically mention what his methodological flaws were. Perhaps he became 'ethically suspicious' for defending the right of other scientists to pursue research in these sensitive areas (Quillette, 2018). In other words, he defended the right of scientists to follow reason, the scientific method, and their mind towards the discovery of the world out there, with reality being the sole arbiter. The bulk of scientific evidence, with which Carl agrees, is that there is no definite evidence of the relationship between a genetic predisposition of different ethnic groups to different levels of IQ. But the fact that any research in the area of group differences in IQ is seen by some as an unacceptable remnant of the Third Reich is bizarre. First, the historical parallel is wrong, as actually the Nazis denounced such research, as the high average scores of many Jewish people would ruin their racist narrative (Carl, 2019). Second, it echoes the days where scientific research was conditional to the approval of some higher authority, based on criteria that have to do more with politics and less with science.

Unfortunately, the story of Noah Carl has no happy end. St Edmunds College in Cambridge terminated his employment, despite the fact that Carl addressed in detail (and in my opinion, in a persuasive way) the accusations against him (idem). One of the questions arising from this sad story is whether it was a free speech issue *per se*. The answer is clearly *no*. Carl was not barred by the state from doing his research, he was not arrested, neither was he sent to a labour camp in the Russian far east tundra like those questioning Lysenkoism. Then why is he seen as another victim of the free speech wars of our time? Because there are many cases that are related to how tolerant a society is to free thought and free expression, even if they are not, strictly speaking, free speech issues. Clarifying the principles that should apply in such cases is a difficult endeavour, but something that needs to be done. For example, what happens when students demand that a public university de-platform a speaker, the views of whom a critical mass considers offensive? Also, many conservatives have raised the issue of large platforms like Twitter, which in a way constitute the modern 'public sphere', de-platforming users with right-wing views like Milo Yiannopoulos, Alex Jones, and even the still then President Donald Trump after the Capitol riots in January 2021. Taking into account how important these platforms have become, is this a violation of these people's free speech rights?

The status of free speech in a public university is very complicated. Who owns the place? The students? The entire public? The trustees and the board of directors? The administration? As it is not private property, coming up with clear rules as to who should have a final say on who gets a microphone is impossible. Yet, there have been cases where the attempts to stop someone from appearing on campus is an assault on free speech: the ones that include the direct use of force. One example is rioting and terrorizing attendees, as happened in Berkeley in 2017, by protesters trying to stop Milo Yiannopoulos from appearing on campus. The rioting caused property damage of $100,000 and at least six people were injured (Park and Lah, 2017). The physical attack on Professor Allison Stanger, who had the bad idea of agreeing to question the author and scholar Charles Murray at an event in Middlebury College, USA, was a use of force against her rights, including her right to free speech. Protesters broke into the event, and assaulted Stanger, grabbing her by the hair and shoving her around. She had to be hospitalized and she under-went physical therapy that lasted for months (Lukianoff and Haidt, 2018, p. 88).

Yet, there are cases where no actual violence is involved, and students only put emotional pressure on the administration to cancel an event. Taking into account the arguments in favour of free speech presented at the beginning of the chapter (the enrich-ment of a public sphere, the exposure to diverse points of view, etc.), the attempts to de-platform speakers can often be rightly condemned. These attempts could be indicative of tendencies that will be examined later in this chapter, such as the prevalence of a victimhood culture and an unearned self-righteousness. Yet, they do not constitute censorship, nor do they deny anyone's right to free speech. The same applies to cases such as Carl's and other shaming campaigns against some person the views of whom are considered offensive or 'unacceptable': 'cancel culture' and putting pressure on someone to lose their job might be wrong, immoral, and a reaction indicating a toxic public sphere; yet, they are not censorship, nor a denial of their right to freedom of speech.

Smith explained that 'the freedom to speak goes hand in hand with the freedom not to speak and not to support speech that one disagrees with' (2017, p. 75). If people think my ideas are bad and campaign to the organizers for me to be dis-invited from speaking at a conference, and the organizers cave in to the demands, no right has been infringed. I can say that the campaigners are intolerant and bad people, I can accuse the conference's organizers of needing to grow a backbone, but I had no right to another people's podium to begin with. Things are even worse when campaigners ask the government to intervene so that Twitter will bring back Milo Yiannopoulos, Alex Jones, or the other de-platformed users. This would negate the right of Twitter's owners to free speech. Their platform is private property, and they should be free to exclude whoever they want for whatever reason.[1] One might criticize them, boycott them, but one cannot ask the state to use coercion so that he or she will have access to someone else's property, despite the latter's wish. One needs to be very careful, as what is seen as a campaign for more freedom might end up undermining the rights that make values such as free expression possible in the first place.

Is free speech a tool of the powerful and privileged?

Today, many on the left consider free speech a privileged concern of the well-off; an abstraction that does little to help the oppressed and the common people. Nothing could be further from truth, and a look at history leaves little doubt about it. All the emancipatory struggles for more freedoms and rights had free speech at their epicentre.

In post-medieval England, 'heretics' who disagreed with the monarch, or who published things that went against allowable opinion, had the arm with which they wrote cut off, or were branded on their cheeks with 'SL', meaning 'Seditious Libeller' (Hume, 2015, p. 80). Since 1275, the law of *Scandalum Magnatum* made it an offence to communicate or publish 'false news' about the king and state authorities. It goes without saying that what counted as false news was interpreted quite flexibly and effectively every criticism of those in power was prohibited (idem, p. 79). It is no surprise then that the Levellers, an early radical liberal movement during the English Revolution of 1649, campaigned, among other things, for an end to the need to receive state licencing in order to print something. As they said, a free press 'appears so essential unto Freedom, as that without it, it's

---

[1]   I will not enter here into the debate around whether social media are 'platforms' or 'publishers', as it is a technical point, but does not alter the principle that their owners should be free to do as they please with their property.

impossible to preserve any Nation from being liable to the worst of bondage' (cited in Hume, 2015, p. 38).

Free speech had also been pivotal for the overcoming of racial discrimination. The iconic figure in the abolitionist movement in the US, former slave Frederick Douglas, was also a free speech advocate, and he claimed that 'liberty is meaningless where the right to utter one's thoughts and opinions has ceased to exist' (cited in Hume, 2015, p. 39). Free speech was also of huge importance to the civil rights movement in the US during the 1950s and 1960s. Quite often, the racist authorities in the south would use libel laws and other legal technicalities to arrest black activists for peaceful actions such as handing out leaflets or publishing ads in the newspapers (Stanley, 2017).

Free speech was also at the centre of feminist struggles for equal rights. Around the time of the First World War, Sylvia Pankhurst and the suffragettes had joined forces with the Free Speech Defence Committee, as they realized that the right to speak for peace, for equal rights, and for whatever opinions were then considered 'unpatriotic' and unpopular was part of their own struggle (Hume, 2015, p. 201). The same applies to other persecuted groups throughout history: their struggle was first and foremost the struggle for their right to speak their mind and express their thoughts. In 1977, *Gay News* magazine was persecuted with a heavy fine and a suspended jail sentence for its publisher, over content that was considered 'blasphemous' (idem). This is useful food for thought for people who believe that freedom of speech is a code for 'hate speech' and means nothing for the less privileged.

Claiming that freedom of speech is merely a 'bourgeois' concern would also be wrong. Karl Marx himself begged to differ, as he mentioned in a polemic titled 'On Freedom of the Press': 'The free press is the ubiquitous vigilant eye of a people's soul, the embodiment of a people's faith in itself, the eloquent link that connects the individual with the state and the world, the embodied culture that transforms material struggles into intellectual struggles and idealises their crude material form' (Marx, 1842). The German revolutionary Rosa Luxemburg agreed and amplified: 'Freedom is always and exclusively freedom for the one who thinks differently' (Luxemburg, 1918). Of course, history has shown that the defence of free speech by most communists has been insincere. As far back as the Lenin days, the Bolsheviks had little patience for free speech. Unsurprisingly, views were persecuted if they'd 'objectively serve the interests of the bourgeois' (Kolakowski, 2005, p. 762). Yet, on the rhetorical level, free speech was celebrated as an achievement of the new socialist state.

Why then, despite its progressive history, does freedom of thought and expression face such hostility today? In one of the most commonly used quotes on the precariousness of freedom, Supreme Court Judge Billings Learned Hand was right to warn us already from the 1940s that 'liberty lies in the hearts of men and women; when it dies there, no constitution, no law, no court can save it'. In the following sections, I will attempt to spot the current tendencies that have caused the idea of free speech to slowly die in the hearts of many people in the West.

Entitled vulnerability

FIRE (the Foundation for Individual Rights in Education) has tried to measure 'disinvitation incidents' at university campuses in the US, meaning 'the controversies on campus that arise throughout the year whenever segments of the campus community demand that an invited speaker not be allowed to speak' (FIRE, 2019). It turns out that from January 2012 until June 2019, there were more than 230 such incidents (idem). So the first takeaway is: the issue is real. The 'problematic' ideas of the speakers ranged from abortion and contraception to the Israeli–Palestinian conflict. Also, it is worth noting that, although the majority of the disinvitations come from students with a left-wing agenda, some also come from the right.

The following has been a commonplace scenario in recent years: a 'problematic' speaker is invited to a university, or a member of staff says something that goes beyond the ever-changing parameters of allowable opinion, and part of the student body engages in protests. The intensity of the activists' reactions — often including tears, emotional breakdowns, and even violence — is noteworthy. It would indicate that the 'perpetrator', who is often a mainstream conservative like Ben Shapiro or even a non-orthodox liberal like Christina Hoff-Sommers, represents the equivalent of an existential threat or an imminent danger. One easy explanation is that the students who are reacting, or those demanding 'safe spaces' to protect them from dangerous thinkers or ideas, or those calling for 'trigger warnings' even for canonical pieces of literature such as *The Great Gatsby* or *The Merchant of Venice* (Flood, 2014), are drunk on their own power and thus want to control the narrative on campus. While this might be the case for some, I believe there is a more plausible, and worrying, hypothesis: the students *actually believe* that they are at risk from words and ideas.

Lukianoff and Haidt have noticed a shift in the rationale that is used for curtailing the free expression of ideas at university campuses and elsewhere. It is no longer a case of one's ideas being wrong or 'dangerous for society', as for example with the no-platforming of far-rightists or fascists from the National Union of Students in the UK in the past. The narrative has shifted from 'your ideas are bad' to 'your ideas will harm me' (Lukianoff and Haidt, 2018, p. 6). In what ways will these ideas harm them? There have been cases where students have claimed that their protests against a speaker had to do with an actual threat some of them felt they faced. The riots at Berkeley in February of 2017 when Milo Yiannopoulos was invited for a talk was a prime example of that. The rationale was that Yiannopoulos would 'out' some students, i.e. reveal their identity as undocumented immigrants. Whether that was his intention remains questionable. But even if Yiannopoulos planned to do so, this wouldn't explain the attempts to shut down events in many other universities with speakers who would never intend to do such thing, such as Ben Shapiro or Jordan Peterson (Campbell and Manning, 2018, p. 232). These students protested against a different kind of harm: a psychological one.

This became clear during the protests against Nicholas and Erika Christakis at Yale, and the reactions to the couple's email (written by Erika, endorsed by both) arguing that students are adults who can negotiate among themselves their Halloween costumes, without the need for an intervention by the university. Among others, Christakis mentioned: 'Talk to each other. Free speech and the ability to tolerate offence are the hallmarks of a free and open society' (Christakis, 2015). Although this statement does not sound like a controversial one, the way many students perceived it was as an endorsement of racist Halloween costumes. Protests erupted, with students mobbing Nicholas Christakis and demanding an apology, intimidating him not to smile or lean his head, and calling him to step down. Someone also wrote 'we know where you live' outside their accommodation on campus. Some of the things shouted by students at Christakis accused him of 'stripping people of their humanity', 'creating an unsafe space', enabling 'violence', and of course that he is 'racist'. A student cried at him: 'It is not about creating an intellectual space! It is not! It's about creating a home here… you should not sleep at night! You are disgusting!' (cited in Lukianoff and Haidt, 2018, p. 56). Some students were also reported to be in such a turmoil because of the Christakis's email that they skipped meals, they couldn't sleep, and they had emotional breakdowns (idem).

To put things into perspective: Nicholas and Erika Christakis are both more or less mainstream liberals, and the students who revolted against them could be considered among the most privileged people who have ever lived, as they got to study at the third best university in the country and the eighth best in the world (Times Higher Education, 2019). Similarly, in the UK it is very often at high-status universities like Cambridge or King's

College London where 'disinvitation incidents' take place. So what explains this narrative of victimization and indignation among students?

The answer needs to be found outside of the university. As Lukianoff and Haidt put it, young people in the Anglo-Saxon world are 'trained to be triggered' from a very young age (2018, p. 10). Claire Fox (2016) was right to argue that instead of merely blaming 'generation snowflake' for today's intellectual atmosphere, we need to see how students got socialized in these attitudes. 'Adult society', she claimed, 'has fed them a diet of anxieties and provided the language of safety and risk aversion that now threatens liberal values of tolerance and resilience' (Fox, 2016, loc. 687). When young people look up to us, they don't see reassurance and conviction anymore; they see risk-averse adults without the self-confidence that the challenges of tomorrow can be met. 'The erstwhile adult role of reassuring the young and telling them not to over-react is replaced by grown-ups reveling in telling horror stories; if once when children had nightmares, we told them not to worry; now we tell them their nightmares are real life' (idem, loc. 846).

Fox (2016) and Furedi (2011) have picked up on some trends in today's society that, taken together, create the perfect storm that we see in the 'free speech wars': risk aversion, the undermining of the ability to cope and be resilient, a sense of vulnerability, a therapeutic lens under which everyday situations (like university exams) are reinterpreted as traumatic challenges, and at the same time an entitlement to a recognition based not on one's achievements, but on a static identity. This worldview is shared by adults. Reported anxiety disorders have gone up by more than 1,200% (yes, one thousand two hundred percent) since 1980 (Fox, 2016, loc. 729). Is our life today objectively 1,200% more challenging and stressful than in 1980? The answer is clearly no. And note that these statistics were gathered before the COVID-19 pandemic and the stress it has caused for so many people. What has changed from 1980 is that, due to some intellectual and cultural tendencies that were presented in previous chapters, things and change are seen as happening *to* us, rather than being guided *by* us. Thus, the present, and even more the future, can look like alien and intimidating forces.

These tendencies are communicated to the new generation from a very young age. At schools, students get introduced very early to 'awareness' about complicated issues like mental health or climate change. Thus, one can see 6-year-old students complaining about their 'well-being' (Fox, 2016, loc. 746), and others suffering from 'eco-anxiety' about the supposed imminent environmental doom by climate change (Scher, 2018). 25% of young adults researched at a US university after the victory of Donald Trump in 2016 reported symptoms that are interpreted by the psychologists who did the study as close to post-traumatic stress disorder (Durkin, 2018). In some Student Unions in the UK, the waving of 'jazz hands' has been encouraged instead of clapping, as the noise of the latter is considered by some as potentially anxiety-triggering (Hosie, 2018). Again, we need to provide perspective here and remember that, in objective terms, this is perhaps the safest era ever for a young person to grow up, especially at a university campus. Everything in life is more controlled than it ever was, and health and safety provisions are at a historic peak (Fox, 2017, loc. 743).

Lukianoff and Haidt (2018) claimed that this 'coddling' of young people is actually detrimental to them. It makes them less resilient to the slightest challenge, and becomes a self-fulfilling prophecy where they eventually see themselves as the vulnerable victims they are taught individuals are. They develop three characteristics by which Campbell and Manning (2018) described the rise of a 'victimhood culture':

- over-sensitivity, which is why the presence of a mainstream conservative like Ben Shapiro on campus can be viewed as a cause for stress;

- a victimhood narrative, which is why they can claim that, although they study in the best and most expensive universities in the world, they are victims of capitalism or patriarchy;
- and an inability to negotiate their challenges without an appeal for outside intervention by some kind of authority, which is why the Christakis email encouraging them to talk to each other when they feel offended was met with indignation and psychological breakdowns.

This vulnerability is then worn as a badge of honour. This is because humans are no longer viewed as rational beings able to understand and tame the world according to their will and face the possible challenges. Instead, they are viewed as beings lost in an incomprehensible chaos, full of risks. But if this is the case, then this disorientation and the failure to stand up to the occasion become the essence of being human. Thus, vulnerability is not to be treated as something to be overcome, but with the respect and honour of an existential truth. Even more, since individuals are bearers of their group identity, as we saw in previous chapters, then this honourable recognition of one as a victim is easily identifiable and automatic: x is member of y group, y group is vulnerable, and thus, x is vulnerable. But what if one is vulnerable based on more than just one identity? This is where intersectionality comes in, with its nexus of relations of power and oppression. According to Cathy Young (2015), this worldview creates 'a reverse caste system in which a person's status and worth depends entirely on their perceived oppression and disadvantage'.

The internalization of vulnerability as a given fact of reality becomes more dangerous for those who accept these ideals and those around them, when it is accompanied by a claim of entitlement that their feelings are to be accepted as an arbiter above everything else. This is why, according to Fox, one sees the contradiction of 'vulnerable' victim-signalling students acting out, throwing tantrums, and writing with chalk on Christakis's wall 'we know where you live'. The primacy of emotions over the old-fashioned idea of objective reason leads to a 'narcissistic self-belief in one's own importance' (Fox, 2016, loc. 1090). Since the earliest days at school, students have been constantly taught the importance of expressing their feelings, irrespective of whether they are rational or not. Primacy of emotions, vulnerability, and the claim to be taken care of creates a personality that, according to Lukianoff and Haidt, is potentially pathological (2018, p. 10). For Fox, it develops a 'pseudo self-esteem', where young people are never challenged, and thus see no reason why they need to change or develop in any way (2016, loc. 1262). Mick Hume saw the attitude of these young people—who should be thirsty for knowledge and intellectual pursuits, but instead think they have everything figured out and the world should uncritically respect that—as 'a cross between helpless toddlers and stuck-in-their-ways pensioners' (2015, p. 285).

Seeing school or, even more importantly, university as a retreat from the real world and as the realm where feelings supersede reality means that these institutions lose their importance as a 'rite of passage' (Fox, 2016, loc. 1125). Looking back to my youth, what made my university years in Greece a life-changing experience was that suddenly I was supposed to be an adult, and deal with 64 modules and professors who took themselves and us seriously. Sometimes, we would be tested via oral exams and the process would look surreal to today's students. We would enter the office of an unimpressed middle-aged professor who would smoke by the window without even looking at us. He would ask questions such as 'tell me the military tactical innovations of von Moltke in the Prussian army', taken from a 400-page book about the history of war from the Byzantine Empire until Operation Desert Storm. In some modules, if the professor was not happy with our first answer, sometimes there was no second question, and he would order us to leave with some disapproving or sarcastic remark. Was this a better pedagogical method? Maybe not. Do I still remember von Moltke's tactical innovations on the battlefield? Not really. Did we become prepared for the world out there, our future employers, and the challenges that we would later face? Definitely.

Also, the fact that young people are asking for an automatic recognition of their claims based on a static and *de facto* vulnerable identity is detrimental to their self-esteem. It provides a short-lived affirmation, but nothing beyond that. In its essence, self-esteem means: I am capable of facing the world, of capturing reality with my mind, and of shaping my life according to my will through my actions (Rand, 1964). Throwing tantrums and demanding the intervention of the authorities to shield someone from an undesirable idea is the exact opposite: the elevation of one's whims above reality, and the confirmation that one is not capable of dealing with a world that makes little sense. As paternalistic as it might sound, people like Fox or Lukianoff and Haidt who criticize those young activists demanding safe spaces and trigger warnings offer them an incalculably better service than their older 'allies' who are eager to throw colleagues under the bus and join them in their protests against 'problematic ideas'.

An assault on objectivity

In October of 2015, a progressive African American student at Williams College in the US attempted to bring to campus Suzanne Venker, a writer who is a critic of feminism and who claims that men and women are happier under traditional gender roles, and 'interrogate' her on her ideas. Predictably, the event was cancelled, due to protests by students. Lukianoff and Haidt (2018, p. 49) cite a statement made by one of the protesters on social media, that is indicative of the tone of the reactions:

> 'When you bring a misogynistic, white supremacist men's right activist to campus in the name of "dialogue" and "the other side", you are not only causing actual mental, social, psychological, and physical harm to students, but you are also

– paying – for the continued dispersal of violent ideologies that kill our black and brown (trans) femme sisters... Know, you are dipping your hands in blood...'

In 2016, Jordan Peterson was the centre of attention in the 'free speech wars', due to his opposition to Bill C-16 in Canada, which according to his opinion would criminalize the refusal to use a trans person's preferred pronouns. Many student unions at the University of Toronto co-authored a letter asking university authorities to discipline Peterson and, among other things, to mandate 'anti-oppression training' for all members of staff. The letter reminded Peterson that 'misgendering a trans person is an act of violence'. They claimed that Peterson 'silences' them, and that their 'existence' and 'realities' are 'refused' (UTMSU, 2016).

Two years later, in 2018, conservative pundit Ben Shapiro was scheduled to give a speech at the University of Southern California. The University's Black Student Assembly, Latinx[2] Student Assembly, and Asian Pacific American Student Assembly released a common statement, which, among other things, mentioned: 'The safety and lives of minority communities on the University of Southern California's campus is in harm's way.' Their reasoning was that Shapiro 'is known to be a purveyor of hate speech, including the eradication of entire races' (cited in Sabes, 2018).

So what we have here is:

– A traditional conservative woman 'causing actual and physical harm' to students, while those who invited her are 'dipping their hands in blood'. What one can assume from all this is that she is beating on students, while the organizers of her speech sit back and enjoy the process.

---

[2] Latinx is a term used by some as a non-binary alternative to the terms Latino and Latina.

- Jordan Peterson enacting 'violence' on students with his words and 'silencing' them. Perhaps his words are transformed into violent action in an undefined way, while at the same time the Canadian professor makes sure that none of the victimized groups he is after has any chance to talk back?
- Ben Shapiro putting lives in harm's way, which is only the prelude to him eradicating 'entire races'; how Shapiro can induce such mass genocide, while at the same time managing to hide the mountains of corpses, remains unclear.

These outrageous exaggerations in the activists' claims are some colourful examples of a wider trend, which is the stretching of words and concepts beyond their actual meaning, in an attempt to create an impression or promote an agenda. Lukianoff and Haidt (2018, p. 85) call this tendency a 'concept creep', and the most prominent examples of it are the concepts of 'harm' and 'violence'. Even its most passionate advocates of free speech would agree that acts of violence that cause harm have nothing to do with free speech. Thus, those who want to see restrictions on what is allowed to be thought or said are stretching the concepts of harm and violence beyond any recognition. According to the Oxford English Dictionary, 'harm' means 'physical injury, especially that which is deliberately inflicted', whereas it can also be used for 'material damage', or 'actual or potential ill-effects or danger'. Interestingly, actual harm is often caused by the pro-testers, as in the riots against Milo Yiannopoulos's speech at Berkeley, or in the assault on Professor Stanger at the Charles Murray event at Middlebury College. Yet, this is not considered noteworthy violence, in the same way as the riots during the summer of 2020 in the USA were portrayed as 'fiery, but mostly peaceful protests' (Concha, 2020).

How are such actions rationalized? In the eyes of the pro-testors, they are just retaliatory force. If Shapiro is 'eradicating races', if people who believe in free speech 'have blood on their hands', and if Peterson is 'denying the right to exist' to entire oppressed groups, then some shoving around and some sucker-punches are the least one could do. This is why re-appreciating the importance of an objective approach to language and definitions is of paramount importance. A relativism that puts emotions and whims over objective reality and says 'violence is whatever I *feel* it is' is not worrisome only in an academic and theoretical way. It will soon have real effects in action, as we have seen above, and as it became apparent with the violence during the summer of 2020.

Furedi saw the over-expansion of the scope of harm as a sign of a time when human subjectivity and our ability to cope with the challenges of life are thought to be diminished. He noticed how 'today's definition of harm is influenced by a therapeutic sensibility that perceives emotions as constantly at risk from a variety of threats' (2011, p. 105). In such a climate, the presence of someone with different opinions on a campus as big as 1,232 acres, like Berkeley, is seen as a threat and as putting students in 'harm's way'. On top of that: in a culture where one's emotions, especially if they belong to a 'victimized group', take precedence over notions of objective reality, such claims are to be treated as self-evidently valid. 'It is so, because I *feel* it to be so, and I *say* it is so' is the underlying assumption of these activists.

Another reason activists can get away with such behaviours is the idea that they are legitimate responses, as they are powerless, whereas their opponents are powerful. There are two problems here. On the one hand, 'power' is too vague a term, and almost never defined. In addition, the already vague definition of 'power' is applied to equally vaguely defined groups of 'oppressors' and 'oppressed'. Of course, being 'powerful' also carries with it an aura of moral inferiority (Lukianoff and Haidt, 2018, p. 64), and thus violence against the 'oppressors' might not be that bad after all. Writer Elan Journo called this tendency the 'Underdog Principle', according to which 'we owe not only our sympathy but our moral backing to the weaker, neediest, most suffering side' (2018, p. 7). He then went on to present how absurd this principle is, and how it lacks any objective reference to justice. After all, groups such as Charles Manson's gang or Al-Qaeda were clearly the underdogs against their opponents, but this says nothing about their moral righteousness. This obviously is not to say that the anti-free speech activists have the moral status of terrorists; it does indicate though that constructing a notion through which an ill-defined powerlessness gives one the green light to commit assault or to riot and to deny the rights of others is wrong and needs to be criticized.

The lack of objectivity and clear definitions takes a form which is way more dangerous and worrying than the relativism of activists at the universities when it is translated into regulations, policies, or law. Claire Fox cited the policy of some councils in the UK that define 'hate speech' as including 'any behaviour, verbal abuse or insults, offensive leaflets, posters, gestures as perceived by the victim or any other person as being motivated by hostility, prejudice or hatred' (2016, loc. 309). Thus, one's subjective experience becomes the arbiter of whether an opinion or a deeply held religious belief becomes an act of hate. A similar approach has been adopted by the UK Home Office when it comes to the definition of hate crime: 'any criminal offence which is perceived, by the victim or any other person, to be motivated by hostility or prejudice towards someone based on a personal characteristic' (Home Office, 2018).

Mick Hume (2015) noted that, when language and one's emotions are elevated above objectivity, we can quickly find ourselves in the territory of irrationality. He presented as an example of this the words that, due to their association with a past of racism and discrimination, today cannot even be uttered. The obvious example is the so-called n-word. In 2018, Netflix fired its head of communications, Jonathan Friedland, for using the n-word twice during meetings (Tapper, 2018). The interesting thing is that there were no allegations that he used the word in a malicious or racist way. Actually, the first meeting was about sensitive words, and Friedland used it as an example of a word that should never be used. Yet, this was enough for him to lose his job.

Hume commented: 'there are words which it is now a mortal sin to utter, regardless of what was meant by them. This sounds like a modern form of mystical mumbo-jumbo, echoing the Old Testament law that anybody would be damned and probably stoned to death if they dared to speak the name of God (Yahweh, if you're interested in tweeting Him)' (2015, p. 207). He linked these forbidden words to the magic chorus of the fairy tales, 'Abracadabra', which interestingly is believed to mean 'I will create with words' (idem, p. 209). This is quite fitting: it is as if the n-word, irrespective of context, aim, or occasion, will unleash evil and destruction on the world. Interestingly, there are more such words that are unspeakable today. In 2018, the academic Gad Saad was banned from Twitter for some hours for using the term 'retarded', henceforth to be known as the 'r-word'. In 2015, Benedict Cumberbatch tried to raise awareness on TV against racial inequalities. Yet, instead of the term 'people of colour', he used by mistake the term 'coloured people'. He got in trouble and had to issue an apology (Selby, 2015). Does it even matter that he was actually trying to fight racism? He pronounced the wrong word, and this is all that counts. Context, intentions, and objectivity need to take a back seat to the modern idea that language is constructing reality.

Yet, anyone who has spent 30 minutes at a gym or a night club will notice that the n-word is used all the time in popular songs, without repercussions. Well, this is not the same. A magic word loses its damning power when used by some groups, and regains it when used by others. Thus, people of colour can use it, irrespective of context or intentions, but everyone else cannot. The argument is that the word uttered by a white person perpetuates a racist past of exploitation, whereas if it is reappropriated by a person of colour, it is an act of empowerment. It is indeed true that a white supremacist saying the n-word is an act of malice and hatred and should be morally condemned. Yet, the fact that different rules apply to different people based solely on their skin colour, irrespective of context or intentions, should raise some eyebrows. Generations have fought racism and, thus, have achieved the honourable result of delegitimizing horrible slurs like the n-word. It is not the other way round though... racism has not been fought because some combinations of letters have been banned. Language does not construct reality; reality is what it is, and language can only describe it and help us grasp it.

The problem is that often nowadays language is used in a different way: not to communicate reality, but to give what Malice (2019, loc. 1486) calls 'in-group signalling' to the other members of a tribe that one is part of them. 'Like the password to some underground club, the right cue is more important than the literal accuracy of what is actually being said' (idem, loc. 1497). If that's the case, we don't even speak the same language anymore, which means we cannot communicate. Therefore, fighting is unavoidable.

Taking scalps in the free speech wars

The Marxist philosopher Slavoj Zizek has done some interesting work in examining the show trials of the 1930s in the Soviet Union and the hysterical climate under which no one was safe. One day someone like Marshal Tukhachevsky was a hero of the socialist fatherland, and the next day he was a traitor, a saboteur, and a fanatic reactionary spy for the Intelligence Service and the fascists. Zizek called it a 'carnival in which today you are a king and tomorrow you are a beggar' (2009, p. 249). Or, during a Central Committee meeting, a life-long prominent Bolshevik like Bukharin would suddenly hear an orchestrated attack against him with phrases like 'Blackmailer!', 'Scoundrel!', ending with shouts along the lines of 'It's time to throw you in prison!' (idem, pp. 234–235). At that time the worst thing a defendant could do would be to attempt to prove his innocence against the imaginary crimes of sabotage, terrorism, and cooperation with fascists. That would constitute defiance towards the wisdom of the Party and thus would make his position worse.

Once the orchestrated attack was under way, a defendant's fate was sealed. All he could do, broken by torture and threats towards the lives of his wife and children, was to play along and apologize. While prosecutors like Vishinsky would refer to them as 'dogs gone mad' and 'jackals', arousing the court audience's standing ovations, and while outside on the streets thousands of enraged people, mobilized by the Party mechanism, would ask for their harsh punishment, the broken defendants would attack themselves to total self-humiliation. Kamenev, the loyal revolutionary and Bolshevik, uttered these words as his closing statement, trying to 'defend' himself in his trial (records and proceedings of the trials can be found at Marxists.org, 1936):

> 'there is a limit to everything, there is a limit to the magnanimity of the proletariat, and that limit we have reached... We are sitting here side by side with the agents of foreign secret-police departments because our weapons were the same, because our arms became intertwined before our fate became intertwined here in this dock... we served fascism, thus we organized counter-revolution against socialism, prepared, paved the way for the interventionists. Such was the path we took, and such was the pit contemptible treachery and all that is loathsome into which we have fallen.'

Berman-Yurin, a communist with international revolutionary action, offered the following closing statement on the made-up accusations against him: 'I do not want to defend myself by any arguments. There are no such arguments. I repented, but too late. Yesterday, in his speech for the prosecution, the citizen State Prosecutor drew the complete picture of my crimes. And the proletarian state will deal with me as I deserve. It is too late for contrition.'

A characteristic of the Moscow trials was their bizarreness: they would ruin someone's life out of the blue, with accusations that everyone knew were completely fabricated. Often, the case against someone was based on a passing comment or a joke made years earlier. Such cases were a spectacle, put on for the consolidation of power by the different echelons of the Party mechanism. No one was safe: prosecutors, like Yagoda and Yezhov, would be the next day's victims, tried and shot for 'sabotage', 'wrecking', 'promiscuity', and whatever else that day's prosecutor's fantasy could come up with. A prosecution would result in the 'unpersoning' of the defendant, who could do nothing to prove his innocence, but was expected to participate in his own destruction with an apology to his perpetrators.

Many of today's public shaming campaigns, often called 'cancelling', share some of the bizarre characteristics of the Moscow trials. Out of the blue, a word, a tweet—sometimes dug up from many years ago, by people Murray called 'offence archaeologists' (2019, p. 180)—a private conversation, or an opinion by someone, or even by someone's partner, is deemed 'offensive' or 'problematic'. Then, taken out of any context or proportion, that person is considered to be an associate in long-standing social problems, and a personification of them. Social media mobs go after the accused person's employers or sources of income, requiring punishment. Also, apologies are demanded, which may or may not appease the rage of the accusers.

The story of the Nobel laureate biologist Tim Hunt is indicative of this tendency. Having made a joke at an academic conference in Seoul about how women in laboratories cause distractions as 'you fall in love with them, they fall in love with you, and when you criticise them, they cry', Hunt entered the plane to get back home unsuspicious of what would follow. By the time he landed, a shaming campaign had taken place, and University College London had asked him to resign his academic position (McKie, 2015). He was already convicted of sexism and apparently he was part of the problem of women's under-representation in STEM fields. As opposed to the Moscow trials, though, his apology or his version of the event was not even required. Many women spoke up about how Hunt was anything but a sexist, and about how he had encouraged and helped them to pursue their careers in science. The question is though: does it even matter? Was this indeed about Hunt being a sexist, or does the fact that he belonged to the wrong group (white, male, 'privileged') qualify him as a scalp to be taken in the culture wars, irrespective of whether he had done something wrong or not?

Hunt's story reminds me of Milan Kundera's fictional hero Ludvik, from his novel *The Joke* (1992). Ludvik, living in socialist Czechoslovakia, engaged in the wrong kind of humour, when he sent a postcard to a girl he liked with the line: 'Optimism is the opium of mankind! A healthy spirit stinks of stupidity! Long live Trotsky!' The postcard fell into the hands of some Party apparatchiks who didn't appreciate Ludvik's humour, and life as he knew it was over. His past as a loyal and enthusiastic communist did not matter. One joke is all it takes.

Or consider the case of Lindsay Shepherd, a young Teaching Assistant at Wilfrid Laurier University, who got in trouble for showing a video in class from a debate between Jordan Peterson and other academics on gender pronouns. She was invited to a meeting with her supervisor, another academic, and the Gendered Violence Prevention and Support Officer, which she secretly recorded (Hopper, 2017). She was accused of presenting arguments 'that are counter to the Canadian Human Rights Code' and 'creating an unsafe environment for students'. Shepherd was not allowed to find out who, or how many students, made the complaint, or why. At some point her accusers revealed that the problem was that she presented Peterson without criticizing him enough. Like the Moscow prosecutors, they dropped the Nazi-card, claiming that Peterson's defence of free speech is also used by white supremacists and that there is always the precedence of the Weimar Republic—apparently too much free speech (!) was a factor in the rise of National Socialism. Shepherd repeatedly asked what she was accused of, and the answers she got were vague. The whole recording and the Kafkaesque 'trial' is uncomfortable to listen to, and was even tougher for Shepherd, who burst into tears unable to understand what was happening and why she was there. She stood her ground though and did not apologise. At the end, a member of the panel asked her 'not to play any more Jordan Peterson videos, or anything of the like'.

The bizarreness of what could cause one's cancelling escalated in the summer of 2020, following the protests and the riots in the USA after the death of George Floyd under the knee of a police officer. The cases of 'cancelling' are too many to keep count, but some characteristic ones include:

- A school principal in Windsor, who lost her job after pointing out in a Facebook post that, although she supports the Black Lives Matter movement, there is also a need to be supportive of law enforcement, and that 'Just because I don't walk around with a BLM sign should not mean I am a racist' (Savage, 2020).
- A data-analyst (sympathetic to the BLM movement) who tweeted an article on research undertaken by a scholar from a BAME[3] background indicating that rioting is politically counter-productive. He was fired from the data company for which he was working, after some of his colleagues complained that his tweet 'threatened their safety' (Chait, 2020).
- A TV commentator in Canada, who expressed the view that Canada is not systematically racist and most Canadians are not racist. He lost his job with CBC News Network, and had to step down from two senior positions with two major companies (Zimonjic, 2020).
- A reporter in Wales who had to step down from being a judge in the Book of the Year awards, as he pointed out in an article that the pro-BLM protests in Cardiff are breaking the government's lockdown rules (BBC, 2020).

---

[3]   BAME stands for 'Black, Asian, and minority ethnic'.

- Footballer Alexander Katai, who had to part ways with LA Galaxy because his wife mocked the protests and the looting that accompanied some of them in an Instagram story (Eurosport, 2020).

In many of the cases that we have seen in this chapter, one can notice that the victims of the shaming campaigns and of the wrath of those offended would not be described as right-wing ideological firebrands, but people with mainstream views that could even be considered parts of the liberal left, like Weinstein or Shepherd (at the time of the event she considered herself a progressive environmentalist) or the Christakis couple. Even Jordan Peterson is quite moderate in his politics. Provocateurs like Milo Yiannopoulos or conservative cultural warriors like Ben Shapiro were the exception and not the rule in the free speech wars. Such events triggered two results: one very positive, the other negative.

The positive outcome is that there has been a new appreciation of the issue of free speech and civility – of the idea that one can passionately disagree with someone but still have a debate. People from different parts of the political spectrum have come together trying to oppose the climate of 'you can't say that' and 'cancel culture'. Lengthy discussions like the ones taking place on the Rubin Report (led by the former leftist journalist Dave Rubin) and on Joe Rogan's show, and online publications like *Quilette* and *Areo* giving voice to 'dissident' voices, have built a new milieu and have made the culture of debate and intellectual pursuits 'trendy' again. It is also very important that there are now various networks of support like the Free Speech Union (2020) that can have the backs of people who are the targets of shaming campaigns, de-platforming, political smearing, etc.

Yet, there is another development, which might prove to be detrimental to the cause of free speech. The 'free speech wars' have solidified and expanded existing divisions, and have been the epicentre of the culture wars. The result of this is many people caring less about how to understand and defend free speech, and more about how to attack and 'own' the other side. Milo Yiannopoulos giving speeches at universities where his only line was 'feminism is cancer' or sending obscene tweets to people he disliked, capitalizing on his appeal as a 'free speech warrior', did very little to actually defend free speech. Even worse, the message for many on the right is that if the left is intent on taking scalps, they need to do the same. Thus, when the comedian Kathy Griffin posed holding a mask depicting the severed head of Donald Trump, there was a campaign of outrage that exacted a heavy toll on her career, including being fired from CNN's New Year's Eve broadcast (Malice, 2019, loc. 2950). Now, this could be unrelated to the culture wars: her posing with a mask of Trump's decapitated head was in really bad taste, and people wanting nothing to do with it can be seen as a rational choice.

Yet, Malice adds an interesting dimension to the story: many of the people who went after Griffin were not actually offended; they just made a calculated decision and estimated that, in the existing climate of 'zero tolerance' to offence, the other side would show hypocrisy if they didn't go after one of their own. After all, if someone were to hold a dummy of Obama's severed head, we'd never hear the end of it. Thus, people on the counter-cultural right decided to go after Griffin not out of being genuinely offended, but 'as an opportunity to get a leftist scalp' (idem). In June 2019, the same happened to Siobhan Prigent, an NHS worker in the UK. Following Trump's visit to London, a group of anti-Trump protesters mobbed a middle-aged Trump supporter in a video that went viral, shouting 'Nazi scum', and somebody threw a milkshake at him, to the roaring approval of many. Prigent did not use physical violence, but she was yelling 'Nazi scum' in the Trump supporter's face, and was laughing at his 'milkshaking'. Soon, a petition appeared online, calling for her to be fired from her job. The petition, which gathered approximately 3,500 signatures, mirrored the language of leftist protesters shaming someone on the other side; yet, now the roles were reversed. As Tom Slater wrote, the petition 'could have been written by a students' union officer incensed that someone used the wrong pronoun' (Slater, 2019). Indeed, Prigent quit her job, and the petition page celebrated 'victory' (Coleman, 2019). Another scalp from the other side was taken.

While some on the right think that the answer to the left's attempt to control the narrative is retaliation of the same kind, others claim to support free speech by asking for government control of the media or the institutions that regulate forms of speech. Twitter and Facebook have de-platformed many on the counter-cultural right (like Yiannopoulos and Alex Jones), have given warnings of misleading content about tweets of the then President Donald Trump (until eventually expelling him as well), whereas YouTube has demonetized many videos of mainstream conservative opinions, like Dennis Prager's 'Prager University', and episodes of the Rubin Report. It is perfectly acceptable to criticize these social media companies for their politically-motivated decisions. Yet, many conservatives have taken it a step further, calling for the state and the then President Trump himself to intervene. The rationale is that such media like Twitter have *de facto* become the new public sphere and, thus, should not discriminate against any views. Prager University has even taken legal action, 'to stop Google and YouTube from unlawfully censoring its educational videos and discriminating against its right to freedom of speech' (PragerU, 2017). As mentioned earlier, these steps might score points in the culture wars, but further undermine the right to free speech. If the owners have no right to choose what is approved on their platform and what is not, and if this decision is dictated by government coercion, then this is by definition censorship.

Thus, it becomes evident that the characteristics mentioned in the last three sections are not exclusively present on the left. The 'taking scalps' mentality has made parts of the right participants in the tango of permanent offence-taking and campaigning to trash the other side. This tango is a dangerous one, and capable of having many unintended consequences. Even though many of the 'free speech controversies' on campuses are not strictly about free speech issues, the values and virtues that make free speech possible are being compromised and are among the first victims of the culture wars. All this becomes even sadder when one takes into account the heavy price that has been paid for standing up for free speech. Thus, coming back to where this chapter started, maybe instead of being awe-struck by his bodyguards, I should have said 'thank you' to Flemming Rose for sticking his neck out for the rest of us. When free speech is denied to one, it is potentially denied to everyone. Courage like his is urgently needed.

The new racial thinking

When I was toying with the idea of a book on the culture wars and tribalism, there was a thought that kept coming back to my mind. Racism has never been more discredited morally, socially, and politically than it is today. And yet, often it looks as if we were never in the recent past as obsessed with race as we are today. Is this really the case, I thought, or is it just me exaggerating, seeing tribalism everywhere? Then, I started paying more attention to various pieces of news here and there; they all seemed to have something in common, so I'd save them in a bookmark folder titled 'racial thinking'. Here are some examples:

- An article in the *Huffington Post* accusing white families as perpetrators of inequality (Daniels, 2018).
- A study about how the diet of white people is 'killing the environment' (Sparks, 2019).
- A report about 'an escalating public debate about the social role of the white writer' (Schulman, 2016).
- A 'healing from internalized whiteness 3-day training', dealing with questions such as 'What do I do with my guilt around having white privilege?' and 'What do I do with my fear that I'll never get it right and that I'll always just mess it up as a white person?' (everydayfeminism.com, 2018).
- A 'shame resilience' workshop for white people, priced at $320.99–$374.20, on how to make productive use of the shame they carry for perpetuating racial and social injustice (Eventbrite, 2019).
- A 'leadership retreat' in Wales, offering a 'dedicated space to deconstruct the denials that sustain racism'. Why should white

'leaders' attend? Because 'those of us who benefit from the status quo need to come to terms with the fact that we *didn't* achieve our positions through "merit" or hard work' (darencof.uk, 2019).
- Criticisms against *Esquire* magazine for featuring a young white boy and the challenges of his life during Black History Month (Eustachewich, 2019).

Keep in mind, these examples are not part of any systematic research. They just popped up on my timeline during the 15–20 minutes I spend every day on twitter, over a period of about four months in 2019. Malice (2019, loc. 923) did a bit more systematic work and gathered a list of things that have been reported in the press recently and were considered as, in one way or another, related to a racist background. Among other things, the list includes:

- milk;
- expecting others to show up on time for an early morning meeting;
- peanut butter and jelly;
- maths;
- a statue of Walt Disney;
- belief in hard work and meritocracy;
- reason.

In April of 2019, some lecture slides went viral on twitter, claiming that characteristics of white supremacy include perfectionism, individualism, objectivity, and the sense of urgency. Such claims are not new, and have been present in the narrative of progressive anti-racist circles for some time now; the inspiration of the list is a report from two decades ago of the Department of Inclusion and Community Engagement of Minnesota Historical Society (2001).

Being in tune with the Black Lives Matter protests in the summer of 2020, the following are only some examples of things problematized as encompassing racist dynamics:

- the term 'master bedroom' (Miller, 2020);
- Uncle Ben's rice—which changed its name to Ben's Original (Booker, 2020);
- jogging (Petrzela, 2020);
- fighting obesity (Strings and Bacon, 2020);
- surfing in California (Zhang, 2020);
- Italian fashion (Bettizza, 2020).

The danger here is to take all these stories light-heartedly and consider them 'political correctness gone mad'. Actually, they are just a few bizarre examples of a tendency that is quite mainstream in today's culture: a tribal outlook that needs to see people as members of groups, and understands the world as a constant conflict between such groups for power and the ability to exploit. Also, farcical stories about how 'everything is racism' can obscure how evil and dangerous a worldview actual racism is. Unfortunately, we have plenty of reminders of it, as really racist ideologies make their presence felt, often resorting to violence and acts of terrorism, like the events at Charlottesville in 2017 and the New Zealand massacre in 2019 by a white supremacist.

There have been many arguments on race and whether it is a biological reality or a social construct. This discussion is long and, due to its politicization, difficult to untangle. There might be differences in things like bone density or vulnerability to specific diseases between people whose ancestors came from different geographical areas, and the reasons could vary. But interpreting such differences in a way that creates hierarchies of political power, or unjustified generalizations, or ethnic and racial segregation, is a social process. In any case, this is a discussion that definitely goes beyond the scope of this book.

Defining racism is influenced by philosophical and political agendas. There are neutral definitions, describing racism as 'the attribution of social significance (meaning) to particular patterns of phenotypical and/or genetic difference' (Banton, 1996, p. 310), leading to the 'racialization' of some groups and the imposition of relations of inferiority–superiority among them, and actual forms of discrimination, like the Nuremberg Laws in the Third Reich, Jim Crow laws, and apartheid (Garner, 2017, p. 21).

Yet, there are more specific definitions, adding to the element of discrimination the element of power (Eddo-Lodge, 2018, p. 89). Such definitions are behind the popular mantra claiming that 'black people or minorities cannot be racist, as they lack power'. Others are even more specific, defining racism as 'cognitions, actions, and procedures that contribute to the development and perpetuation of a system in which Whites dominate Blacks' (Essed, 2002, p. 181). Pluckrose and Lindsay claim that dominant today in the public sphere is a definition of racism that is influenced by postmodern critical theories and does not see the phenomenon as a prejudice based on race, but as a vaguely defined 'system' that 'permeates all interactions in society yet is largely invisible except to those who experience it or who have been trained in the proper "critical" methods that train them to see it' (2020, p. 21).

A vague and clumsy understanding of racism following a political agenda is, in my opinion, dangerous. Racism has very real and horrific consequences, and history is full of them: lynching, torture, rape, segregation, concentrations camps, and the Holocaust. Yet, to prevent such horrors, we need to understand the kind of thinking that gives rise to racism. I consider racism a derivative of tribal thinking. Perhaps its most horrific derivative, but a derivative nonetheless. Thus, I endorse Rand's definition of racism, which highlights its epistemological aspect:

> 'Racism is the lowest, most crudely primitive form of collectivism. It is the notion of ascribing moral, social or political significance to a man's genetic lineage—the notion that a man's intellectual and characterological traits are

produced and transmitted by his internal body chemistry...
Like every form of determinism, racism invalidates the specific
attribute which distinguishes man from all other living
species: his rational faculty. Racism negates two aspects of
man's life: reason and choice, or mind and morality, replacing
them with chemical predestination.' (Rand, 1964, p. 147)

Thus, racism is a way of thinking that is not only wrong for the
victim, but also for the perpetrator, as it does not offer an accurate
understanding of reality. It is also an act of intellectual laziness. 'It
is a quest for automatic knowledge — for an automatic evaluation
of men's characters that bypasses the responsibility of exercising
rational or moral judgment' (idem, p. 149).

Trying to focus on the epistemological element of racism, but
without denying its actual political effects, I will use the term
'racial thinking' in this chapter. As tribalism is prevalent in both
the left and the right, predictably so is racial thinking.

Progressive racial thinking

Do groups underachieve because of discrimination?
This section will examine how and why many who consider
themselves progressives or who position themselves on the wider
left have contributed to bringing race back to the forefront of
today's public sphere, even under the best of intentions to
eradicate racism, or to highlight its persistence. The idea of
including people one could loosely categorize as leftists or progressive liberals in a chapter about racial thinking might be
considered outrageous by some. Yet, this should not be the case.
No political ideology, and no good intentions, can protect someone from the consequences of bad ideas and premises.

Thomas Sowell (1984), an African American sociologist and
economist of conservative political persuasions who has done a
lot of work on modern racial thinking, summed up the position of

the wider left on racism in the US and elsewhere in the West (and the same scheme could apply to other issues, such as sexism):

(1) Statistical disparities in various metrics between different groups are seen as proof of discrimination and structural injustice.

(2) The solution is believed to reside in political initiatives, quotas, affirmative action, etc.

(3) Negation of points 1) and 2) is seen as a proof of a stubborn overt or covert racism.

Sowell has spent his decades-long intellectual career trying to offer a different point of view regarding racial relations and disparities. His point is that considering discrimination and racism as the main (if not the sole) reason behind the underachieving of many African Americans in the US is destructive first and foremost for the black community itself (Sowell, 1984; 1994; 2013). He provided various international comparisons and historical data that exhibit that discrimination against ethnic groups does not always coincide with underachievement (the Jewish and Chinese people in various societies on different continents are an example), which indicates that there might be other factors, such as individual choices and preferences, or cultural patterns within the underachieving group that also need to be examined. Yet, such views are quite marginal in social sciences and among the academic and non-academic left. The prevailing view is that disparities are a result of racism that is still alive and kicking, and this inhibits the life prospects of minority groups.

From the analysis of chapter 3, one could understand the insistence of the left on such a worldview. History is seen as an everlasting struggle between groups of oppressors and oppressed. Also, in an age celebrating the importance of identity in providing epistemological certainty, it makes sense for people to see themselves through the lenses of their ethnic group. Thus, a simplistic worldview where whites are the exploiters and BAME groups are the exploited is intellectually convenient. Yet, what we will see happening is such a view providing a gateway for *more* preoccupation with race, not less.

Whiteness as a root of social evils

By objective measures, we live in the least racist times of the last many centuries, as evident by various historical moments: from the long overdue formal equality of rights through the Civil Rights Act of 1964 (despite its shortcomings) to the election of the first African American US President in 2008. Yet, racism is still evident in the thoughts and actions of many people, and often of state agents, as indicated by some cases of police brutality against black people. For many, such incidents are indicative beyond doubt of a racism that is institutional in US society. Such a view is prominent among scholars of disciplines such as critical race, legal, feminist, postcolonial, queer, and intersectional studies, for whom it is considered a given that we are still living in a predominantly racist society, where racism is a constant undercurrent, even when it's not visible to the untrained eye.

The key to understanding the theory about the institutional nature of racism is the notion of 'whiteness' and 'white supremacy'. A scholar explained the rise of such disciplines as a reaction to 'colour blindness' and the false perception that 'race no longer matters' (Andersen, 2003). A reader not familiar with these critical theories might get confused here. Isn't 'colour blindness' supposed to be a good thing? Didn't Dr Martin Luther King inspire millions with his dream about a world where his kids 'will one day live in a nation where they will not be judged by the colour of their skin but by the content of their character' (King, 1963)? This is simplistic, according to ideas prevalent in critical race studies, if not a direct expression of white supremacy (DiAngelo, 2018, p. 89). The claim is that colour blindness fails to acknowledge the omnipresent hegemony of 'whiteness': the way that white identity's domination is diffused in all the power structures and social relations in the USA.

Trying to understand whiteness and white privilege leads to some definitions that obscure, rather than clarify, the issue. For Andersen, the concept of whiteness is about 'the development of white identity and white privilege' and can help us see 'how white racial identity is constructed and how systems of white privilege operate' (2003, p. 21). For Pluckrose and Lindsay, white privilege is used by critical race theorists to indicate a 'complicity in perpetuating systemic racism simply by being white' (2020, p. 237). For Eddo-Lodge, white privilege is 'an absence of structural discrimination, an absence of your race being viewed as a problem first and foremost, an absence of "less likely to succeed because of my race"' (2018, p. 86). A definition based on a negative (absences) might not be very illuminating, so here is a third definitional attempt: 'all actors socially regarded as "white" —, and I shall argue later, as "near white" — receive systemic privileges by virtue of wearing the white — or virtually white — outfit, whereas those regarded as nonwhite are denied these privileges' (Bonilla-Silva, 2003, p. 271).

Here we see how race is viewed not as a static 'biological' category, but as an open social construct subject to constant renegotiation based on one's position in the intersectional structures of power. Under this prism, Japanese Americans or Asian Indians in the US are part of the 'near white' category (idem, p. 278). Still though, the definition of white privilege is problematic. Whites (and allies) receive 'systematic privileges'... of what kind and from whom? Also, notice the passive voice: other groups are 'denied these privileges'. By whom? Does a critical mass of individual whites deny such privileges to non-whites, or are they passing discriminatory laws? Clearly no, so the answer needs to be that the perpetrator of injustices is a vaguely defined system, which, as it is constructed by white people, has a blind spot for racial inequalities.

This system, according to some critical race scholars, is capitalism, and thus a struggle against racism needs to include a global battle against capitalism (Andersen, 2003, p. 25). This argument harkens back to pre-World War II America, where many on the left claimed that racism lies not only in the hearts of people and discriminatory legislations, but on social structures and the power relations of the capitalist system. This is why this milieu was never convinced by the expansion of individual rights and of educational awareness as a remedy to racism (Gordon, 2015).

Yet, there is a problem with the idea that a vaguely defined racism runs deep in the system, and it is twofold:

(a) it fails to provide a smoking gun to exhibit how exactly this is still the case;
(b) more importantly, it establishes racial thinking as a permanent way of viewing the world and sees individuals as static avatars of their racial identity.

Putting individuals in racial boxes

Policies like affirmative action and positive discrimination 'quotas' are examples that could enhance, rather than alleviate, racial tensions. In 2018, a group representing students of Asian ethnic background brought a lawsuit against Harvard University, challenging 'race-conscious admissions policies that give minority students a better shot at getting accepted' (Wood, 2018). Similar policies are followed by many other Ivy League universities. According to some estimates, admissions policies implemented to guarantee diversity and the acceptance of students from less privileged backgrounds mean that around half of the percentage of Asian-Americans that would have been accepted in the absence of such policies (and if admissions were based on a colour blind basis such as test scores) are not accepted (Xu, 2018). Harvard claims that this is not anti-Asian racism, as such policies support diversity. For anyone believing in individual achievement and meritocracy, such a system is clearly unfair. Yet, as we saw earlier, for some, terms such as 'individualism' and 'meritocracy' are smokescreens for the continuation of white supremacy — or in this case, supremacy of 'near whites' high on the intersectional axis of power, such as Asian Americans.

Racial quotas have been the subject of controversy beyond universities. In 2016, during the Academy Awards the hashtag #OscarsSoWhite trended on twitter, supporting the need for more diversity in Hollywood. There are now diversity standards that need to be reached for a movie to be considered for a BAFTA award in the UK, including among other things 'on-screen representation, themes & narratives' (BAFTA, 2018). But this results in art being seen under the suspicious prism of racial thinking. In 2017, there were claims that Adele won the Album of the Year award in the Grammys over Beyoncé because of racism — without much evidence as to why this was the case (Chua, 2018, p. 32). Instead of celebrating two beautiful voices, according to progressive racial thinking one could see two women as representatives of their racial identities.

What percentage of BAME actors and creators would it take for the Oscars to stop being so white? Sowell has made the case that expecting the representation of an ethnic group in an institution to be exactly analogous to its percentage in the population goes against the rules of statistical variance and, thus, is a wrong indicator of discrimination, unless there is hard data suggesting otherwise (1984, pp. 54–55). Interestingly, some on the side of critical race theory agree, though coming from a different angle. In the best-selling book *Why I'm No Longer Talking to White People About Race* (a title sounding slightly discriminatory), Reni Eddo-Lodge mentioned: 'When pressed on lack of representation, some like to cite the racial demographics in Britain, saying that because the minority of the population isn't white, that percentage and that percentage only should be represented in organisations. This mathematical approach is the new tokenism. It is an obsession with bodies in the room rather than recruiting the right people who will work in the interests of the marginalised' (2018, pp. 79–80). This is confusing. So it is not about percentages? So what is then the proper basis for quotas? And who are the 'right people' who can represent the collective entity of the 'marginalized'?

We can definitely assume who are *not* 'the right people' though. Many claim that the rise of African Americans like Colin Powell, Condoleezza Rice, or the Supreme Court Justice Clarence Thomas in positions of power is a sign of the US society moving beyond white supremacy. Wrong, says Bonilla-Silva: such figures are 'safe minorities' (which probably means 'they are conservatives') and thus only mask a new type of racism (2003, p. 272). In July of 2019, the then new Prime Minister of the UK Boris Johnson appointed a uniquely diverse cabinet, with almost one fifth of his ministers coming from an ethnic minority background. The reactions from the progressive milieu were quite vocal: these ministers were accused by prominent commentators and politicians of 'selling their soul' for a position, of 'tokenism', of being products of 'internalised whiteness', and of not being a person of colour anymore (cited in Myers, 2019). In 2018, Kanye West was characterised as Uncle Tom and a collaborator by a variety of commentators for his sympathy for Donald Trump (Mohamed, 2018). The tribal thinking here is evident: all black people, as avatars of their identity, are expected to think in the same way and hold the same beliefs (perhaps beliefs decided by the 'right people' who 'work in the interests of the marginalized'). To suggest otherwise would mean to see them as individuals with their own judgment. Under this narrative, being black is becoming more a political ideology, and less a skin colour or an ethnic background (Murray, 2019, p. 156).

Racial thinking vs. individual agency

This racial outlook undermines the capacity of BAME people for agency. An interesting read is another best-seller, Ta-Nehisi Coates' *Between the World and Me* (2015). There, the author recalled his life and the hardships he has witnessed growing up and living in the US as a black person. In the neighbourhood he grew up in, there was a predominance of violence, drugs, beatings, and guns.

Yet, what is conspicuous by its absence is the reference to anyone white. He described violence as giving a sense of security to 'black bodies' (as black people are referred to by many who ascribe to critical race theories): 'They would break your jaw, stomp your face, and shoot you down to feel that power, to revel in the might of their own bodies' (2015, p. 22). Yet, the suggestion that white supremacy is not evident there (as there are literally no white people involved) is problematic for Coates: '"Black-on-black crime" is jargon, violence to language, which vanishes the men who engineered the covenants, who fixed the loans, who planned the projects, who built the streets and sold red ink by the barrel... To yell "black-on-black crime" is to shoot a man and then shame him for bleeding' (idem, pp. 110–111).

There should be no surprise for such claims. Even if Coates cannot name a single occasion of a wrongdoing against him from a white person, or even if he had never met a single white person in his life, according to a narrative that is very powerful today he would still be a victim of racism. This is because, based on critical race theory, racism is a diffused system of power without particular points of reference. Thus, advocates of this theory claim that one could be the victim of racism even if no individual around is a racist. After all, according to this worldview, society and power relations are not constituted by autonomous individuals, but by groups in hierarchical relationships to each other (Pluckrose and Lindsay, 2000, p. 41). Asking for empirical evidence and hard data for the existence of an objectively defined racism would also be unacceptable under such a theoretical prism, as it would deny the lived experience of someone from a marginalized view and thus promote a western-centric (and according to others, white supremacist) way of thinking.

I claim that Coates' view is actually quite disempowering for black individuals. Whatever they do, what happens in their life is never within their control or responsibility. The malice of white supremacy is everywhere for them, and there is no escape. Individuals cannot take life into their own hands. Coates' disdain for the notion of individual responsibility (idem, p. 33) is evident even when he mentions the achievements of African Americans. He is uneasy with 'history books that spoke of black people only as sentimental "firsts" — first black five star general, first black congressman, first black mayor — always presented in the bemused manner of a category of Trivial Pursuit' (idem, p. 43). Thus, denying the history and contribution of black people is an element of white supremacy, and celebrating them is tokenism. It is as if there can be no reconciliation, which Coates openly stated later in the book, as he claimed that without racial supremacy there is no American Dream (idem, p. 105).

Some of the cases Coates gave as landmarks for solidifying his rage and his belief that racism is central and permanent in the US are the deaths of Prince Jones in 2000, who was unjustifiably shot by a police officer, the shooting of Michael Brown in Ferguson in 2014 by a police officer, and the fatal shooting of Trayvon Martin by neighbourhood watch volunteer George Zimmerman in 2012. The last two cases were central in the rise of the Black Lives Matter movement, together with the death of Eric Garner in 2014, following a headlock grip by a police officer (the officer was eventually found innocent). Each one of these cases is a tragedy, and might raise various issues on law enforcement in the US. Yet, it is a stretch to qualify them as expressions of white supremacy. The officer who shot Prince Jones was himself black. The evidence in court suggested that Michael Brown had attacked the police officer and grasped his gun, and the officer was acquitted by a grand jury that was 30% African American. Zimmerman was also acquitted, as it was evidenced that, before being shot, Martin had attacked him and was pounding his head on the pavement; also, the fact that Zimmerman was of Hispanic origin makes the 'crime of white supremacy' narrative weaker. The fact that Coates did not feel the need to examine each one of these cases on their own merit, and even included in his narrative a case where the perpetrator was a black officer, shows how his view of the USA as a white supremacist society is unfalsifiable.

The prevalence of the idea that the USA is an institutionally racist society became even more evident in the summer of 2020. George Floyd, a black man, died while being constrained by a white officer who had his knee on Floyd's neck for more than eight minutes. His death was attributed to heart failure, probably aggravated by previous use of drugs (according to the official autopsy). According to a separate autopsy by the family, his death could have been caused by asphyxia. Whichever of these versions one wishes to follow, there is no doubt that the manner of Floyd's arrest contributed to his tragic death (Read, 2020). What followed was the biggest wave of protests the US has ever seen, despite the lockdowns that were in place due to the COVID-19 pandemic. Often the protests turned to riots, but most commentators were lenient and did not wave their support for the Black Lives Matter movement: after all, America was finally facing the problem of institutional racism.

A question that was barely ever asked was the obvious one: is there any evidence that the death of George Floyd had anything to do with racism? There is little doubt that the police officer who kneeled on his neck acted in an unforgivable way, but did he do so moved by racism? There is no evidence of any previous racist indications in his life or behaviour. Also, two of the four members of the police squad that were present on the scene were BAME. In addition, a similar incident in 2018, when a white man died under identical conditions—under arrest and having a police officer's knee on his neck—barely made the news (Associated Press, 2020). But all these are the wrong questions, the proponents of critical race theory would point out. In their worldview, someone not being consciously racist is not enough to alleviate them from the accusation of racism. As an influential anti-racist scholar-activist put it: 'The question is not "Did racism take place?" for that is to be assumed, but rather "How did racism manifest in that situation?"' (cited in Pluckrose and Lindsay, 2020, p. 157). Even if the police officer who kneeled on Floyd was not racist himself, as a white man in a position of power he was the embodiment of a white supremacist system, the presence of which is not to be questioned, and acted as an avatar and an embodiment of his identity.

Racial thinking as prejudice

A belief in such a narrative that views the whole of society as being under the hegemony of white supremacy can lead to bitterness and a prejudiced outlook. Coates admitted that when 9/11 happened, he could not feel sorrow for the police officers and the fire fighters who lost their lives: 'looking out upon the ruins of white America, my heart was cold' (2015, p. 86). In his eyes, the dead men and women in uniform symbolized 'the sword of American citizenry' (idem). 'But I did know that Bin Laden was not the first man to bring terror to that section of the city. I never forget that. Neither should you. In the days after, I watched the ridiculous pageantry of flags, the machismo of firemen, the overwrought slogans. Damn it all. Prince Jones was dead' (idem, p. 87). Again, the fact that Jones was shot by a black officer does not mitigate Coates' hate for (white) America. Elsewhere in the book, he referred to white Americans as 'the heirs of these Virginia planters' (idem, p. 43). Referring to 197 million people as a group, and seeing them as heirs of slave owners, is textbook racism: it refuses to evaluate them as individuals, and characterizes them by the actions of people of the same skin colour from centuries ago. And such an outlook does not come from an extremist voice: the book was celebrated, among others, by *The Guardian*, *Slate*, *New York Times*, *Washington Post*, and other mainstream media, besides winning the National Book Award.

Eddo-Lodge also saw whites as a group. Referring to white kids in education, she mentioned how they 'effortlessly transition from student booze-culture-loving lager louts to slick-young-professional status' (2018, p. 68). This is racial stereotyping, pure and simple. Such views are not unusual among critical race theorists. Bonilla-Silva mentioned how many of them see whiteness as a 'moral problem' (2003, p. 271). Robin DiAngelo, whose book *White Fragility: Why It's So Hard for White People to Talk About Racism* (2018) was central in the pro-Black Lives Matter narrative in the summer of 2020, expressed a wish to be 'a little less white, which means a little less oppressive, oblivious, defensive, ignorant and arrogant' (cited in Soriano, 2019). Andersen pointed out the claim that racial justice means that whiteness needs renunciation (2003, p. 25). Fox mentioned how often white people expressing strong opinions are dismissed for exhibiting 'white confidence' (2016, loc. 1485). Chua claimed that mentions of 'whiteness' as something constant and relating to all white people is resembling anti-Semitism and the image of the 'eternal Jew' (2018, p. 199). Lukianoff and Heidt highlighted how, during the protests in Evergreen College (see previous chapter), white 'allies' were expected to sit at the back of the room and to listen, but not talk (2018, p. 116). This sounds suspiciously like segregation based on race. Indeed, in the summer of 2020 students supportive of Black Lives Matter requested — unsuccessfully — New York University to stand by its support for the movement and create separate accommodation for black and 'black-identifying' students (Soave, 2020).

Racial thinking needs to be seen for what it is, irrespective of which ethnic group it comes from or where it is directed, and it needs to be denounced. Also, as mentioned earlier in this chapter, the gap between racial thinking and overt racism is often a small one. Speaking of overt racism and being obsessed with 'whiteness' brings us to some people who proudly embrace such a racialist worldview: the new white nationalists and the alt-right.

White nationalism and the alt-right

Alt-right: what it is and what it isn't

Few words have been so misused in the political vocabulary over the last years as the term 'alt-right'. It has been used as a smear for people in or around the conservative milieu, and among others for people so different to each other such as Jordan Peterson, Ben

Shapiro, Alex Jones, and Milo Yiannopoulos. Actually, none of these people are alt-right. The misuse of the term is not only wrong and disingenuous; it is actually dangerous. It undermines how bad and distinctive from all other shades of the right and of conservatism the alt-right actually is. Also, it reveals a failure to go deep into and understand the alt-right. Most of its proponents are not knuckle-dragger old-style skinheads with KKK or neo-Nazi tattoos. The movement includes more sophisticated, often well-educated individuals who are good speakers and writers. This makes the movement more dangerous; it also makes undermining it or misreading it more inexcusable.

Alt-right is an abbreviation for alternative right. The name can be claimed by two people: by paleoconservative Paul Gottfried, who used it around 2008 to refer to the non-mainstream strands of the conservative movement (and mostly to paleoconservatives), and by Richard Spencer. Eventually, Spencer became more associated with the term, as he has been the organizer of the network that made the alt-right more noisy, and established it as a white nationalist movement. When I refer to the term, I refer to it in the way Spencer meant it, i.e. as a white nationalist milieu in the USA. In this chapter, I will focus more on the ideas of the movement, and less on its history and the people who comprise it —for the latter, I refer the reader to the edited work of Mark Sedwick, *Key Thinkers of the Radical Right: Behind the New Threat to Liberal Democracy* (2019).

The editor of the white nationalist website *Counter-Currents*, Greg Johnson (2018), presented the main tenets of the alt-right:

- Whiteness is a central pillar of European civilization and legacy.
- Immigration and policies that affect 'white fertility' push whites into becoming a minority in their lands.
- The solution is the promotion of white ethno-states, which, among other things, will follow policies enabling the white population to reverse such a trend.

As for the movements upon which the alt-right builds, they are the following: 'race realism, White Nationalism, the European New Right, the Conservative Revolution,[1] Traditionalism, neo-paganism, agrarianism, Third Positionism,[2] anti-feminism, and right-wing anti-capitalists, ecologists, bioregionalists, and small-is-beautiful types' (idem, loc. 204). Common in these movements are trends that we have seen earlier in this book: anti-liberalism, anti-egalitarianism, anti-capitalism, traditionalism, and identitarian-ism. Thus, although the movement is prevalent in the United States, its ideological roots are located mostly in Europe. The tradition of white supremacy, along with the transgressive ethos that we saw in the US counter-cultural right, add up to the eclectic mix of the alt-right. It is the emphasis on race that is the main thing that distinguishes the alt-right from the European New Right. European identitarians focus on identity and culture, whereas their American counterparts focus on race. Also, anti-Semitism is prevalent in the US movement, but not so much in Europe (Macklin, 2019, pp. 213–214).

The racialism of the alt-right

The central worldview of the movement can be summarized in the words of a European, Guillaume Faye: 'The base of everything is biocultural identity and demographic renewal' (2001, p. 37). Thus, the struggle is about 'the necessity to defend the biological and cultural identity of one's people' (idem, p. 100). The alt-right would wear tribalism as a badge of honour. As a white nationalist writer mentioned: 'Human equality is a myth; our world is tribal; the white tribe is being suppressed in its own nations' (Bell, 2018, loc. 2067). Who is the opponent, the 'other'? The 'alien', i.e. 'those who are culturally and biologically of non-indigenous origin' (Faye, 2001, p. 75).

---

[1] A German nationalist conservative movement active between the end of the First World War and the rise of the National Socialists.
[2] This means opposition to both capitalism and communism.

Their emphasis on race is the reason the alt-right is presented as a separate case from the counter-cultural and anti-establishment right. One of the movement's intellectuals is Jared Taylor, who since 1990 has been running the (now online) *American Renaissance* magazine. He considers himself a 'race realist', i.e. he believes race has a biological base and that races are different. Taylor understands the alt-right as being 'united in contempt for the idea that race is only a "social construct"' (2018, loc. 572). As an identitarian, he sees race as 'central to group and individual identity' (idem, loc. 594). For him, the normal status of race relations anywhere in the world is summed up in one word: conflict (Taylor, 2013). Thus, a racially homogeneous society is seen as having more potential to be peaceful. Moreover, he wants such a society to come up by peaceful means, assisted by social policy, such as freedom of association, and stricter immigration laws. For him, Jews are welcome in a white ethno-state. Maybe even *some* blacks? As Taylor mentioned in an interview, in tune with Evola's view that race lies also in one's heart, 'if Thomas Sowell decides he's white, I'd have a hard time telling him no' (mentioned in Malice, 2019, loc. 3898). Taylor is an example of how new white identitarianism is a different phenomenon from old-style 'redneck' KKK racism. He is a Yale graduate who lived in Japan for many years and who is a connoisseur of Asian culture. He is ready to admit that Asians and Ashkenazi Jews have on average a higher IQ than white people. Then, why is he aiming for a coherent white ethno-state? Because he believes 'there is no higher morality than to work for the survival and prosperity of one's people' (idem, loc. 643).

Anti-Semitism and the 1488ers

Taylor's view of the Jews as potential allies of whites is not shared by many other figures of the alt-right. Many within the movement focus on the 'Jewish question', and exhibit overt anti-Semitism. Jews are considered enemies of whites, for three reasons: (a) their supposed impact on 'white dispossession', i.e. the compromise of western cultures by multiculturalism and ethnic diversity, which is predicted (according to the milieu) to lead to something close to a 'white genocide'; (b) their supposed influence on US foreign policy in the Middle East, which is seen as pro-Israel and contrary to the US interests; (c) their supposed effect on culture and the media, leading to the promotion of 'homosexuality, premarital sex, pornography, and adultery' (MacDonald, 2018, loc. 767). Thus, we see a new version of the old anti-Semitic stereotype of the 'oversexed Jew'. Of course, rational consistency was never a characteristic of anti-Semites; others in the movement who are more tolerant towards homosexuality (appreciating the pagan tradition of male bonding and admiration) consider homophobia 'a Jewish invention' (cited in Lyons, 2019, p. 251). Another revival of vulgar old anti-Semitism is the projection on the Jew as untrustworthy and unfaithful. According to an alt-rightist: 'When any element of the organized Jewish community is the counterparty in an agreement, like the fable of the frog and the scorpion, the compulsion towards betrayal, even against allies, is irresistible for the Jew' (Le Brun, 2018, loc. 1936).

This open anti-Semitism is one of the reasons many in the movement have a positive evaluation of Hitler and the legacy of German National Socialism. A writer on the white nationalist site *Counter-Currents* elaborated:

> 'The legacy of German National Socialism inspires, and its symbolism rouses many racially conscious whites today regardless of their nationality. Whatever one thinks of National Socialism and whether or not one believes the official narrative about it, it is part of the common history of the movement to which the modern-day alt right belongs, and it represented the same aspirations and longings that animate all racially conscious whites today.' (Durand, 2018, loc. 2873).

The part of the movement sympathetic to the Nazis is often referred to as the '1488ers', in reference to the symbolism of the numbers 14 and 88 for the movement. 14 is the number of words in a white supremacist slogan ('we must secure the existence of our people and a future for white children'), whereas 88 stands for 'Heil Hitler' (H is the eighth letter in the alphabet). It has to be mentioned, though, that not everyone on the alt-right is supportive of the legacy of National Socialism, and it is an issue of constant arguments within the movement.

Richard Spencer, and the white ethno-state as safe space

The 'face' of the alt-right in the media and for most people outside of the movement has been Richard Spencer. Spencer, like Taylor, also deviates from the image of the skinhead thug. With a degree in English Literature and Music and a BA in Humanities, Spencer is well-spoken, and well-dressed, as he claims that belonging to a transgressive group means that 'we have to look good' (cited in Bar-On, 2019, p. 227). Spencer rose from the wider paleo-conservative milieu, as he was involved with the editing of *American Conservative* (from which it is believed he was fired for his extremist ideas) and *Taki Magazine,* the site of political and social commentary of the eccentric ultra-conservative Greek author Taki Theodorakopoulos. Then, Spencer went on to operate a succession of sites that became the main online 'home' of the alt-right: *Alternative Right, Radix Journal,* and *AltRight.com.* He also runs the think-tank National Policy Institute (NPI).

At the centre of Spencer's worldview is race. In a 'Manifesto of the Alt-Right', Spencer (2017) declared: 'Race is real. Race matters. Race is the foundation of identity.' He considers white identity as related to peoples 'derived from the Indo-European race, often called Aryan', including Celts, Germans, Slavs, Hellenes, Latins, Nordics, but *not* Jews. 'Jews are an ethno-religious people distinct from Europeans. At various times, they have existed within European societies, without being of them. The preservation of their identity as Jews was and is contingent on resistance to assimilation, sometimes expressed as hostility towards their hosts' (idem). Spencer's goal is the foundation of 'racially or ethnically defined states' (idem), i.e. ethno-states. Thus, despite his dismissal of Jewish people as non-whites, he considers Israel a model of an ethno-state. Spencer claims that these ethno-states will be formed peacefully and voluntarily. Yet, when pushed during an interview by author Angela Nagle on what will happen if this requires a violent confrontation, Spencer replied: 'The existence of my people is not negotiable' (ABC News, 2018).

Spencer's biggest talent, probably a result of his engagement with mainstream ideas in academia, is understanding how to present and sell his white nationalism in the current intellectual atmosphere. He saw two significant tendencies in identity politics today: the claim for 'recognition' and the status of 'vulnerability'. In a video (now removed from YouTube, as is most of the material of the alt-right) called 'Who Are We', which was used as an introduction to the Alt-Right channel, Spencer called on (white) people to 'become who they are'. Once more in this book, we see group identity considered as the final horizon of an individual's life. Who 'we' are is our ancestors, our history, our culture, and our identity. This identity is supposedly under threat. Thus, Spencer puts forward not an image of white superiority, but of white *vulnerability*. Like Taylor, he claims that whites indeed have on average a lower IQ than Asians. Also, he sees them under threat from 'dispossession' through immigration, etc. Thus, he is (literally) calling for a 'safe space'[3] for white people; though this safe space will not be a room in a university with soothing music and furry toys to cuddle, but a whole ethno-state.

Despite his early socializing with circles close to paleolibertarians, Spencer is an opponent of capitalism and freedom, as they lead to a mixing of races and cultures, and what he sees as a soul-destroying consumerism and social disintegration. As he said in the 'Who Are We' video, 'a nation based on freedom is just

---

[3]   As, for example, in his interview with Garry Younge of *The Guardian* that went viral in 2017.

another place to go shopping'. Elsewhere, he said that 'the interests of businessmen and global merchants should never take precedence over the well-being of workers, families, and the natural world' (Spencer, 2017). In tweets he has challenged the merits of free speech, as he believes it is a faux-freedom in an unequal and incohesive society; yet, free speech appears as a value to be respected in the 2017 manifesto. He has supported universal healthcare, but preferably within a white ethno-state, and voted for Joe Biden in the 2020 elections. Also, he is, predictably, opposed to individualism: 'We need to be willing to take care of people and not simply think of ourselves as individuals who can acquire as much wealth as possible' (cited in Mirkowitz, 2017). Thus, Spencer is, at the end of the day, close to what we would call a small n and s national socialist.

This brings us to a peculiar characteristic of the alt-right: its *un-Americanism*. As Bar-On mentions, the alt-right 'rejects two sacred American values, namely, equality and liberty' (2019, p. 226). White nationalists would answer that the Founding Fathers were *de facto* white supremacists and some of them slave owners. Yet, this can be challenged when taking into account the ideas that gave rise to the founding of the country. Yet, they were also the ones who conceived and wrote the Declaration of Independence and the Constitution, two radical texts that express the spirit of the country. They make the revolutionary point that rights belong to individuals, not to groups or races. One's freedom is recognized as essential due to one's nature as a human being; not because one is American, or white. The state is there to recognize and serve one's rights — not to create them. Thus, a government is legitimate not because it expresses 'the will of the people', but only as long as it fulfils its mission: the defence of individual rights. This is the foundation of Americanism (Hoenig, 2018). Furthermore, the white nationalists' belief that the civilization that gave birth to the USA is compatible only with specific races goes against the history of the country, and the idea of the 'melting pot'. At its core, the melting pot is an individualistic and anti-collectivist idea; it recognizes that what should make different individuals members of a free country is their adherence to specific ideas, rather than a tribalist allegiance. Such a worldview is alien to the alt-right.

The rise and fall (?) of the alt-right

The golden era of the alt-right was the period around 2015–16. Trump's campaign and the energy it generated within the anti-establishment right created a space where the voices of white nationalism merged into the incoherent whole. It is not that Trump was necessarily aware of the movement—Greg Johnson called the alt-right's relationship with him a 'one-way man-crush' (cited in Macklin, 2019, p. 212). Trump's campaign 'encouraged cooperation and collegiality within the movement and provided a steady stream of new targets for creative memes and trolling' (Johnson, 2018, loc. 264). Johnson considered the dispersion of the term 'cuckservative' that was dismissively used for Trump's opponents within the GOP a cultural win for the alt-right (idem).

The two events that signified the alt-right's 'fall' took place within nine months. The first was what became known within the movement as 'hailgate': at an event of the National Policy Institute in November 2016, following Trump's victory, Spencer finished his speech by toasting 'hail Trump, hail our people, hail victory!', raising a whiskey glass. Some people in the audience reacted with Nazi salutes, and they were caught on camera by a reporter of *The Atlantic* who was present there (Lombroso and Appelbaum, 2016). The second event was the tragedy in Charlottesville a few months later. Many white nationalist groups, including Spencer's NPI, organized a 'Unite The Right' rally in Charlottesville, Virginia, to protest the removal of Confederate monuments, but also to display the movement's power—though it actually verified how small the movement was, as no more than 700 people attended. The two-day gathering in Charlottesville, 11th and 12th August 2017, was a freak show: neo-Nazis, klansmen, militias with confederate symbols, chants about how 'Jews will not replace us', and marches with torches at night, resembling the National Socialists in 1930s Germany. The worst was yet to come. Antifascists had organized counter-protests for 12th August, and soon violence erupted. As a result of the clashes, an antifascist protester lost her life when she was run over by a white nationalist. To add to the tragedy, two state troopers lost their lives when a police helicopter crashed outside of Charlottesville.

Nothing was the same after Charlottesville. Many in the anti-establishment right completely disassociated themselves from the alt-right. They would be known as the 'alt-lite', meaning the pole of the anti-establishment conservatives that were not (or at least not predominantly) white nationalists. Trump was heavily criticized for his mild denouncing of the rally, and in later months he disassociated himself further from the whole milieu. Many prominent individuals, groups, and works of the alt-right were kicked off of Twitter, YouTube, Amazon, and other platforms. It would be safe to say that the movement as it was known in 2015–17 is mostly done for. Yet, the reasons that allowed the beast of racial nationalism to wake up need to be understood, as they are still in effect.

The prevalent explanation for the rise of white nationalism is that racism and white supremacy have always had roots in American society. While this might be the case, this would over-look the special character of the alt-right, which needs to be seen as a distinctively 21st-century phenomenon. The alt-right is not the KKK for our times. This is not a moral evaluation of it; it might not be as bad, or it might be worse. The alt-right, at its core, is identity politics in its ugliest and most primitive form. It is a product of a zeitgeist that constantly reminds us that our identity is the prism through which we see the world, that society is a con-stant struggle among different groups, and that our environment and culture are conditioning us. It is the product of a society obsessed with race, even under the noble intention to extinguish the poison of racism. White identitarians are proud of seeing themselves as another tribe in the identity politics war. Spencer pointed out how 'Conservatives like to demean such things as "identity politics", as just another car on the gravy train. But the reality is that leftists are engaging in the kind of ideological project that traditionalists should be hard at work on—the formation of "meta-politics"' (2015). By meta-politics, Spencer meant the war for cultural hegemony; in other words, the culture wars.

If after Charlottesville there can be no misunderstandings about the alt-right, it is important to apprehend why it initially had an appeal for people who aren't comfortable with Nazi paraphernalia or 1488 tattoos. A comment by a reader in the *American Conservative* steered sensation in early 2017, so it is worth quoting an important part of it, as it sheds light on the sentiment of many who view themselves as disenfranchised:

'I'm a white guy. I'm a well-educated intellectual who enjoys small arthouse movies, coffeehouses and classic blues. If you didn't know any better, you'd probably mistake me for a lefty urban hipster.

And yet. I find some of the alt-right stuff exerts a pull even on me. Even though I'm smart and informed enough to see through it. It's seductive because I am not a person with any power or privilege, and yet I am constantly bombarded with messages telling me that I'm a cancer, I'm a problem, everything is my fault.

I am very lower middle class. I've never owned a new car, and do my own home repairs as much as I can to save money. I cut my own grass, wash my own dishes, buy my clothes from Walmart. I have no clue how I will ever be able to retire. But oh, brother, to hear the media tell it, I am just drowning in unearned power and privilege, and America will be a much brighter, more loving, more peaceful nation when I finally just keel over and die.

Trust me: After all that, some of the alt-right stuff feels like a warm, soothing bath. A "safe space," if you will. I recoil from the uglier stuff, but some of it—the "hey, white guys are

actually okay, you know! Be proud of yourself, white man!"
stuff is really VERY seductive, and it is only with some
intellectual effort that I can resist the pull.' (cited in Dreher,
2017)

This person closed his ears to the sirens of white nationalism.
There would be no excuse whatsoever in denouncing one type of
prejudice and tribalism by joining another tribe and engaging in a
campaign of collectivistic hate. Yet, the fact that tribal thinking is
the new norm is used expertly by white nationalists. Taylor tends
to use lines such as the following one: 'What do you call a black
person who prefers to be around other black people, and likes
black music and culture? A black person. What do you call a
white person who listens to classical music, likes European
culture, and prefers to be around white people? A Nazi. All non-
whites are expected to have a strong racial identity; only whites
must not' (2018, loc. 594). The narrative that we saw in the previous section, viewing whiteness as a moral problem and something we need to renunciate, only strengthens the alt-right's
message.

One could object here: 'Does this mean that the 1488ers or the
white supremacists read the critical race theories of the left and
this is what radicalized them? And do you claim the two sides are
moral equals?' The answer is no to both. Yet, intellectuals do
contribute to the *leitmotif* of a culture. And the *leitmotif* of our
culture is one where identity and struggles among groups are
elevated as the prism through which the world makes sense. The
fact that all identities will eventually adjust to such a worldview is
something to be expected. Irrespective of one's aims, fuelling
identity politics and resentment among different tribes is actually
playing with fire. Fortunately, this version of the alt-right was not
good enough to consolidate further significance and momentum
in this zeitgeist. But our luck might run out when a next wave of
racial tribalism comes along, maybe more sophisticated and in a
less vulgar outfit (and, thus, more dangerous).

The gender wars

During our educational trips in early primary school, while on the bus, we boys would chant at the top of our voice jingles at the girls such as 'boys are knights, girls are chickens' (it rhymes in Greek). The girls, far from being distressed, would reply back with their own rhymes, such as 'girls are Greece, boys are marmalade' (it rhymes as well). Understandably, today this would be condemned as wrong, but back then it was considered a bonding experience. The not-so-popular girls and boys, by partici-pating in the ritual, would become, while it lasted, part of some-thing bigger, brought together by the presence of a common 'other'. Effectively, we were already little tribalists.

If people indeed have a tendency for in-group preference, then gender tribalism comes as an easy and convenient option. On the perceptual level, it is a simple differentiation that splits the population almost at 50–50. One part of this equation, women, have diachronically had every right to be angry, because in the vast majority of societies and for the vast majority of human history they were relegated to the status of second-class citizens and lived mostly in the shadow of men. Yet, today's standing of gender politics reminds us of the situation we encountered in the previous chapter on race relations. While there are still prejudices and the remnants of a discriminatory past, by all measurable metrics equality among the sexes is at a historical high in the West. Nevertheless, we see that tensions have risen around gender politics, which are often the field of bitter altercations. As Williams mentioned, 'feminism has been a remarkable success story. But what's striking is the absence of celebrations' (2017, p. 95). Actually, feminism today is more vocal and omnipresent as a movement than ever before, a fact acknowledged and celebrated by prominent feminists (David, 2016, p. 143). But they are not alone, as the last few years have brought the rise of an incoherent milieu that has been forming around the narrative that it is men who are now the gender discriminated against and left behind.

Researching this chapter, what I found remarkable is how someone immersed in only one of these movements could be totally convinced that justice is on their side and, thus, incapable of understanding what the other side is talking about. Feminists would highlight the patriarchal roots of modern societies, the gap in the average income of men and women, the disproportionally small presence of women in positions of power (from governments to executive boards), the threat of sexual violence they face, the patronizing or undignified attitude of many men against them, their sexual objectification in popular culture, etc. Some men, on the other side, point out that being a man means facing a significantly higher risk of suicide, of being the victim of violent crime, of getting a harsher prison sentence, of losing one's child in a custody court, of falling behind in school, of doing the most dangerous jobs, of being portrayed as a psychopathic criminal or a goofy loser in popular culture, etc. How we should make sense of these many (real or alleged) inequities is beyond the scope of this work. What matters is that more people than ever (a) see their life through the prism of their gender, (b) consider their gender to be in a disadvantaged position, and (c) require social or political change to mitigate that.

As with the previous chapter, I will not get into the debate of whether gender is rooted mostly in biological reality or if it is a social construct. I agree with Camille Paglia that 'gender roles are malleable and dynamically shaped by culture' (2018, p. 220). Yet, as she immediately points out, the historical persistence across centuries and societies of some characteristic elements in gender polarity probably indicates that 'there is something fundamentally constant in gender' (idem). Biology does provide a frame and some constraints, but this should not lead to a deterministic and static view that takes away human agency.

Since most people are familiar with feminism and its central tenets, I will mostly focus on an analytical evaluation of some of its expressions that are relevant to the themes of the book. However, the section on the 'manosphere' will be more descriptive, as it is a relatively new phenomenon and most people have little familiarity with it. I will finish with a reference to the Kavanaugh case that polarized public opinion in the US in the autumn of 2018, as it encapsulated many of the characteristics of modern tribalism.

Feminism

This section will deal with some aspects of modern feminism that I consider manifestations of the wider ideological trends that have been presented earlier in the book: a mindset categorizing people into groups, a diminished belief in individual agency, and a questioning of objective and universal reason. To begin with, there is no doubt that throughout history women have not enjoyed equal rights (whenever and wherever the term 'rights' had any meaning), and have been subjected to demeaning behaviours or beliefs, some of which survive even today. Any truly progressive and freedom-minded person would recognize this and stand against such injustices. At the same time, there has been more to feminism as a movement in its various 'waves' than a commitment to equal rights. Thus, it is open to criticism like any other movement we addressed in this book.

Generalizations and stereotyping

One of the characteristics of various strands of modern feminism is a worldview that sees society as divided into groups that are adversary to each other, and the construction of generalizations based on such group characteristics. This is important, because it could compromise feminism's emancipatory potential, like we've seen happening with other movements. Of course, this is not because there is something inherently problematic with feminism, or because women suddenly became greedy for more power and control. There is a less dramatic explanation: in recent decades, the majority of social and political movements have revolved around a tribalist worldview, and feminism has just played along.

We can see signs of this divisive ideology even in some feminist authors who attempt to be inclusive of men in their emancipatory narrative. I will use as an example bell hooks (pen name, intentionally lower-cased, of academic and feminist Gloria Watkins) and her popular book *Feminism is for Everybody* (2015). Hooks tried to make the case for the common interests of men and women in achieving a world of sexual equality — an unquestionably noble endeavour. There, she mentioned: 'Men as a group have and do benefit from patriarchy, from the assumption that they are superior to females and should rule over us... Most men are disturbed by hatred and fear of women, by male violence against women, even the men who perpetuate this violence. But they fear letting go of the benefits' (Hooks, 2015, p. xiii). Thus, even when the author is willing to give the benefit of the doubt to men, the end result is that merely by being a man one is a participant in, and maybe even a contributor to, patriarchy.

Yet, how exactly *all men* benefit from patriarchy, if such a term would even be clearly defined and proven to exist, remains unclear. Rational people, irrespective of their gender, do not benefit from injustices; they recognize that even if there might be a short-term advantage to their group, in the long term everyone is losing in a society where all individuals are not free to reach their productive and creative potential.[1] What tends to happen with the construction of 'privileges' such as being male or being white is that what is problematized is not always discrimination or injustice, but also the absence of them (Pluckrose and Lindsay, 2020, p. 182). Such identities like male and white, because they are not discriminated against and are part of supposedly dominant

---

[1]   I owe this insight to a private communication with Dr Greg Salmieri.

groups, carry with them a burden similar to that of an original sin, as they 'are problematized for the alleged implications of their very existence' (idem, p. 188).

Another poorly defined generalization in today's popular narrative around gender relations is the prevalent notion of 'toxic masculinity'. Toxic masculinity, we are told, can be a contributing factor to such a variety of phenomena such as climate change, the Brexit vote, Trump's victory in 2016, crime, racism, and wars (Salter, 2019). It is a term that has spilled out from academia or radical feminist circles and is now even used by institutions such as the United Nations (UN Women, 2020) and the World Health Organization (PAHO/WHO, 2019). The American Psychological Association did not explicitly use the term, but characterized traits traditionally identified as masculine, like stoicism or an urge for risk and constant achievement, as potentially harmful (Pappas, 2019). Thus, 'toxic masculinity' is dealt with as an issue to be solved and requiring intervention.

Yet, like 'whiteness' in the previous chapter, the term toxic masculinity is quite vague in its definition, and seems to be encompassing different aspects. Indeed, some traditional notions of masculinity, met in various times and societies, have been demeaning for women and tyrannical for other men. Some of the phenomena the term attempts to describe, such as unprovoked violence or bullying, are condemnable. Yet, there are also other traits considered traditionally masculine, like the cultivation of strength, a competitive spirit, and a stoic attitude to pain, which should, within most contexts, be celebrated as virtues. More importantly, there should be nothing inherently 'masculine' about these trends: especially the good ones should be celebrated and promoted as virtues for everyone, men *and* women, rather than stigmatized. Thus, constructing a narrative where masculine traits are seen with suspicion, whereas their opposites are seen as feminine values, creates a static and disempowering view, first of all for women.

The female and the male mind

As tribalism is a prism through which the world is perceived, its adoption by parts of modern feminism has also some epistemological implications on how they view the acquisition of knowledge. In parts of feminist scholarship there is a celebration of 'positionality' or 'standpoint', i.e. of the privileged access to reality by a person's identity, or, even better, the various inter-secting identities of oppression (Pluckrose and Lindsay, 2000, p. 164). Thus, it is oppression that offers a more direct link to truth, or to 'one's truth', as many prefer to call it. This could imply that knowledge does not come from one's mind, but from their lived experience, their environment, and their position within a structure. These factors can indeed be important in understanding the world in a better way; yet, they are not necessarily the main, and they are definitely not the only, factor to be taken into accordance when judging whose view is the correct one on an occasion, or who is to voice an opinion and who is to remain quiet.

There are some further implications to this view. If we live in a structurally sexist society, as many feminists claim we do, and if oppression can include anything from a sexually objectifying commercial to sexual harassment and heinous crimes like rape, then women *as a group* are oppressed (Williams, 2017, p. 97). Thus, according to this view, women, as part of the oppressed group, are to be listened to more, and the knowledge they produce is more valid. Paglia saw this tendency present in women's studies disciplines (now mostly called 'gender studies') and thus she called them 'institutionalized sexism' (2018, p. 58). Somebody (even worse, a man) might bring dry statistics and objective argumentation in challenging, for example, the gender pay gap, but then they are to be dismissed as they do not take into account the lived experience of women. By this logic, positionality and lived experience appear as more credible claims than a universally applicable objectivity, and feelings as more valid than reason.

A question arises here: what if a 'marginalized' or 'oppressed' group was to promote a discriminatory or unethical view? For example, what if an ethnic or religious minority, claiming its own 'form of knowledge', thought that a more just equilibrium would be a 'separate but equal' segregation, or even worse the physical removal of the 'dominant' group from society once the tables are turned? Should such views be respected, since dismissing them would deny the lived experience of a marginalized group, or should they openly be fought as wrong? What tools would one have to oppose these views if universal reason is not an option? Under critical theory and the epistemology accepted by many feminist scholars, the answer is not obvious. This is why I claim that positionality is not a tool better situated to provide justice and the overcoming of prejudice than dry reason and objectivity.

Many feminists often openly consider claims in favour of universality and objective reason as tools for the perpetuation of a knowledge created by and for men (in the same way these values have been viewed by some critical race theorists as contributing to the perpetuation of white supremacy). For example, bell hooks talked about the importance of spirituality in feminism, and its uneasiness with 'black or white' binary categories, such as good or bad, which are seen as by-products of a Judeo-Christian tradition that facilitated various forms of oppression (2015, pp. 105–106). It is indeed true that quite often racist and sexist exploitation had at their root pseudo-theories about the supremacy of whites or men. Yet, such false ideas do not constitute the triumph of reason, but its *negation*. The fact that a rationalistic-sounding scheme was used to subjugate some groups constitutes a false application of the principles of reason and objectivity. Actually, it was under the flag of reason that the great abolitionists and the suffragettes waged the victorious battle for the equality of all races and sexes. It is *more* dry reason and objectivity that will make us all better off, not less.

Actually, the epistemological tribalism of positionality and intersectionality makes meaningful ties of solidarity more and more difficult to achieve. Supposedly, as a white heterosexual male, I am incapable of understanding the struggles of a black lesbian woman, even after I have heard her experiences, just because we occupy different spaces in the nexus of power. Also, this would indicate that she cannot understand my experiences. But then, if we are speaking a language that reaches the ears but not the minds of those outside the group, what is left of our common humanity? Not much. As Williams is right to mention, even among women there can be no common struggle under the auspices of intersectionality. For example, a white college professor might be oppressed as a woman, but she is on a different epistemological frequency than another woman who is part of another more oppressed group. Under this worldview, even the feminist idea of the 'sisterhood' is jeopardized (Williams, 2017, p. 217).

This epistemological Tower of Babel adds fuel to the fire of controversies such as the existence or not of a 'rape culture' in our societies. The definition of rape culture is vague. According to the popular site Everyday Feminism, it is about cultural practices and situations where sexual violence and rape are 'ignored, trivialized, normalized, or made into jokes' (Ridgway, 2014). There are indeed cases where rapists slip through the justice system (like many other criminals), or where some fraternities sing chants promoting unacceptable behaviour towards women, or where some people find rape a laughing matter—which is also the case with male rape and the 'drop the soap' prison jokes. Yet, such tendencies tend to be condemned by the institutions that set the tempo of a society, such as the media, universities, or big businesses. It is difficult to comprehend how we may live in a rape culture if a rape joke could pretty much toss someone out of polite society.

Marshal's University Women's Centre (nd) defined rape culture as 'an environment in which rape is prevalent and in which sexual violence against women is normalized and excused in the media and popular culture'. This definition is also vague.

Matters become even more unclear when examples of rape culture are given, including sexually explicit jokes, pressure on men 'to score', and 'teaching women to avoid getting raped instead of teaching men not to rape'. None of these situations necessarily indicate though that this is a society characterized by a tolerance for rape. Victim blaming has been and still is an unacceptable tendency, expressed in remarks such as 'she asked for it' or 'she was dressed provocatively'. However, the claim that warning girls and women about the dangers of rape is evidence of a rape culture is bizarre. In the Krav Maga class where I train, we quite often do drills for defence against knife attacks (although the odds even for a trained defender against an armed attacker are extremely low). As a matter of fact, some people join the class explicitly due to their fear over the rising prevalence of knife crimes in the UK. The fact that we spend our time and money to prepare for the possibility of an attack does not indicate our contribution to the prevalence of a 'knife culture'. Neither can the main solution be to teach men not to butcher others. Our willingness to train is an acknowledgment that there are some evil people out there, and one should better be prepared for the worst-case scenario. This is the reality; it is *not* victim blaming.

Also, if in the USA there is a rape culture, then how would we characterize the culture in some Islamic theocracies, or other misogynistic cultures in the past and the present? An answer some feminists give is that they are also a rape culture. But putting a culture where some individuals unacceptably joke about rape or blame the victim for 'bringing it upon herself' under the same umbrella with a culture where the victims of rape are punished with lashes defies the standards of what a reasonable comparison is.

Every rape or every person who sanctions anything having to do with rape is one too much. The problem is that often the debate around rape culture is underpinned by a tribal partisanship where the one side considers the issue a fantasy, whereas the other side considers any questions or objections of its arguments as 'denial'. Thus, it becomes more difficult for all to embark on the more productive debate: how to make sure that the heinous crime of rape will be more successfully addressed, and how will the unacceptable tolerance of some people towards wrong views around rape be further delegitimized.

Campbell and Manning have made a very interesting observation: rape culture is not clearly defined, nor has there been a consensus about its existence; yet, it has reached the level of a truth the dispute of which supposedly reveals someone's 'problematic' premises. We are not entirely sure what exactly a rape culture is, but those who question the validity of the term, among them female dissenting voices like Christina Hoff Sommers or the individualist feminist Wendy McElroy, are rape denialists and are 'no-platformed' from university campuses (2018, p. 128). Lukianoff and Haidt (2018, p 27) brought the issue back to epistemology and mentioned that actually the disagreement on whether we live in a rape culture or not would not be solved if we all agreed on an objective definition of what such a culture is. If the determining factor is the lived experiences of some women, especially if they have been the victims of rape, then challenging the existence of rape culture would be unacceptable. To do so would be to invalidate their experience. This was the argument of some students who protested the presence of McElroy at a university campus: her 'rape culture denial' would be an assault on the victims' lived experience (idem). Interestingly, the fact that McElroy herself had been the victim of rape did not play a role in the protesters' dismissal of her views.

Victim feminism and powerful women

A lot of feminism's critics have talked about the movement becoming more like 'victim feminism', where the default position is that women are under threat and in need of some form of intervention to cope (Williams, 2017). This can be seen in a variety of initiatives, from affirmative action quotas for women, to the construction of the act of sex as a threatening experience, to the ban of 'objectifying advertising'. This view of women as victimized subjects who need institutional support deserves to be criticized, not from an anti-feminist but from a pro-women's agency angle.

The discussion around sex and the #MeToo movement is a good place to start. The #MeToo campaign shed light on the extent of sexual harassment in various circles, and contributed to bringing down some evil individuals. For that, it should be celebrated. Yet, there has also been another narrative gaining ground, which could complicate the discussion in the public sphere about sexual assault. According to it, any unpleasant experience, such as a comment by a stranger on the street, or a clumsy flirtation, or the touching of a knee, is put under the same umbrella as sexual violence, thus creating a picture where women are collectively viewed as powerless agents (Berlinski, 2017). There are indeed cases where power imbalances make such situations difficult to manage for women: the story of a US President and a White House intern having a sexual affair is such an example. Yet, the idea that women cannot put in his place a goofy or a creepy flirtatious co-worker is anything but empower-ing. An interesting contrast is provided by journalist Julia Hartley-Brewer and her reaction to a politician who repeatedly touched her knee back in 2002 at a party conference. As she described, 'I calmly and politely explained to him that, if he did it again, I would punch him in the face. He withdrew his hand and that was the end of the matter' (cited in Tolhurst, 2017).

Society's post-#MeToo approach to sex is indicative of the uncertain times we live in. For Williams, a big victory of the feminist movement in the 1960s with the sexual revolution was to re-appropriate sex as enjoyment in itself, rather than as a duty linked to marriage or motherhood (2017, p. 123). Yet, sex has been reconstructed by some feminists as something which is potentially dangerous for women, as it is seen as a tool for male domination. Radical feminist Catharine MacKinnon has been interpreted to claim that *all* acts of sex are actually rape. In an interview, she explained that what she meant was that often even when women consent to sex, due to the structural power imbalances in (what she sees as) our patriarchal society, this consent is actually coerced. Thus, MacKinnon problematized all acts of heterosexual sex that 'that take place under conditions of sex inequality' (cited in Jeffries, 2006). Whether this means *all* acts of sex in a society like ours remains uncertain. The view of sex as a tool for patriarchal domination is why another prominent feminist, Andrea Dworkin, problematized pornography, as she saw it as institutionalizing the sexual dominance of men over women (Dworkin, 1991). This view of an inherent power imbalance in sex is seen nowadays in various cases at university campuses in the US, when, following sexual intercourse where both parties had presumably consented but were under the influence of alcohol, only the man is punished (Harris, 2017). For Paglia, such an approach to sex and inter-gender relations is actually bringing back the worst anti-feminist prejudices of previous eras, setting 'a reactionary double standard that defines women as somehow weaker, frailer, or purer than men' (2018, p. 132).

I claim that a similar disempowering view of women is behind initiatives like the one by London Mayor Sadiq Khan to ban adverts from the tube that promote an 'unrealistic body image' and might make women feel 'physically inferior' (Jackson, 2016). What that tells us is that women, far from having the agency to face any challenge in life, cannot cope with the spectacle of a well-toned model in a bikini. This is a demeaning view of women. And yet, it is celebrated as 'empowering'.

When I come across such stories and views, I think of women like Golda Meir, the Prime Minister of Israel from 1969–1974. In the morning of 6th October 1973, during the holy day of Yom Kippur, she received an ominous telegraph by the head of Mossad: 'The Egyptian army and the Syrian army are about to launch an attack on Israel… in the early evening' (Tsoref, 2018). Over the next 20 days, she led her country in a war that threatened the very existence of Israel, and which in its early stages looked destined for defeat. Often, she had to impose her will on her war cabinet. This included the legendary eye-patch wearer Moshe Dayan who served as Defence Minister, and various generals and army commanders tested in battle; to say that these men were strongly opinionated would be an understatement. Yet, irrespective of how one evaluates her command in the Yom Kippur war, Golda Meir faced all the challenges and led Israel to a victory that was decisive for its survival.

Or, I think of the novelist and philosopher Ayn Rand, and how she viewed women. In her novel *Atlas Shrugged*, the heroine is Dagny Taggart, a railway executive who broke the 'glass ceiling' way before the prevalence of modern feminism. In a scene, Rand described Dagny in her youth as follows: 'She was twelve years old when she told Eddie Willers [Dagny's childhood friend] that she would run the railroad when they grew up. She was fifteen when it occurred to her for the first time that women did not run railroads and that people might object. To hell with that, she thought — and never worried about it again' (Rand, 2007, p. 51). I wonder what Golda Meir and Ayn Rand would think about the modern view that women need protection from posters or from a flirtatious remark.

Interestingly though, such powerful women are seldomly celebrated by the feminist movement. A characteristic example is Margaret Thatcher: the daughter of a grocer who went on to be accepted to Oxford University to study chemistry, then she became the youngest female candidate for a national election, then she became an MP, then the leader of the Conservative Party, and eventually the first female Prime Minister in the history of the UK. And yet, she is nowhere to be found in the feminist pantheon. Prominent feminist Mariam David, referring to Thatcher, mentioned that she is 'not concerned with women like her' (2016, p. 88). The reason? Thatcher represents 'rampant competitive individualism' (idem) rather than the sisterhood. Thatcher declined to see herself as a success story for feminism, and saw herself instead as an individual. Also, her leadership style was 'masculinized' (Childs, 2013). Former Labour MP and actress Glenda Jackson, in a speech she gave to parliament some days after Thatcher's death, said that it is questionable whether the Iron Lady even qualifies as a woman, at least according to her standards (BBC News, 2013).

Two observations need to be made here. First, this is a familiar tendency in identity politics. In the previous chapter, we saw how for many on the left and for critical race scholars, conservatives like Condoleezza Rice or Colin Powell are 'safe minorities', i.e. people who have betrayed their essence as members of a group. Also, many women who are critical of feminism are considered to have 'internalized misogyny'. This is the essence of tribalism: considering that the individuals ought to have a worldview based not on their own judgment, but on the consensus of the group. It would be interesting though to find out who decides what that consensus should be, and by what standards. Thus, Cobley made the interesting point that being female does not guarantee automatic admission to the protection of the tribe. There are boxes to be ticked, such as following the tribe's line (2018, p. 104). For the outsiders, there is no sympathy. It is safe to assume that if the spiteful and sexist attacks towards women of the opposite tribe, such as Sarah Palin or Melania Trump, were directed at progressives like Nancy Pelosi or Michelle Obama, the condemnations and outrage would be at a whole different level.

But there is another problem with the 'Thatcher was not a victory for women' mantra. It implies that traits like authority, an uncompromising attitude, and imposing one's will under difficult circumstances are 'masculine' traits, and that women should not have to resort to them to have a chance in politics. As the prominent feminist Germaine Greer put it: 'If women understand by emancipation the adoption of the masculine role then we are lost indeed' (cited in Williams, 2017, p. 196). This risks essentializing the view of women as a weaker and more agreeable sex, and thus repackaging old anti-feminist myths. An often-told story about Thatcher is the one where during a policy meeting she banged

Hayek's book *The Constitution of Liberty* on the table saying 'this is what we believe', and thus imposed order on the snobbish and elitist male Tory ministers who were not used to being bossed around by a woman. This is an iconic feminist moment, if there ever was one.

Feminism as central planning

We have seen how many of the elements that one can criticize modern feminism for are actually trends that have been prevalent in other movements, across the left and the right in recent decades: a distrust in the ability of human subjectivity to cope with the challenges of life, the questioning of universal reason, and the promotion of the idea that different groups come into contact with reality in different ways. Yet, such ideas produce very real and material results. In the name of equality and diversity, one can see universities giving one-off pay rises to female members of staff (Pells, 2016), and others opening vacancies only for women in the STEM fields (Botzas, 2019). This means that the women who got the pay rise were not seen as individuals who were underpaid. As their group was, on average, paid less than the other group, its members got a pay rise precisely for being members of that group. By the same token, the university hiring only women clearly did not evaluate the candidates as individuals; the reason for hiring them was the need for a more equal representation of groups in STEM.

A concerning aspect of this tribal worldview, keeping in mind how politics are consistently downstream from culture and philosophy, is what is its end game. Such an egalitarianism that pushes for preferential group treatment and quotas requires constant interventions and social engineering. Keep in mind that, for many modern feminists, gender disparities and inequalities are seen in all aspects of life, from posters on the tube to inter-gender relationships at the office, and from the salary of athletes to representation on executive boards. But then, feminism applied with political means would look like central planning at large, covering all aspects of public and private life. Second wave feminists argued that the personal is political; the logical conclusion then is that everything is political, and thus everything is up for the intervention of some powers that be. This is not a very promising future to look forward to.

The manosphere

In the two previous chapters, we have come across the trend where the narrative of one side of the culture wars gains prominence, thus creating a reaction from another milieu. While that reaction might have some credible points, it also evolves into a tribalist worldview that adds extra vitriol to the culture wars. The case could not be different with the gender wars. In this section, I will talk about the manosphere, the loose network of men coming together in search of meaning and in reaction to what is perceived as the cultural, social, and political dominance of feminism.

The manosphere is mostly about online spaces where men meet and interact, or consume content. I will define it as having two characteristics:

(a) A will of the men that are part of it to develop into what they perceive as a better version of themselves, according to some form of masculine ideal, and through sharing information and tips on life skills.

(b) An effort to make sense of a world that is perceived as unwelcome or hostile to expressions of masculinity. Often, the blame for this development is cast on feminism.

According to these criteria, there are various sub-tribes in the manosphere, and some of them are of interest for this book, as they either have a presence in the culture wars or they are related to themes covered in previous chapters.

The charm of the game

Many people associate the manosphere with pick-up artists (PUAs) and other experts in giving dating advice to men. These experts do not even have to be men; for example, dating coach Kezia Noble is a woman, but her YouTube channel has more subscribers (by October 2020, 410,000) than most popular male seduction experts. The popularity of seduction experts has to do with two elements. First, it is an area where, judging by the numbers, many men feel they need to seek support, as they appear clueless as to how to pursue romance with women. The high percentage of celibate millennials is an indication of it (Julian, 2018). At the same time, it is a subculture that has become prominent and notorious even in mainstream circles, mostly due to the book *The Game* (Strauss, 2005) in the mid-2000s.

In *The Game*, writer Neill Strauss followed the magician-turned-seduction expert Erik von Markovik, aka 'Mystery', in his romantic and sexual endeavours. The 'Mystery method' included seduction tricks such as 'negging' (a teasing critical remark), 'peacocking' (having something in one's appearance that will attract the attention and invite a comment by women), and 'DHVing' (demonstrating higher value, such as by entering the club with female company). Strauss turned from an awkward and shy guy who had zero success with women to an expert in seduction, becoming Mystery's 'wingman' nicknamed 'Style'. This created a buzz: if a skinny and bald awkward guy like Strauss can reach such levels of seduction mastery that he can 'game' celebrities like Britney Spears, then so can the average Joe who has been struggling to ask a girl out on a date. But beyond the 'keys to seduction' element, *The Game* is a book that is fun to read. Strauss guides the reader through the pick-up community's rise in fame in Southern California, but also through its absurdity, its inner conflicts, and the constant existential dead-ends of Mystery, who, it turns out, is a romantic at heart craving affection and getting in deep downward spirals of heartache when facing unrequited love (Strauss, 2005).

PUAs' technique of 'cold approaching' unsuspecting 'targets' in bars can be annoying or creepy for many women. Yet, Nagle is right to point out that this very early version of the manosphere in retrospect looks innocent and mostly devoid of the misogynistic and reactionary elements that have inhabited it since then (2017, p. 88). In fact, Strauss himself denied the persona of Style and distanced himself from the milieu, whereas notable early PUAs like Eben Pegan (formerly known as David DeAngelo) and Owen Cook (aka RSD Tyler in the PUA community) have turned their businesses towards self-development. Cook has also been careful to navigate the waters in the post-#MeToo era, and now goes out of his way to educate men on constantly seeking consent and never making women feel uncomfortable. His approach is based less on the pre-scripted tricks of Mystery and more on the ideas of spiritual guru Eckhart Tolle (2001) on 'being present in the moment' and on sharing 'abundance' and 'high-vibration energy', providing value and making everyone around happier. One of Cook's company's seduction experts is Julien Blanc, who back in 2014 was accused of encouraging his students to get aggressively physical with women, embroiling him in a media scandal and banning him from entering the UK and Australia (Travis, 2014). Since then, Blanc has also rediscovered himself as a teacher of self-development and healing. Thus, 'game' has developed from doing rehearsed tricks to get the attention and affection of women to developing confidence and self-esteem, and thus attracting women organically.

Overall, the vast majority of men consuming dating advice and pick-up artistry material seem to be socially awkward and shy people. As many dating experts have said, most of their clients just want to find a woman to have a relationship with, and one of the most usual reasons they join the community is to win their ex-girlfriend back. The old guard of PUAs might be among the most well-known representatives of what many perceive as the manosphere, but in truth it is questionable if they are even part of it, as they have mostly been a 'single-issue' milieu without

wider ideological claims. Also, many among the rest of the manosphere's participants consider them naïve and too immersed in a
'feminine-primacy mindset'. In other words, they consider them
'blue-pill conditioned', and still miles away from 'red pill'
wisdom.

The red pill, MGTOWs, and incels

The red pill metaphor from the film *The Matrix* is important in
understanding the manosphere. The blue pill symbolizes
accepting the dominant ideology and fitting into the existing
world, which is seen as accommodating the needs of women and
as being supported by effeminate men. The red pill represents the
bitter shock of seeing the world for what it actually is, the understanding of women and of their mindset, and the intellectual
arming of oneself for navigating this reality with the proper
knowledge and masculine values as defence. As male identity
politics, the manosphere's starting point is accepting the red pill.
Its godfathers are the so-called three Rs: blogger Roissy, creator of
the blog and forum Chateau Heartiste (now taken down from
WordPress), Rollo Tomassi, early moderator of the pick-up forum
SoSuave and blogger and author of *The Rational Male* series, and
pick-up artist turned alt-right fellow-traveller and traditionalist
Roosh V.

Tomassi's books (2013, 2015, 2017) all start with a line from *The
Matrix* that exemplifies the process of getting red-pilled:

'– Why do my eyes hurt?
– You've never used them before.'

The Matrix metaphors are also indicative of how the manosphere
members see themselves: as cultural rebels who fight a social
order hostile to men. Also, reactionary traditionalism is added to
the mix, as many men in the manosphere yearn for a patriarchal
period where supposedly everything was simpler and better,
including inter-gender dynamics. This period, before the rise of

feminism and progressive liberalism, is seen as the golden era for both men and women. In the absence of a hook-up culture of casual sex, monogamy and strong communities guaranteed two things: (a) that everyone would get a chance at romantic and sexual happiness, and (b) solid family ties that strengthened the roots of each culture. It is clear how these ideas are compatible with the radical traditionalism of the identitarian right.

Roosh Valizadeh (aka Roosh V) had been a prominent PUA, travelling around the world and writing 'travel guides' on how to have casual sex with women. Yet, recently some introspection led him to the conclusion that all this casual sex was soul-destroying and meaningless. Then he posted a lengthy set of new rules on his site's forum. Among the topics that are *not* welcome anymore are:

'– Meeting women with the intention of fornicating with them
…
– Physical intimacy with women you're not married to beyond the act of kissing
– Maintaining relationships with multiple women (i.e. spinning plates)
– Cheating on significant others (adultery)
…
– Stories of sexual activity while not married
– Promoting masturbation, oral sex, anal sex, etc.' (Roosh V, 2019)

What has filled Roosh's existential gap is traditionalism. Another R of the manosphere, blogger Roissy, also fused his pick-up artistry advice and gender theories with race realism and white nationalism.[2] Like many on the identitarian right and the manosphere, Roosh V considers Eastern Europe as a good place to meet women with traditional values and start a family. As a traditional-

---

[2] Further analysis on the views of Roissy is impossible, as his website was taken down by WordPress and there are few traces left.

ist, he despises 'neoliberal' capitalism, but his rationale includes an extra spin. In a discussion with white nationalist Richard Spencer, Roosh V explained that capitalism creates a 'free market' for romance. Just like with the economy, free competition will (supposedly) inevitably lead to monopolies (NPI/Radix, 2019). This is because, according to the manosphere, there is a natural hierarchy where 20% of males (termed as Alphas) monopolize the resources (including women), leaving little if nothing to the remaining 80% (labelled as Betas or as Average Frustrated Chumps — AFCs — in the red pill lingo).

This emphasis on hierarchies might bring to mind Jordan Peterson and his now infamous metaphor of the lobsters. Peterson saw lobsters as a typical example of natural hierarchies, and explained how some of them exhibit behaviours and form rituals that establish domination vis-à-vis the rest of the lobsters (2018, pp. 1–8). Peterson has never actually claimed that we are like lobsters, but made the point that unequal distribution of resources and skills is a normal state everywhere in nature. Peterson has unwillingly been an influence in parts of the manosphere; yet, various fields of psychology (and mostly evolutionary theories) had been present in these circles many years before his rise to infamy.

It is now time to examine the 'red pill maxims' of the manosphere, as presented by Rollo Tomassi in his blog posts and books. For Tomassi, the red pill is based on sociology, evolutionary psychology, behaviourism, and the collective observations of thousands of men (2013). Later, he upgraded it to an objective science: praxeology (Tomassi, 2017). The term has been historically used by some economists of the Austrian School to study economics as a science of human action, based on the premises of purposeful human behaviour. Tomassi built the red pill on such an approach, as he considers it neutral and impossible to be subjected to biases or preconception. This means we ought to judge humans by what they do, rather than what they say or proclaim to believe, and thus we can reach objective and universal conclusions, when some patterns repeat themselves (Tomassi, 2017, pp. 21–22). Based on such an approach, these are some of the main tenets of the red pill (Tomassi, 2013):

- 'Women will make rules for Betas, and break rules for Alphas.'
- 'Women want a man who other men want to be and other women want to fuck.'
- 'Nothing is as simultaneously fear inspiring and arousing for women as a Man she suspects is self-aware of his own value.'
- 'Genuine desire cannot be negotiated.'
- 'For one gender to realize their sexual imperative the other must sacrifice their own.' The sexual imperative for men is unlimited access to unlimited sexuality, whereas for women it is 'hypergamy'. Hypergamy is about a dual sexual strategy: mating with Alphas and obtaining satisfying sex and their superior genes, and then getting the provisioning, resources, and unconditional love from a Beta male.

One may consider such a deterministic view of masculine and feminine nature as an idiosyncrasy confined within the misogynistic echo chamber of the manosphere. Yet, such ideas stem from a worldview that has deep roots in today's mainstream culture. The specifics might vary, but the view that our environment and our biology determine us, that free will is an illusion, that we are servants of powers we cannot control, and that our identity is the end-point of our horizon, enjoy widespread credibility and respectability in polite society. It is to be expected that each tribe is going to repackage these ideas and create its own narrative, which is then used as ammunition in the culture wars. Thus, merely dismissing the manosphere as a misogynistic gathering of weirdos or creeps is a superficial reading of it. The manosphere is a child of its time, and a predictable one.

The red pill ideology has led some men to attempt to find fulfilment in life and improve themselves while having minimum or zero interactions with women: they are the Men Going Their Own Way (MGTOWs). Judging from the number of viewers on

YouTube for some prominent MGTOWs, like a guy named Sandman who often has hundreds of thousands of views, it is one of the most popular sub-tribes in the manosphere. MGTOWs are often close to more mainstream Men's Rights Activists, who claim, among other things, that the court system is skewed against men and share sad stories from divorce, alimony, and child custody courts (Innes-Smith, 2018).

A bleak worldview is even stronger among another subset of men, who feel that there is no escape for them from the bottom of the sexual hierarchy. Thus, they embrace their predicament as Betas and make it the distinguishing characteristic of their identity. This bleak view is known as the 'black pill', and is a characteristic among many of the so-called 'incels', i.e. involuntary celibate men. On forums and websites, they seek affirmation of their misery and often resort to anti-social attitudes and rampant misogyny. The world became aware of incels in 2014 when a young man named Elliot Rogers killed six people in a shooting rampage, as he targeted a girls' sorority house at the University of California, Santa Barbara. He left behind a manifesto, where he explained at length his hatred for women, which is derived from their constant rejection of him (Futrelle, 2018).

It is true that the misogyny found among incels is also widespread in other parts of the manosphere. Yet, incels are also ideological children of their time. Their self-righteous entitlement, their need for recognition and affirmation of their vulnerability, and their tribalist view of women as the enemy are not exclusive to the manosphere. Myers is right to say that 'far from upholding masculine values like stoicism and self-reliance, the incel subculture is imbued with today's therapeutic sensibility' (2018). It has to be mentioned, though, that obviously not every involuntarily sexually inactive man is part of the incel tribe; also, not every incel has violent or misogynistic fantasies. Most of the incels, however, share a static view of their identity as a prison, and thus internalize a worldview based on vulnerability.

Jack Donovan and the masculine way of the tribe

An opposite worldview is promoted by a figure of the manosphere who would proudly carry the title of a tribalist: blogger and author Jack Donovan. Donovan is a very unusual person. He has a degree in Arts, and has a background in dancing, but now spends much of his time with small groups of other men training and competing in the wilderness, and bonding through ancient pagan rituals (Lyons, 2019). At times, he sounds like an anarchist, yet his writings on the existential reality of violence are consumed by far rightists. His most well-known book, *The Way of Men* (2012), has been endorsed by the alt-right leader Richard Spencer, who said that while others in the manosphere 'theorize about the best way to pick up unstable women at bars', Donovan is asking 'who "the Man" really is'. Nevertheless, although he has appeared at events of white nationalists in the past, Donovan denounced white nationalism and Spencer himself; the latter after the violence in Charlottesville, the former because he considers a tribalism that includes a whole race of people with little else in common as unsustainable (Donovan, 2017). Donovan is a particularly good writer, with clear Nietzschean influences. Undercutting the sum of his work is his belief in our existential need for tribalism.

Donovan sees tribalism as 'a commitment to one group of people above and potentially at the expense of all others' (2016, p. 13). Writing on what it means to be a man, Donovan said that 'the way of men is the way of the gang' (idem, p. 1), i.e. the way of the tribe. The gang is 'the kernel of masculine identity' and the existential horizon of a man (Donovan, 2012, p. 162). In a primal condition, or, as Donovan put it, when shit hits the fan, the gang helps men to 'protect the perimeter' and establish their will. In times of peace, the competition between men within the gang helps them build character and skills. The skills that make a man 'good at being a man', which is different to merely being 'a good man', are strength, courage, mastery, and honour (idem). For Donovan, these skills are universal and amoral; they are crucial

for physical survival, which is the precondition for the construction of philosophy and morality.

Donovan argued that in our times, being good at being a man
is not a necessity, but a lifestyle option and a value commitment.
It is a gesture of defiance and resistance against what he called
'the empire of nothing'. He is an avowed enemy of 'neoliberal'
globalization and multiculturalism, as he thinks that they're
taking away the diversity of different cultures and stripping life of
meaning (Donovan, 2016). A way I could describe Donovan is as a
'universalist tribalist'. He wants all cultures, races, and identities
to have their own tribes, which have to be small and homogeneous. Thus, he denounces race as the sole criterion for tribal
affiliation. He considers white nationalism as a movement
inspired by resentment, and he said that 'I'm not a White
Nationalist because I don't think people are worth saving just
because they're white' (2017). Donovan sees masculinity as the
path to excellency, but this can only happen through a group of
men who push each other to become better. Thus, racial entitlement based on an unchosen characteristic like skin colour will not
do it for him.

Therefore, we have seen how the manosphere is quite a complex and diverse phenomenon. Considering it a monolithic bloc
united by misogyny, as the media usually sees it, is overlooking
many of its aspects. In some ways, it is a male version resembling
some aspects of modern feminism; this is especially the case with
Men's Rights Activists and the 'grievance' parts of the milieu that
put emphasis on male vulnerability and gender injustice. In other
ways, it differs from feminism. While the latter focuses more on
transformation on a social level, a key characteristic of most parts
of the manosphere is the call for self-development. Taking into
account the number of men spending their lives in inaction and a
downward spiral of unfulfilled potential, such a message can be
beneficial. The problem is that there can be no complete and
fulfilling self-development when it is accompanied by a worldview that is deterministic, that undermines free will, and sees

women *as a group* as a potential enemy to be feared or avoided. To close the section with the words of a woman, to be free and to realize our potential, both men and women need to liberate ourselves from the gender wars (Williams, 2017, p. 261).

Bringing it all together: the Kavanaugh case

Coming from Greece, I have grown quite familiar with a toxic political atmosphere. We have seen political assassinations, bombings, attacks with rocket-propelled grenades, and the public beatings and lynching of politicians and public figures. Even so, I have rarely experienced such a tense and polarized climate of suspicion and hostility as the one around the nomination of Judge Brett Kavanaugh for the Supreme Court of the USA from August to October of 2018.

The story should be more or less known to everyone who follows the news. Towards the end of the Senate Judiciary Committee's procedures to evaluate Kavanaugh's nomination—a choice made by Donald Trump—a Democrat Congresswoman made public the private complaint she received from a woman who claimed that Kavanaugh had sexually assaulted her 36 years earlier, in 1982. The accuser revealed herself to be Dr Christine Blasey Ford, and the Senate suspended any further procedures until the case was clarified, and the FBI had conducted a supplementary investigation. Both Dr Ford and Kavanaugh testified in an emotional and tense public hearing on 27th September (Krieg, 2018). Dr Ford's allegations were not corroborated, and Kavanaugh's nomination was approved in early October by a margin of two votes in the Senate. During the process, Senators and conservatives who supported Kavanaugh were intimidated by protesters, whereas Dr Ford also received heinous threats (Cole, 2018; Arnold, 2018).

The polarization that the whole process created and the various reactions in the public sphere sum up many of the worrying tendencies addressed in this book. In a way, it was the perfect storm: a white powerful conservative man accused of using his privilege to get away with assaulting a courageous woman who revealed his violent acts. Or, viewed from a different angle, an innocent man's reputation ruined by a woman, the Democrats, and the partisan media class that wanted to stick it to the enemy: white conservative men and Republicans. The case is also quite revealing about the methods through which many people reach their conclusions nowadays, which is why I have chosen it as the closing section of the book's case studies.

Commenting on the specifics of the case can be tempting. Most commentators agreed that Dr Ford seemed like a credible person who would not make up such a serious allegation. At the same time, Judge Kavanaugh's side had a valid point that the accuser could not provide some crucial information regarding her allegations, whereas people she mentioned as potential witnesses have denied any knowledge of the incident.

Yet, the complicated nature of the case did not stop people from picking sides. Hashtags that became popular on social media such as #believewomen or #believehim leave a very significant question open: believe *based on what*? What is the process through which people have reached a conclusion? In most cases, it seems to be some form of group identification. Women believing women, men believing men, women not believing white men, Republicans not believing a Democrat, and so on. The Kavanaugh case became merely the canvas on which they projected their pre-existing views.

At some point, it was not even about Kavanaugh anymore. The organizer of the Women's March, Linda Sarsour, said that the rage about Kavanaugh's nomination is also 'about immigration, refugees, the rights of people of color, voting rights, reproductive rights, Native American rights' (cited in Walter and Durkin, 2018). She also expressed her disappointment with conservative women who did not outright believe Dr Ford: 'There is a longstanding problem that a majority of white women voted for Donald Trump and have supported Kavanaugh—they put their proximity to power over their own interests' (idem). Apparently, these women's interests are unknown to them and have to do with the allegiance they should show to the sisterhood.

Another commentator detached the case even more from its factual basis, commenting on how it provided her with a spiritual experience: 'On Wednesday, with the hearing looming, and an army of enraged maenads already in full battle cry on Twitter, I quit therapy in triumph' (Harris, 2018). Feminist author Jill Filipovic encouraged, via a tweet, women to divorce their Republican husbands. Another feminist said that the case showed how 'survivors of sexual violence are still, within rape culture, not being heard and not being listened to' (cited in Walters and Durkin, 2018). But Dr Ford was listened to. The process of the nomination was halted and the Senate entered the impossible process of having to evaluate what happened in a room 36 years ago. It seems like the premise here is that to listen should also mean to believe. Not on a case-by-case basis and based on objective criteria, but based on the accuser's gender and status as a victim.

A tribalist outlook means that Kavanaugh was not any longer judged as an individual with his life and reputation on the line, but as a representative of his group. According to a feminist writer's article titled 'The Manipulative Power of White Man's Tears', Kavanaugh's emotional testimony was not convincing, as 'abusive men are enacting systemic emotional manipulation that enables them to stay in power' (Froio, 2018). Another feminist activist commented that Kavanaugh's defence of himself in the Senate 'was a temper tantrum from someone who has never been told no in his life' (cited in Walter and Durkin, 2018). So how is a white male like me supposed to judge the merits of the Kavanaugh case? 'Good men who want to be on the right side of history will follow the leadership of women, they will listen to us, they will believe us, they will join us, or they can get out of the way' (idem).

Of course, similar approaches, with the genders and the roles reversed, could be found on the other side. The tribalist elevation of feelings above objective judgment reached its apogee with the countless numbers of tweets during the hearings, from both sides, openly declaring that the case is clear to them because they formed an opinion by psychologizing on Dr Ford's or Judge Kavanaugh's appearance from thousands of miles away and the comfort of their living room while staring at a screen. Thus, the arbiter of truth seems to be tribal identification, or gut feeling. This is a worrying tendency that goes beyond politics, and has to do with the criteria that people use when trying to approach truth.

The proper attitude towards this case, which due to its serious-ness has already stigmatized the lives of those directly involved in it, is that we do not know who is right. Even more, *it is not possible* for us, the spectators, to know who is right. The only way to reach the truth would be through the objective process of a court of law, assisted by a thorough investigation by the authorities. What would be needed is the systematic examination of evidence, the cross-examining of those involved and of possible witnesses, and the principles that have been used in societies respecting the indi-vidual rights of the defendant and the accused. However, and understandably, due to the passing of time, the statute of limita-tions would not allow such a process. Thus, the case cannot be further investigated by a court and Kavanaugh can claim the presumption of innocence.

We might never find out who is right and who is wrong in the Kavanaugh affair, but at least let us revalidate how we pursue truth. When lives, reputations, and the delivery of justice is on the line, we cannot merely go by gut feeling. The only means to pass judgment is reason, and it needs to be compatible with the facts of reality and evidence. But what the Kavanaugh case did show, and in accordance with the verdict of this book, is that for a critical mass of people the arbiter of truth is gender, race, emotions, political allegiances, or other tribal affiliations.

Conclusion

'The worse the coming future, the more it should motivate its opponents.' – Leonard Peikoff

From tribalism...

Someone who has read a book presenting the omnipresence of tribalism in our society, or who merely pays attention to the latest news cycle, can easily be led to pessimism, cynicism, or fatalism. On one level, this reaction is understandable: things are indeed bad in many respects, and they can get worse. They probably *will* get worse.

Even so, a person loving life can and should find many reasons to be thrilled about our era. Furthermore, we cannot give up on this unprecedentedly fascinating and exciting world we are blessed to live in. Standing on the shoulders of giants, we are richer, we live longer, and the possibilities should be endless. Even during a pandemic and strict lockdowns, due to technology and human ingenuity, life went on without major disruptions as far as production and supply chains were concerned, whereas we got various vaccines in record time. We have the sum of human knowledge and creativity just clicks away from us, usually for free. Challenges such as beating diseases, the radical expansion of life expectancy, the abundance of affordable and clean energy, and space exploration make the future exciting and promising.

Thus, we should not let go of this world without a fight. The solution is not to give up the field of ideas and retreat; after all, ideas will still determine what kind of world we will live in. Nor is the solution to merely join the tribe closest to us, as a means of self-protection and of choosing the lesser evil. Buying some time is a short-sighted approach, especially if there is no clear road towards what we want to achieve.

Where to begin though? How do we fight this intellectual atmosphere of bitterness, tribalism, and low horizons? The first thing to do is spot the common denominator in the things that are going wrong out there, in the troubling phenomena that this book has covered. The root of the problem, *and* its solutions, are to be located in the sphere of ideas. And the most dangerous idea behind many of the world's problems is *the loss of our belief in individual agency*. Or, put differently, the loss of our belief that the sovereign individual can make sense of the world and tame it, cope with the challenges of life, and overcome the unavoidable blows that lie in front of us. The image of human the achiever has given way to the image of a human in an existential crisis, seeking the safety of the tribe, constantly in need of intervention and support, and overwhelmed by powers that seem outside of our control.

Such a view of human beings is unavoidable in a world where the volitional mind and reason are dismissed as chimeras. One's mind is one's main tool of survival. It is the navigating instrument and the most powerful weapon in one's arsenal. If one's mind is indeed incapable of understanding reality, if it is constantly at the mercy of environmental influences, psychological predispositions, or other deterministic factors, then indeed there is little one can do. Without navigation and stripped of tools, an individual is lost and in a state of constant angst, like the terrified subject in the famous painting by Edvard Munch, *The Scream*.

Under such a mindset, achievement and a sense of control over the world out there become impossible, or even undesirable. Thus, vulnerability becomes our *de facto* existential position; the normal and expected state that we find ourselves in. Then, it is not a surprise that in today's dominant view almost everyone is seen as belonging to a vulnerable group: women, ethnic and religious minorities, the young, the old, the poor, and even the rich, who are supposedly greedy and constantly on the spinning wheel of the rat race. A point I tried to make clear in this book is that this view, in most cases, is not a manufactured plot in order to give power to the bureaucrats or the intellectual leaders who want to exercise control over these vulnerable groups—though during the draconian lockdowns of 2020 many policy makers might have capitalized on this tendency. The point is, when we undermine the image of the rational sovereign individual, then this vulnerability is the only possible view of life.

But once vulnerability establishes itself as an existential view, it doesn't take long until it becomes an existential *need*. If productive achievement is seen as impossible, accessible only to a privileged few, or even as imposing an insurmountable toll on our planet and the environment, then the lack of it can become a badge of honour. Then, being a victim and vulnerable becomes the norm and even something to be pursued. As we saw earlier in the case studies, this might explain why there are grievances by more and more groups to be recognized as disenfranchised and victimized.

In a world of existential disenfranchisement, where the individual is viewed as at constant risk in an indecipherable reality, the group appears as a safe heaven. If existential security cannot be provided by the rational mind and individual agency, then group identity becomes a lifeboat. Through it, the constantly-at-risk individual becomes part of something bigger. The predicament of the one becomes the predicament of the group. There is not only strength in numbers, but also a louder outcry about how the group is the victim of wrongdoing by another, supposedly more dominant, group. As we have seen, this is where tribalism comes along—when the group provides the prism through which oneself, others, and reality in general are perceived.

According to this narrative, I am not predominantly Nikos anymore, but a member of my various groups, in the intersectional web of power. Thus, an attack on the group is an attack on me, and vice versa. We often come across various comments in the public sphere and on social media, such as: 'If you don't like feminism, you hate women', 'if you voted for Brexit, you tell me I am not welcome here', or 'if you stand against Trump, you don't want working class American people to do well', and the list goes on. As we have seen, the culture wars are constantly expanding such arguments beyond politics, to areas like sport, entertainment, advertising, our consumption choices, etc. The personal becomes political, and the political becomes personal.

However, if more and more things are political, then more and more things become a field of struggle. Let us remember what it means when something is 'political': it means it is an issue that is to be addressed by political action, which means, ultimately, by the implicit or explicit use of force. Through this prism, the public sphere becomes the arena of an everlasting struggle of basically all against all, in a zero-sum game where a gain for one group means a loss for another. And if reason and reality are no longer the arbiter—since we are told that one group's experience and perception of reality and of good and evil is not the same as of other groups—sooner or later the means available to solve our differences will be force and coercion.

Whilst we fight in the trenches of the culture wars, divided into the opposite camps of our various identities, communication and understanding between us become more and more difficult. Solidarity, benevolence, and cohesion through values that we can share become hard to achieve in our current epistemological Tower of Babel. Denying our universal common core of the rational mind, human subjectivity loses its sanctity. We are seen as personifications of our group identity, put into tribal boxes where any communication with other groups needs to be cautious, mediated by rules and bureaucratic procedures, and akin to walking on eggshells. Under such a miserable mindset, we are all losing. Instead of interacting freely and taking the best from each culture, we are told to be aware of 'cultural appropriation' and of overstepping the boundaries of other groups. In this worldview, cultures and their practitioners are static, like museum artefacts. Individuals are seen as passive avatars, rather than active shapers of history and creators of new worlds.

The past, rather than being our common heritage or at least a useful experience to draw lessons from, becomes a prison that determines our present and our future. Instead of striving to view members of groups who have long been subject to injustice as individuals capable of great achievement, we view them only as bearers of their collective identity and, thus, as perpetual victims. Such a worldview can preserve a fractious environment that breeds such injustices. The zeal by many activists of today to bring down statues not only of villains who were on the wrong side of history, but also of heroes (though, surely, with flaws) like Thomas Jefferson and Winston Churchill, is also symbolic of our preoccupation with the past. The present and the future appear bleak, and the pursuit of heroic endeavours that will inspire the erection of new statues is seen as too hard to achieve. With no positive vision about the present and the future, the past becomes a privileged terrain for struggle and disputes over meaning.

Here is the situation in a nutshell: tribal thinking is dominating the public sphere, and is pouring gasoline on the fire of the culture wars. In a social space that resembles more and more a battlefield, existential security is pursued at the level of the group. This makes tribal conflicts even fiercer, and the process is perpetuated in a downward spiral. Tribalism is expressed in various aspects of life, from universities to Hollywood and from inter-gender relations to politics. Yet, the root lies in our mind and the way we view the world. This is why I characterized tribalism first and foremost as an epistemology, i.e. as a way of acquiring information about the world out there.

Nowhere is this more obvious than in the way in which many people today preface a statement by putting forward their identity: 'as a transgender woman, I think x'; 'as a working-class man, my view on the topic is...'; 'as a person of colour, I believe y'; and so on. Often the experiences of some people indeed provide them with more direct knowledge on some issues. But epistemologically, what does it mean if I say 'as a heterosexual white Greek male, I believe x'? Do I make sense of the world through my genitalia, my chromosomes, or my passport? Obviously not. There is only one valid way to make sense of the world, and this is through my mind, using reason and having reality as my point of reference. There can be no 'as a member of x group, I think y'; the only option is 'as a rational individual, I think x', and the only alternative is 'I don't think'. This provides the key to understanding what is the only viable alternative to tribalism: the independent thinking of the sovereign rational individual.

...towards intellectual independence

The worst possible reaction to the toxic public sphere is to fight one kind of tribalism with another. This is not only because doing so perpetuates the culture wars and group warfare, but mostly because it limits the horizons of people. By definition, it is the independent rational mind of the individual that is the antidote to tribalism.

- Tribalism sees the world through the prism of belonging to a group; the rational individual uses his/her own judgment.
- Tribalism sees other people as avatars of their group identity; the rational individual judges other people on their own merit, to the best of his/her knowledge.
- For the tribal mind, the world is a place of existential angst that imposes things on vulnerable subjects; for the rational individual, reality is accessible via reason and thus the world can make sense and can be successfully navigated. The subjects are not passive spectators that just have things happening to them, but active shapers of their destiny.

This is why I call these people sovereign individuals: by the use of their rational faculty, they can independently make sense of the world. This is a first step towards taking control of their destiny and towards standing up to the challenges of life. Of course, tragedies and failures are still possible, but the worldview is one of confidence and of seeing the individual subject as capable of success, of overcoming calamities, and even of history-making.

Such a positive view of the potential of human beings was beautifully sketched in the novels and the philosophical work of Ayn Rand (see for example: Rand, 2007; 1984; 1964). She summed up her worldview in an afterword in her magnum opus *Atlas Shrugged* as follows: 'My philosophy, in essence, is the concept of man as a heroic being, with his own happiness as the moral purpose of his life, with productive achievement as his noblest activity, and reason as his only absolute' (Rand, 2007, p. 1171). This is a view of life that is the exact opposite in every respect to the tribalist tenets we saw in this book. In existential terms, it says we live in a world that can make sense; thus, we can be happy and prosperous (and it is moral to be so), if we make the right choices. The tool for all this is reason, which is a faculty accessible to all individuals, irrespective of their group. It is up to individuals whether they use it or not, which is a testament to their free will. To use it is the right and moral choice.

Thus, the epistemological nemesis of tribalism is intellectual independence. Rand defined independence as 'one's acceptance of the responsibility of forming one's own judgments and of living by the work of one's mind' (1964, p. 28). Uncritically following the tenets of others is a denial of what the nature of human thinking is. As philosopher Tara Smith mentioned, 'to fail to think for oneself is, truly, to fail to think' (2007, p. 287). But how can people know that their judgment is right? How can the virtue of independence avoid the predicament of descending into subjectivism and the blind following of one's whims or irrational desires? By having objective reality as an arbiter and the 'supreme court' of one's choices. 'The independent person's attitude is not "me first", but "reality first"' (idem, p. 286). Thus, blindly following one's unexamined whims or caprices is equally as bad as blindly following the 'line' of the tribe. Rational thinking, objectivity, and having reality as a point of reference are the antidotes to both of the above negative mindsets.

When it comes to how one can relate to other people, they can be of tremendous value to one's life; though only under the proper conditions. One can learn from others, benefit from them, assist them, cooperate, and build strong bonds of friendship, solidarity, and exultant romantic love, which are key for one's happiness. But none of these things negate the existential need for independence of the mind. Even when one person has to rely on the advice of an expert, there is still the responsibility to make his or her own judgment on whether that person is indeed an authority, to link any new information with previous knowledge, to maybe take more informed opinions on board before an important decision is made, and so on. Thus, one should never sacrifice one's judgment for the blind following of the judgment of others (Gotthelf, 2016, p. 92).

Many of the 'villains' we met in this book say that we live in an atomized society and, thus, without tribal links life is boring, alienating, and without meaning. But it is only by using your mind, making your own choices, and choosing your own values that life gets its meaning. Being invested in your own vision and building your own character is a prerequisite for emotions of passion, dedication, and exaltation. It requires the use of reason to choose the values one will go after, which can then lead to the forming of bonds with people who by their own choice share the same values (Locke and Kenner, 2011; Salmieri, 2016). In that case, those you *choose* to associate with are your brothers and sisters in spirit and in arms; they are not your victims, nor are you a tool in their grand plans because by default you happened to be part of the same or of opposing groups, as tribalism dictates.

As Ghate (2016) put it, the path towards becoming an intellectually independent sovereign individual begins by seizing the reins of your mind. This means, by exerting 'the full mental effort required to initiate and sustain one's conceptual awareness of the world' (idem, p. 108). By being conscious of your mental procedures, you can recognize and decipher any tendencies towards irrationality and the lazy option of tribalism. You can then bring your mind back to context, and fight such deviations. This is how you make yourself 'the author of your soul' (idem, p. 125) with your own rational judgment, your own values, and your own goals. Then the world can make sense, and reality is not a hostile place, nor does it require tribalism to provide existential reassurance.

This process of thinking independently and rationally is a complex one, a difficult one, and requires constant effort. Yet, having such high expectations of human beings means seeing in them the possibility of a hero. It means seeing yourself and fellow individuals as people who can overcome difficult challenges and ultimately prevail in their struggle by being faithful to rational and positive values. Such an existential view of people is not harsh or inhuman. Properly understood, heroes are not super-humans; on the contrary, they are humans *par excellence*, because they put forward the uniquely human form of survival: the uncompromising use of their mind and the passionate pursuit of their values, despite any obstacles (Bernstein, 2019). A consistent use of reason is within everyone's grasp, which is why the heroic is an ideal within everyone's reach.

This view of life is at odds with the current intellectual climate we find ourselves in, and yet it is achievable. It is true that tribal thinking is present on various levels of our societies, from institutional bureaucracies to popular culture and politics. Yet, it is a mostly amorphous system with weak convictions. The consistent and ideological firebrands of the various tribes that we met in the book are still mostly a minority. The zeitgeist is tribal, but a lot of people are uncomfortable with it and crave a different worldview.

The situation is similar on the political level. The culture wars between the right and the left have offered us a service: they have successfully demonstrated how both share the tribalist premises. They lack a positive vision for the future, and they mostly mobilize their bases around fear and the 'at least we are not as bad as the others' creed. Their exhausted non-vision for the future means that the field is open and everything is up for grabs. But the fight cannot begin from politics.

As we saw, tribalism is first and foremost a worldview, and secondly its political expressions. Thus, we first need to fight the battle of ideas. Because it is on the level of ideas that we make the crucial decisions as to how to view the world and how to view ourselves. Do we consider the responsibility to make our own decisions, to live our life as we want to live it, and to espouse the truth whatever the consequences may be, an unbearable weight? In that case, maybe we should stick to what others are doing and thinking, and we should not rock the boat.

But if we do dare to rationally think for ourselves, if we do choose to name things as we see them, and if we are not afraid to go against allowable opinion when reality and our mind are telling us that the majority is wrong and we are right, then we experience our agency and humanity at their fullest. It is the responsibility of reason, of making up our own mind and of living our own life, that tribalism finds so dreadful. It is exactly this responsibility that makes us human, and can make us history-makers.

Bibliography

Abramson, A. and Shuster, S. (2018) Steve Bannon says time's up and right-wing populism are on a collision course, *Time.com*, [Online], https://time.com/5185798/steve-bannon-says-times-up-and-right-wing-populism-are-on-a-collision-course/ [23 Dec 2019].

Adams, R. (2018) Cambridge gives role to academic accused of racist stereotyping, *The Guardian*, [Online], https://www.theguardian.com/world/2018/dec/07/cambridge-gives-role-to-academic-accused-of-racist-stereotyping [25 Dec 2019].

Adorno, T. and Horkheimer, M. (1997) *Dialectic of Enlightenment*, London and New York: Verso.

Alain, B. (2010) *The Communist Hypothesis*, London and New York: Verso.

Althusser, L. (1966) On the cultural revolution, *Decaleges*, [Online], https://scholar.oxy.edu/cgi/viewcontent.cgi?referer=https://www.google.com/&httpsredir=1&article=1003&context=decalages [29 Apr 2019].

Althusser, L. (2001) *Lenin and Philosophy and Other Essays*, New York: Monthly Review Press.

Andersen, M.L. (2003) Whitewashing race: A critical perspective on whiteness, in Doane, A.W. and Bonilla-Silva, E. (eds.) *White Out: The Continuing Significance of Racism*, pp. 21–34, New York and London: Routledge.

Anderson, W.L. (2000) Rethinking Carter, *Mises.org*, [Online], https://mises.org/library/rethinking-carter [23 Dec 2019].

Arnold, A. (2018) Christine Blasey Ford speaks out about the threats she's faced, *The Cut*, [Online], https://www.thecut.com/2018/11/christine-blasey-ford-threats-gofundme.html [26 Dec 2019].

Associated Press (2020) Lawyer: Officer's knee to neck killed man during 2018 arrest, *ABC News*, [Online], https://abcnews.go.com/US/wireStory/lawyer-officers-knee-neck-killed-man-2018-arrest-71347397 [25 Oct 2020].

BAFTA (2018) BAFTA introduces new diversity requirement to film awards.

Bar-On, T. (2019) Richard B. Spencer and the alt right, in Sedwick, M. (ed.) *Key Thinkers of the Radical Right: Behind the New Threat to Liberal Democracy*, pp. 224–241, New York: Oxford University Press.

BBC (2020) Black Lives Matter: Book judge axed over Twitter remarks, *BBC*, [Online], https://www.bbc.co.uk/news/uk-52940249 14 Oct 2020].

Beaumont-Thomas, B. (2019) Katy Perry shoes removed from stores over blackface design, *The Guardian*, [Online], https://www.theguardian.com/music/2019/feb/12/katy-perry-shoes-removed-from-stores-over-blackface-design [31 Jul 2019].

Beevor, A. (2006) *The Battle for Spain: The Spanish Civil War 1936–1939*, New York: Penguin Books.

Berlet, C. and Lyons, M.N. (2000) *Right-Wing Populism in America: Too Close for Comfort*, New York and London: The Guilford Press.

Berlinski, C. (2017) The warlock hunt, *The American Interest*, [Online], https://www.the-american-interest.com/2017/12/06/the-warlock-hunt/ [25 Dec 2019].

Berman, R. (2020) The United States vs Steve Bannon, *The Atlantic*, [Online], https://www.theatlantic.com/politics/archive/2020/08/steve-bannon-fraud-trump/615523/ [12 Oct 2020].

Bernstein, A. (2019) *Heroes, Legends, Champions: Why Heroism Matters*, New York: Union Square Publishing.

Bettizza, S. (2020) Is Italian fashion racist?, *BBC*, [Online], https://www.bbc.co.uk/news/av/world-europe-54061928 [27 Oct 2020].

Biddle, C. (2018) William F. Buckley: Cowardly, dishonest, unjust, racist, and loved by conservatives, *The Objective Standard*, [Online], https://www.theobjectivestandard.com/2018/02/william-f-buckley-cowardly-dishonest-unjust-racist-and-loved-by-conservatives/ [23 Dec 2019].

Billig, M. (1995) *Banal Nationalism*, London, Thousand Oaks, New Delhi, and Singapore: Sage.

Binswanger, H. (2014) *How We Know: Epistemology on an Objectivist Foundation*, New York: TOF Publications.

Birsteim, V.J. (2008) *The Perversion of Knowledge: The True Story of Soviet Science*, Cambridge, MA: Basic Books.

Blake, A. (2019) A key witness in the Brett Kavanaugh saga comes down on his side, *The Washington Post*, [Online], https://www.washington post.com/politics/2019/09/17/key-witness-brett-kavanaugh-saga-comes-down-his-side/ [26 Dec 2019].

Booker, B. (2020) Uncle Ben's changing name to Ben's Original after criticism of racial stereotyping, *NPR*, [Online], https://www.npr.org/sections/live-updates-protests-for-racial-justice/2020/09/23/916012582/uncle-bens-changing-name-to-ben-s-original-after-criticism-of-racial-stereotypin [27 Oct 2020].

Boztas, S. (2019) Top European technical university to open jobs exclusively to women, *The Telegraph*, [Online], https://www.telegraph.co.uk/news/2019/06/18/top-european-technical-university-open-jobs-exclusively-women/ [10 Aug 2019].

Branden, N. (1967) Alienation, in Rand, A. (ed.) *Capitalism: The Unknown Ideal*, pp. 308–339, New York: Signet.

Breitbart, A. (2012) *Righteous Indignation: Excuse Me While I Save the World!*, New York: Grand Central Publishing.

Bronze Age Pervert (2018) *Bronze Age Mindset*, Independently Published.

Buchanan, P.J. (1992) *1992 Republican National Convention Speech*, *Patrick J. Buchanan Official Website*, [Online], https://buchanan.org/blog/1992-republican-national-convention-speech-148 [5 Apr 2019].

Buchanan, P.J. (2002) *The Death of the West: How Dying Populations and Immigrant Invasions Imperil Our Country and Civilization*, New York: St Martin's Press.

Calton, C. (2018) Romanticizing Reagan, *Mises Wire*, [Online], https://mises.org/wire/romanticizing-reagan [28 May 2019].

Campbell, B. and Manning, J. (2018) *The Rise of Victimhood Culture: Micro-aggressions, Safe Spaces, and the New Culture Wars*, London: Palgrave.

Carden, J. (2019) Steve Bannon's foreign policy crusade against China, *The Nation*, [Online], https://www.thenation.com/article/steve-bannon-foreign-policy-crusade-china/ [23 Dec 2019].

Carl, N. (2019) Noah Carl controversy: FAQ, *Medium*, [Online], https://blog.usejournal.com/noah-carl-controversy-faq-ad967834b12d [18 Jun 2019].

Carlyle, T. (2015) *On Heroes, Hero-Worship, and the Heroic in History*, Scotts Valley, CA: CreateSpace Independent Publishing Platform.

Center, M.U.W. (nd) Rape culture, *Marshall University*, [Online], https://www.marshall.edu/wcenter/sexual-assault/rape-culture/ [9 Aug 2019].

Chait, J. (2020) The still-vital case for liberalism in a radical age, *NY Mag.com*, [Online], https://nymag.com/intelligencer/amp/2020/06/case-for-liberalism-tom-cotton-new-york-times-james-bennet.html [14 Oct 2020].

Chakelian, A. (2018) 'He changed — all his nastiness suddenly came out': Meet the people breaking up over Brexit, *New Statesman*, [Online], https://www.newstatesman.com/politics/brexit/2018/12/he-changed-all-his-nastiness-suddenly-came-out-meet-people-breaking-over [3 Apr 2019].

Chambers, W. (2005) Big Sister is watching you, *National Review*, [Online], https://www.nationalreview.com/2005/01/big-sister-watching-you-whittaker-chambers/ [26 May 2019].

Chasmar, J. (2017) Allison Stanger, professor injured by Middlebury College mob: 'I feared for my life', *The Washington Times*, [Online], https://www.washingtontimes.com/news/2017/mar/6/allison-stanger-professor-injured-by-middlebury-co/ [3 Apr 2019].

Childs, S. (2013) Thatcher's gender trouble: Ambivalence and the Thatcher legacy, *Political Studies Association*, [Online], https://www.psa.ac.uk/political-insight/blog/thatcher%E2%80%99s-gender-trouble-ambivalence-and-thatcher-legacy [11 Aug 2019].

Christakis, E. (2015) Email from Erika Christakis: 'Dressing yourselves', *Fire*, [Online], https://www.thefire.org/email-from-erika-christakis-dressing-yourselves-email-to-silliman-college-yale-students-on-halloween-costumes/ [21 Jun 2019].

Chua, A. (2018) *Political Tribes: Group Instinct and the Fate of Nations*, London, Oxford, New York, New Delhi, and Sydney: Bloomsbury.

Cineas, F. (2020) Critical race theory, and Trump's war on it, explained, *Vox.com*, [Online], https://www.vox.com/2020/9/24/21451220/critical-race-theory-diversity-training-trump [9 Oct 2020].

Clinch, M. (2017) The 'party of Davos' wakes up to the new, new world order, *CNBC.com*, [Online], https://www.cnbc.com/2017/01/09/davos-wakes-up-to-the-trump-new-world-order.html [23 Dec 2017].

Coates, T.-N. (2015) *Between the World and Me*, Melbourne: Text Publishing.

Cobley, B. (2018) *The Tribe: The Liberal-Left and the System of Diversity*, Exeter: Imprint Academic.

Cole, D. (2018) Ted Cruz forced from restaurant amid Kavanaugh drama, *CNN*, [Online], https://edition.cnn.com/2018/09/25/politics/ted-cruz-heckled-restaurant-brett-kavanaugh/index.html [26 Dec 2019].

Coleman, J. (2019) NHS worker Siobhan Prigent should be sacked, *Change.org*, [Online], https://www.change.org/p/nhs-nhs-worker-siobhan-prigent-should-be-sacked [30 Jun 2019].

Concha, J. (2020) CNN ridiculed for 'Fiery But Mostly Peaceful' caption with video of burning building in Kenosha, *TheHill.com*, [Online], https://thehill.com/homenews/media/513902-cnn-ridiculed-for-fiery-but-mostly-peaceful-caption-with-video-of-burning [12 Oct 2020].

Coulter, A. (2015) *¡Adios, America!: The Left's Plan to Turn Our Country Into a Third World Hellhole*, Washington, DC: Regnery Publishing.

Daniels, J. (2018) White families are engines of inequality, *Huffington Post*, [Online], https://www.huffpost.com/entry/opinion-daniels-white-black-wealth-gap_n_5a947f91e4b02cb368c4bf48?guccounter=1 [31 Jul 2019].

#DareConf (2019) Facing up to race, power and privilege, *Dareconf.uk*, [Online], https://dareconf.uk/retreat [31 Jul 2019].

David, M.E. (2016) *Reclaiming Feminism: Challenging Everyday Misogyny*, Bristol: Policy Press.

Day, V. (2017) Soiled! Soiled, I say!, *Vox Popoli*, [Online], https://voxday.blogspot.com/2017/06/soiled-soiled-i-say.html [21 May 2019].

Dearden, L. (2018) Man who taught girlfriend's pet pug dog to perform Nazi salutes fined £800, *The Independent*, [Online], https://www.independent.co.uk/news/uk/crime/count-dankula-nazi-pug-salutes-mark-meechan-fine-sentenced-a8317751.html [24 Dec 2019].

Dept of Inclusion and Community Engagement and the Minnesota Historical Society (2001) *White Supremacy Culture*, [Online], https://www.thc.texas.gov/public/upload/preserve/museums/files/White_Supremacy_Culture.pdf [31 Jul 2019].

DiAngelo, D. (2018) *White Fragility: Why It's So Hard for White People to Talk about Racism*, Boston, MA: Beacon Press.

Doherty, B. (2000) Manufactured vulnerability, in Doherty, B., Paterson, M. and Seel, B. (eds.) *Direct Action in British Environmentalism*, pp. 62–78, London: Routledge.

Doherty, B. (2007) *Radicals for Capitalism: A Freewheeling History of the Modern American Libertarian Movement*, New York: Public Affairs.

Doherty, B. (2012) *Ron Paul's Revolution: The Man and the Movement he Inspired*, New York: Broadside Books.

Donovan, J. (2012) *The Way of Men*, Milwaukie, OR: Dissonant Hum.

Donovan, J. (2016) *Becoming a Barbarian*, Milwaukie, OR: Dissonant Hum.

Donovan, J. (2017) Why I am not a white nationalist, *JackDonovan.com*, [Online], https://www.jack-donovan.com/axis/2017/05/why-i-am-not-a-white-nationalist/ [14 Aug 2019].

Dreher, R. (2017) Creating the white tribe, *American Conservative*, [Online], https://www.theamericanconservative.com/dreher/creating-the-white-tribe/comment-page-1/ [2 Aug 2019].

Durand, E. (2018) Nazism and the alt right: At peace with ourselves, in Johnson, G. (ed.) *The Alternative Right*, loc. 2813–2892, San Francisco, CA: Counter-Currents Publishing Ltd.

Durkin, E. (2018) Trump-Clinton election battle left students with PTSD symptoms, study finds, *The Guardian*, [Online], https://www.theguardian.com/us-news/2018/oct/23/trump-clinton-2016-election-ptsd-students-stressful-experience- [23 Jun 2019].

Dworkin, A. (1991) *Pornography: Men Possessing Women*, New York: Plume.

Eddo-Lodge, R. (2018) *Why I'm No Longer Talking to White People About Race*, London, Oxford, New York, New Delhi, and Sydney: Bloomsbury.

Eduardo, B.-S. (2003) 'New racism', colour-blind racism, and the future of whiteness in America, in Doane, A.W. and Bonilla-Silva, E. (eds.) *White Out: The Continuing Significance of Racism*, pp. 271–284, New York and London: Routledge.

Times Higher Education (2019) World university rankings, *Times Higher Education*, [Online], https://www.timeshighereducation.com/world-university-rankings/yale-university [21 Jun 2019].

Essed, P. (2002) Everyday racism: A new approach to the study of racism, in Essed, P. and Goldberg, D.T. (eds.) *Race Critical Theories*, pp. 176–191, Oxford: Blackwell.

Eurosport (2020) LA Galaxy part with midfielder Katai after wife's 'racist' posts, *EuroSport*, [Online], https://www.eurosport.co.uk/football/la-galaxy-part-with-midfielder-katai-after-wife-s-racist-posts_sto7767596/story.shtml [14 Oct 2020].

Eustachewich, L. (2019) Esquire criticized for cover on white boy's struggles during Black History Month, *New York Post*, [Online], https://nypost.com/2019/02/12/esquire-criticized-for-cover-on-white-boys-struggles-during-black-history-month/?utm_source=NYPTwitter&utm_campaign=SocialFlow&utm_medium=SocialFlow [31 Jul 2019].

Eventbrite (2019) Shame resilience for white people, Eventbrite, [Online], https://www.eventbrite.com/e/shame-resilience-for-white-people-tickets-62895928415 [31 Jul 2019].

Evola, J. (1995) *Revolt Against the Modern World*, Rochester, VT: Inner Traditions.

Evola, J. (2003) *Ride the Tiger: A Survival Manual for the Aristocrats of the Soul*, Rochester, VT: Inner Traditions.

Faye, G. (2011) *Why We Fight: Manifesto of the European Resistance*, London: Arktos.

Feder, J.L. (2016) This is how Steve Bannon sees the entire world, *BuzzFeed News*, [Online], https://www.buzzfeednews.com/article/lesterfeder

/this-is-how-steve-bannon-sees-the-entire-world#.nso36vN6l [3 Jun 2019].

FIRE (nd) User's guide to FIRE's disinvitation database, *The Fire*, [Online], https://www.thefire.org/how-to-use-the-disinvitation-database/ [21 Jun 2019].

Flood, A. (2014) US students request 'trigger warnings' on literature, *The Guardian*, [Online], https://www.theguardian.com/books/2014/may/19/us-students-request-trigger-warnings-in-literature [20 Jun 2019].

Fox, C. (2016) *'I Find That Offensive'*, London: Biteback Publishing.

Free Speech Union (2020) About, *FreeSpeechUnion.org*, [Online], https://freespeechunion.org/about/ [14 Oct 2020].

Friedersdorf, C. (2015) Why it matters that the Charleston attack was terrorism, *The Atlantic*, [Online], https://www.theatlantic.com/politics/archive/2015/06/was-the-charleston-attack-terrorism/396329/ [3 Apr 2019].

Froio, N. (2018) The manipulative power of white men's tears, *Bitch Media*, [Online], https://www.bitchmedia.org/article/the-manipulative-power-of-brett-kavanaugh-crying [14 Aug 2019].

Frostrup, M. (2016) 'My partner and I are at breaking point over Brexit', *The Guardian*, 31 July, [Online], https://www.theguardian.com/lifeandstyle/2016/jul/31/my-partner-and-i-are-at-breaking-point-over-brexit [3 Apr 2019].

Furedi, F. (1990) Introduction, in Jakubowski, F. (ed.) *Ideology and Super-structure in Historical Materialism*, pp. vii–xxxiii, London and Winchester: Pluto Press.

Furedi, F. (2017) The hidden history of identity politics, *Spiked Online*, [Online], https://www.spiked-online.com/2017/12/01/the-hidden-history-of-identity-politics/20596/#.WiUcjkbyhhE [26 May 2019].

Futrelle, D. (2018) When a mass murderer has a cult following, *The Cut*, [Online], https://www.thecut.com/2018/04/incel-meaning-rebellion-alex-minassian-elliot-rodger-reddit.html [26 Dec 2019].

Garner, S. (2017) *Racisms: An Introduction*, Los Angeles, London, New Delhi, Singapore, Washington DC, and Melbourne: Sage.

Ghate, O. (2007) The basic motivation of the creators and the masses in The Fountainhead, in Mayhew, R. (ed.) *Essays on Ayn Rand's The Fountainhead*, pp. 243–284, Lanham, Boulder, New York, Toronto, and Plymouth: Lexington Books.

Ghate, O. (2016) A being of self-made soul, in Gotthelf, A. and Salmiery, G. (eds.) *A Companion to Ayn Rand*, pp. 105–129, Oxford: Wiley Blackwell.

Gitlin, T. (1993) *The Sixties: Years of Hope, Days of Rage*, New York, Toronto, Sydney, Auckland, and London: Bantam Books.

Gordon, L. (2015) *From Power to Prejudice: The Rise of Racial Individualism in Midcentury America*, Chicago and London: University of Chicago Press.

Gotthelf, A. (2016) The morality of life, in Gotthelf, A. and Salmiery, G. (eds.) *A Companion to Ayn Rand*, pp. 73–104, Oxford: Wiley Blackwell.

Greene, J. (2015) *Moral Tribes: Emotion, Reason and the Gap Between Us and Them*, London: Atlantic Books.

Haidt, J. (2013) *The Righteous Mind: Why Good People Are Divided by Politics and Religion*, New York: Vintage.

Harris, D. (1997) Dwight Eisenhower and the New Deal: The politics of pre-emption, *Presidential Studies Quarterly*, 27 (2), pp. 333–342.

Harris, L. (2018) Brett Kavanaugh and the power of public trauma, *Medium.com*, [Online], https://medium.com/s/powertrip/the-power-of-public-trauma-ecf72bd52bf3 [14 Aug 2019].

Harris, S. (2017) After 'inebriated' hook up, student gets expelled without due process, *Reason*, [Online], https://reason.com/2017/06/20/campus-sex-due-process/ [10 Aug 2019].

Hartman, A. (2015) *A War for the Soul of America: A History of the Culture Wars*, Chicago and London: University of Chicago Press.

Haynes, J. (2019) *From Huntington to Trump: Thirty Years of the Clash of Civilizations*, London: Lexington Books.

Everyday Feminism (2018) Healing from internalized whiteness, *Everydayfeminism.com*, [Online], https://everydayfeminism.com/healing-from-internalized-whiteness/ [5 Sep 2019].

Hecken, T. and Grzenia, A. (2008) Situationism, in Klimke, M. and Scharloth, J. (eds.) *1968 in Europe: A History of Protest and Activism, 1956–1977*, pp. 23–32, Basingstoke and New York: Palgrave.

Heim, J. (2017) How a rally of white nationalists and supremacists at the University of Virginia turned into a 'tragic, tragic weekend', *Washington Post*, [Online], https://www.washingtonpost.com/ graphics/2017/local/charlottesville-timeline/ [3 Apr 2019].

Hentoff, N. (1992) *Free Speech for Me – But Not for Thee: How the American Left and Right Relentlessly Censor Each Other*, New York: HarperCollins.

Heritage.org (nd) 2019 Index of Economic Freedom: Rwanda, *Heritage.org*, [Online], https://www.heritage.org/index/country/rwanda [17 Dec 2019].

Hetherington, K. (1998) *Expressions of Identity: Space, Performance, Politics*, London and Thousand Oaks: Sage.

Higgens, D. (2016) Thomas Mair: The far-right extremist who murdered MP Jo Cox, *The Independent*, [Online], http://www.independent.co. uk/news/uk/crime/thomas-mair-guilty-tommy-verdict-jo-cox-mp-murder-trial-court-latest-quiet-neighbour-a7434011.html [3 Apr 2019].

Hoenig, J. (2018) *A New Textbook of Americanism: The Politics of Ayn Rand*, Chicago, IL: Capitalistpig Publications.

Hoff Sommers, C. (2013) *Freedom Feminism: Its Surprising History and Why It Matters Today*, Washington, DC: AEI Press.

Home Office (2018) Hate crime, England and Wales, 2017/18, *Gov.UK*, [Online], https://assets.publishing.service.gov.uk/government/ uploads/system/uploads/attachment_data/file/748598/hate-crime-1718-hosb2018.pdf [27 Jun 2019].

Hooks, B. (2015) *Feminism is for Everybody: Passionate Politics*, New York and London: Routledge.

Hopper, T. (2017) Here's the full recording of Wilfrid Laurier repri-manding Lindsay Shepherd for showing a Jordan Peterson video, *National Post*, [Online], https://nationalpost.com/news/canada/ heres-the-full-recording-of-wilfrid-laurier-reprimanding-lindsay-shepherd-for-showing-a-jordan-peterson-video.

Horowitz, J. (2017) Steve Bannon cited Italian thinker who inspired fascists, *The New York Times*, [Online], https://www.nytimes.com/

2017/02/10/world/europe/bannon-vatican-julius-evola-fascism. html [26 May 2019].

Horwitz, R.B. (2013) *America's Right: Anti-Establishment Conservatism from Goldwater to the Tea Party*, Cambridge: Polity.

Hosie, R. (2018) Clapping replaced with jazz hands: Where did the action come from and what other alternatives are there?, *The Independent*, [Online] https://www.independent.co.uk/life-style/clapping-banned-manchester-university-students-union-jazz-hands-applause-a8566531.html [23 Jun 2019].

Hume, M. (2015) *Trigger Warning: Is the Fear of Being Offensive Killing Free Speech?*, London: William Collins.

Innes-Smith, J. (2018) What's the truth about men's rights activists?, *The Spectator*, [Online], https://blogs.spectator.co.uk/2018/08/whats-the-truth-about-mens-rights-activists/ [26 Dec 2019].

Isserman, M. and Kazin, M. (2008) *America Divided: The Civil War of the 1960s*, New York and Oxford: Oxford University Press.

Jackson, J. (2016) Sadiq Khan moves to ban body-shaming ads from London transport, *The Guardian*, [Online], https://www.theguardian.com/media/2016/jun/13/sadiq-khan-moves-to-ban-body-shaming-ads-from-london-transport [10 Aug 2019].

BBC News (2013) Jackson: Thatcher was 'a woman, but not on my terms', *BBC*, [Online], https://www.bbc.co.uk/news/av/uk-politics-22100011/jackson-thatcher-was-a-woman-but-not-on-my-terms [11 Aug 2019].

Jared, T. (2013) A brief history of US race relations: A lecture to the Property and Freedom Society 2013 Conference, *Property and Freedom Society*, [Online], https://www.youtube.com/watch?v=rIcugsixfow [3 Aug 2019].

Jebsen Moore, K. (2019) A witch-hunt on Instagram, *Quillette*, [Online], https://quillette.com/2019/02/17/a-witch-hunt-on-instagram/ [31 Jul 2019].

Jeffries, S. (2006) Are women human?, *The Guardian*, [Online], https://www.theguardian.com/world/2006/apr/12/gender.politics philosophyandsociety [10 Aug 2019].

Johnson, G. (2018) What is the alternative right?, in Johnson, G. (ed.) *The Alternative Right*, loc. 116–560, San Francisco, CA: Counter-Currents Publishing Ltd.

Journo, E. (2018) *What Justice Demands: America and the Israeli-Palestinian Conflict*, New York and Nashville: Post-Hill Press.

Julian, K. (2018) Why are young people having so little sex?, *The Atlantic*, [Online], https://www.theatlantic.com/magazine/archive/2018/12/the-sex-recession/573949/ [26 Dec 2019].

Kean, S. (2017) The Soviet era's deadliest scientist is regaining popularity in Russia, *The Atlantic*, [Online], https://www.theatlantic.com/science/archive/2017/12/trofim-lysenko-soviet-union-russia/548786/ [18 Jun 2019].

Kilgore, E. (2018) Trump now trails only Reagan among recent presidents in GOP esteem, *New York Magazine*, [Online], http://nymag.com/intelligencer/2018/02/trump-trails-only-reagan-among-recent-presidents-in-gop-love.html [23 Dec 2019].

King, M.L. (1963) I have a dream…, *National Archives*, [Online], https://www.archives.gov/files/press/exhibits/dream-speech.pdf [25 Dec 2019].

Klimke, M. and Scharloth, J. (2008) 1968 in Europe: An introduction, in Klimke, M. and Scharloth, J. (eds.) *1968 in Europe: A History of Protest and Activism, 1956–1977*, pp. 1–9, New York: Palgrave Macmillan.

Kolakowski, L. (2008) *Main Currents of Marxism: The Founders, The Golden Age, The Breakdown*, New York and London: W.W. Norton & Co.

Krieg, G. (2018) The moments that defined the Christine Blasey Ford-Brett Kavanaugh hearing, *CNN*, [Online], https://edition.cnn.com/2018/09/27/politics/blasey-ford-kavanaugh-hearing-notable-moments/index.html [26 Dec 2019].

Kundera, M. (1992) *The Joke*, London: Bloomsbury House.

Langmuir, M. (2018) Donald Trump is destroying my marriage, *New York Magazine*, [Online], http://nymag.com/intelligencer/2018/11/donald-trump-is-destroying-my-marriage.html [3 Apr 2019].

Lasch, C. (1979) *The Culture of Narcissism: American Life in an Age of Diminishing Expectations*, New York and London: W.W. Norton & Co.

Le Brun, P. (2018) What the alt right isn't, in Johnson, G. (ed.) *The Alternative Right*, loc. 1822–2032, San Francisco, CA: Counter-Currents Publishing Ltd.

Lerner, M. (1971) Anarchism and the American counter-culture, in Apter, D. and Joll, J. (eds.) *Anarchism Today*, pp. 34–59, London: Palgrave Macmillan.

Locke, E. and Kenner, E. (2011) *The Selfish Path to Romance: How to Love with Passion and Reason*, Doylestown, PA: Platform Press.

Lombroso, D. and Appelbaum, Y. (2016) 'Hail Trump!': White nationalists salute the president-elect, *The Atlantic*, [Online], https://www.theatlantic.com/politics/archive/2016/11/richard-spencer-speech-npi/508379/ [2 Aug 2019].

Lotringer, S. and Marazzi, C. (2008) *Autonomia: Post-Political Politics*, Los Angeles, CA: Semiotexte.

Lukianoff, G. and Haidt, J. (2018) *The Coddling of the American Mind: How Good Intentions and Bad Ideas Are Setting Up a Generation for Failure*, New York: Penguin.

Luxemburg, R. (1918) The Russian Revolution, *Marxists.org*, [Online], https://www.marxists.org/archive/luxemburg/1918/russian-revolution/ [19 Jun 2019].

Lyons, M.N. (2019) Jack Donovan and male tribalism, in Sedwick, M. (ed.) *Key Thinkers of the Radical Right: Behind the New Threat to Liberal Democracy*, pp. 242–258, New York: Oxford University Press.

MacDonald, K. (2018) Jews and the alt right, in Johnson, G. (ed.) *The Alternative Right*, loc. 663–855, San Francisco, CA: Counter-Currents Publishing Ltd.

Macklin, G. (2019) Greg Johnson and Counter-Currents, in Sedwick, M. (ed.) *Key Thinkers of the Radical Right: Behind the New Threat to Liberal Democracy*, pp. 224–241, New York: Oxford University Press.

Maffesoli, M. (1995) *The Time of the Tribes: The Decline of Individualism in Mass Society*, London, Thousand Oaks, and New Delhi: Sage.

Maher, R. (2019) How realistic is Steve Bannon's vision for populist 'revolt' against European Union?, *The Globe Post*, [Online], https://theglobepost.com/2019/02/21/bannon-movement-eu/ [23 Dec 2019].

Malice, M. (2019) *The New Right: a Journey to the Fringe of American Politics*, New York: All Points Books.

Malik, K. (2019) The history and politics of white identity, *Pandaemonium*, [Online], https://kenanmalik.com/2019/03/16/the-history-and-politics-of-white-identity/ [3 May 2019].

Mangan, L. (2016) 'He's Out, I'm In: Can our relationship survive the Brexit argument?', *The Guardian*, 18 June, [Online], https://www.theguardian.com/politics/2016/jun/18/husband-votes-leave-wife-votes-remain-eu-referendum-relationships [3 Apr 2019].

Marcuse, H. (1965) Repressive tolerance, *Marcuse.org*, [Online], https://www.marcuse.org/herbert/pubs/60spubs/65repressivetolerance.htm [20 Jun 2019].

Marcuse, H. (2002) *One-Dimensional Man*, London and New York: Routledge.

Marx, K. (1842) On freedom of the press, *Marxists.org*, [Online], https://www.marxists.org/archive/marx/works/1842/free-press/ [19 Jun 2019].

Marx, K. (1990) *Capital, Volume 1*, London: Penguin Classics.

Marx, K. (1991) *Capital: Volume. 3*, London: Penguin Classics.

Marx, K. and Engels, F. (1970) *The German Ideology*, London: Lawrence & Wishart.

Marx, K. and Engels, F. (2007) *Manifesto of the Communist Party*, Radford: Wilder.

Marxists.org (1936) Report of court proceedings: The Case of the Trotskyite-Zinovievite Terrorist Centre, *Marxists.org*, [Online], https://www.marxists.org/history/ussr/government/law/1936/moscow-trials/index.htm [30 Jun 2019].

May, A. (2018) Antifa at Tucker Carlson's home: Group breaks door, chants at Fox host, *USA Today*, [Online], https://www.usatoday.com/story/news/politics/2018/11/08/mob-tucker-carlsons-home-antifa-break-door-chant-fox-host/1927868002/ [3 Apr 2019].

McCluskey, M. (2019) Gillette makes waves with controversial new ad highlighting 'toxic masculinity', *Time.com*, [Online], https://time.com/5503156/gillette-razors-toxic-masculinity/ [30 Dec 2019].

McElroy, W. (2014) The big lie of a 'rape culture', *The Future of Freedom Foundation*, [Online], https://www.fff.org/explore-freedom/article/the-big-lie-of-a-rape-culture/ [9 Aug 2019].

McKelvey, T. (2016) Dallas shooting: Gunman 'wanted to kill whites' says police chief, *BBC*, 8 July, [Online], https://www.bbc.com/news/world-us-canada-36745862 [3 Apr 2019].

McKie, R. (2015) Shamed Nobel laureate Tim Hunt 'ruined by rush to judgment after stupid remarks', *The Guardian*, [Online], https://www.theguardian.com/science/2015/jun/13/tim-hunt-forced-to-resign [30 Jun 2019].

McLellan, D. (2000) *Karl Marx: Selected Writings*, Oxford: Oxford University Press.

McManus, M. (2017) Post-modern conservatism, *The Philosophical Salon*, [Online], https://thephilosophicalsalon.com/post-modern-conservatism/ [2019].

McManus, M. (2018) The emergence and rise of postmodern conservatism, *Quillette*, [Online], https://quillette.com/2018/05/17/emergence-rise-postmodern-conservatism/ [4 May 2019].

McVeigh, R. (2001) Power devaluation, the Ku Klux Klan, and the Democratic National Convention of 1924, *Sociological Forum*, 1 (16), pp. 1–30.

Melucci, A. (1996) *Challenging Codes: Collective Action in the Information Age*, Cambridge: Cambridge University Press.

Meszaros, I. (2005) *Marx's Theory of Alienation*, London: The Merlin Press.

Miller, K. (2020) From 'master bedroom' to 'blacklist': What will it take to change racist terms in our everyday language?, *Yahoo News*, [Online], https://uk.news.yahoo.com/from-master-bedrooms-to-blacklists-what-will-it-take-to-change-racist-terms-in-our-everyday-language-193858660.html [27 Oct 2020].

Milstein, C. (2012) Occupy anarchism, in Khatib, K., Killjoy, M. and McGuire, M. (eds.) *We Are Many: Reflections on Movement Strategy from Occupation to Liberation*, pp. 291–305, Oakland and Edinburgh: AK Press.

Mirkowitz, D. (2017) The racist right looks left: At Richard Spencer's secret conference, white supremacists denounce corporate capitalism,

The Nation, [Online], https://www.thenation.com/article/the-racist-right-looks-left/ [3 Aug 2019].

Mohamed, N. (2018) Does Kanye West deserve to be called an Uncle Tom?, *The Guardian*, [Online], https://www.theguardian.com/commentisfree/2018/oct/15/kanye-west-uncle-tom-slavery-donald-trump [25 Dec 2019].

Moldbug, M. (2009) A gentle introduction to Unqualified Reservations, *Unqualified Reservations*, [Online], https://www.unqualified-reservations.org/2009/01/gentle-introduction-to-unqualified/ [31 May 2019].

Murray, D. (2019) *The Madness of Crowds: Gender, Race and Identity*, London, Oxford, New York, New Delhi, and Sydney: Bloomsbury.

Myers, F. (2018) Incels: The ugly truth, *Spiked Online*, [Online], https://www.spiked-online.com/2018/07/06/incels-the-ugly-truth/ [12 Aug 2019].

Myers, F. (2019) Uncle Tom's cabinet, *Spiked Online*, [Online], https://www.spiked-online.com/2019/07/28/uncle-toms-cabinet/ [31 Jul 2019].

Nagle, A. (2017) *Kill All Normies: Online Culture Wars from 4Chan and Tumblr to Trump and the Alt-Right*, Washington and Winchester: Zero Books.

O'Farrell, C. (2019) Highly cited researchers (h100); Foucault at number 1, *Foucault News*, [Online], https://michel-foucault.com/2019/05/01/highly-cited-researchers-h100-foucault-at-number-1-2019/ [27 Jun 2019].

O'Neill, B. (2009) Too many people? No, too many Malthusians, *Spiked Online*, [Online], https://www.spiked-online.com/2009/11/19/too-many-people-no-too-many-malthusians/ [26 May 2019].

Paglia, C. (2018) *Free Women, Free Men: Sex – Gender – Feminism*, Edinburgh: Canongate.

PAHO/WHO (2019) 1 in 5 men will not reach the age of 50 in the Americas, due to issues relating to toxic masculinity, *PAHO.org*, [Online], https://www.paho.org/hq/index.php?option=com_content&view=article&id=15599:1-in-5-men-will-not-reach-the-age-of-50-in-

the-americas-due-to-issues-relating-to-toxic-masculinity&Itemid=1926 &lang=en [16 Oct 2020].

Pakulski, J. (1991) *Social Movements: The Politics of Moral Protest*, Melbourne: Longman Cheshire.

Palahniuk, C. (2006) *Fight Club*, London: Vintage.

Pappas, S. (2019) APA issues first-ever guidelines for practice with men and boys, *American Psychological Association*, [Online], https://www. apa.org/monitor/2019/01/ce-corner [9 Aug 2019].

Park, M. and Lah, K. (2017) Berkeley protests of Yiannopoulos caused $100,000 in damage, *CNN.com*, [Online], https://edition.cnn.com/ 2017/02/01/us/milo-yiannopoulos-berkeley/index.html [27 Jun 2019].

Payne, S. (1995) *A History of Fascism, 1914–1945*, New York: Routledge.

Peikoff, L. (1983) *The Ominous Parallels*, New York: Meridian.

Peikoff, L. (2012) *The DIM Hypothesis: Why the Lights of the West are Going Out*, New York: New American Library

Pells, R. (2016) Essex University gives female staff one-off pay rises in order to close gender pay gap, *The Independent*, [Online], https:// www.independent.co.uk/news/education/education-news/essex-university-gives-female-staff-one-off-pay-rises-to-close-gender-pay-gap-a7063446.html [10 Aug 2016].

Peterson, J. (2018) *12 Rules for Life: An Antidote to Chaos*, London: Penguin Books.

Petrzela, N. (2020) Jogging has always excluded black people, *The New York Times*, [Online], https://www.nytimes.com/2020/05/12/ opinion/running-jogging-race-ahmaud-arbery.html [27 Oct 2020].

Pluckrose, H. and Lindsay, J. (2020) *Cynical Theories: How Activist Scholarship Made Everything about Race, Gender, and Identity – and Why This Harms Everybody*, Chicago, IL: Pitchstone Publishing.

PragerU (2017) PragerU takes legal action against Google and YouTube for discrimination, *PragerU*, [Online], https://www.prageru.com/ press-release/prageru-takes-legal-action-against-google-and-youtube-for-discrimination/ [30 Jun 2019].

Pran, D. (1999) *Children of Cambodia's Killing Fields: Memoirs by Survivors*, New Haven and London: Yale University Press.

Quillette (2018) Academics' mobbing of a young scholar must be denounced, *Quillette,* [Online], https://quillette.com/2018/12/07/academics-mobbing-of-a-young-scholar-must-be-denounced/ [18 Jun 2019].

RADIX, N. / (2019) The bride gathering cult with Roosh V., *YouTube,* [Online], https://www.youtube.com/watch?v=GS8HjDbiEmM [12 Aug 2019].

Rand, A. (1964) *The Virtue of Selfishness,* Rand, A. (ed.), New York: Signet.

Rand, A. (1967) Conservatism: An obituary, in *Capitalism: the Unknown Ideal,* pp. 214–225, New York: Signet.

Rand, A. (1990) Global Balkanization, in Rand, A. and Peikoff, L. (eds.) *The Voice of Reason: Essays in Objectivist Thought,* pp. 115–129, New York: Meridian.

Rand, A. (1999) *Return of the Primitive: The Anti-Industrial Revolution,* New York: Meridian.

Rand, A. (2000) *Philosophy: Who Needs It,* New York: Signet.

Rand, A. (2007) *Atlas Shrugged,* London: Penguin.

Raed, R. (2020) Attorney for Minneapolis police officer says he'll argue George Floyd died of an overdose and a heart condition, *Los Angeles Times,* [Online], https://www.latimes.com/world-nation/story/2020-08-20/george-floyd-derek-chauvin-defense [25 Oct 2020].

Reilly, K. (2016) Read Hillary Clinton's 'basket of deplorables' remarks about Donald Trump supporters, *Time,* [Online], https://time.com/4486502/hillary-clinton-basket-of-deplorables-transcript/ [23 Dec 2019].

Revel, F.J. (2009) *Last Exit to Utopia: The Survival of Socialism in a Post-Soviet Era,* New York: Encounter Books.

Ridgway, S. (2014) 25 everyday examples of rape culture, *Everyday Feminism,* [Online], https://everydayfeminism.com/2014/03/examples-of-rape-culture/ [9 Aug 2019].

Rodriguez, O.R. (2018) 4 hurt in campus riot over Milo Yiannopoulos speech sue Cal, *NBC Bay Area,* [Online], http://www.nbcbayarea.com/news/local/Four-Injured-at-Campus-Riot-Over-Milo-Yiannopoulos-Speech-Sue-Berkeley-UC-Berkeley-469598203.html [3 Apr 2019].

Roosh, V. (2019a) NEW RULES: Casual sex and hooking up can no longer be discussed on the forum, *Roosh V forum*, [Online], https://www.rooshvforum.com/thread-73256.html [12 Aug 2019].

Roosh, V. (2019b) Rules of the forum, *Roosh V forum*, [Online], https://www.rooshvforum.com/thread-13005.html [26 Dec 2019].

Roszak, T. (1995) *The Making of a Counter Culture: Reflections on the Technocratic Society and Its Youthful Opposition*, Berkeley, CA: University of California Press.

Roy, E.A. and Martin, L. (2019) 49 shot dead in attack on two Christchurch mosques, *The Guardian*.

Sabes, A. (2018) USC students falsely claim Ben Shapiro touts 'eradication of entire races', *Campus Reform*, [Online], https://www.campusreform.org/?ID=11357 [26 Jun 2019].

Salmiery, G. (2016) The act of valuing (and the objectivity of values), in Gotthelf, A. and Salmiery, G. (eds.) *A Companion to Ayn Rand*, pp. 49–72, Malden and Oxford: Wiley Blackwell.

Salter, M. (2019) The problem with a fight against toxic masculinity, *The Atlantic*, [Online], https://www.theatlantic.com/health/archive/2019/02/toxic-masculinity-history/583411/ [25 Dec 2019].

Savage, K. (2020) Windsor principal on leave after Black Lives Matter comments stir controversy, *VTDigger*, [Online], https://vtdigger.org/2020/06/14/windsor-principal-on-leave-after-black-lives-matter-comments-stir-controversy/ [14 Oct 2020].

Schäfer, A.R. (2011) *Countercultural Conservatives: American Evangelicalism from the Postwar Revival to the New Christian Right*, Wisconsin and London: The University of Wisconsin Press.

Scher, A. (2018) 'Climate grief': The growing emotional toll of climate change, *NBC News*, [Online], https://www.nbcnews.com/health/mental-health/climate-grief-growing-emotional-toll-climate-change-n946751 [23 Jun 2019].

Schulman, S. (2016) White writer, *The New Yorker*, [Online], https://www.newyorker.com/culture/cultural-comment/white-writer [31 Jul 2019].

Scruton, R. (2016) *Fools, Frauds and Firebrands: Thinkers of the New Left*, London, Oxford, New York, New Delhi, and Sydney: Bloomsbury.

Seife, C. (2000) Vatican regrets burning cosmologist, *Science Magazine*, [Online], https://web.archive.org/web/20130608054739/http://news.sciencemag.org/sciencenow/2000/03/01-04.html [18 Jun 2019].

Selby, J. (2015) Benedict Cumberbatch criticised for using term 'coloured' to describe black actors, *The Independent*, [Online], https://www.independent.co.uk/news/people/benedict-cumberbatch-criticised-for-using-term-coloured-to-describe-black-actors-in-conversation-10003113.html [27 Jun 2019].

Shapiro, B. (2016) I know Trump's new campaign chairman, Steve Bannon. Here's what you need to know, *The Daily Wire*, [Online], https://www.dailywire.com/news/8441/i-know-trumps-new-campaign-chairman-steve-bannon-ben-shapiro [3 Jun 2019].

Slater, T. (2019) The right-wing snowflakes strike again, *Spiked Online*, [Online], https://www.spiked-online.com/2019/06/07/the-right-wing-snowflakes-strike-again/ [2019].

Smith, T. (2007) Unborrowed vision: Independence and egoism in The Fountainhead, in Mayhew, R. (ed.) *Essays on Ayn Rand's The Fountainhead*, pp. 285–304, Lanham, Boulder, New York, Toronto, and Plymouth: Lexington Books.

Smith, T. (2017) The free speech vernacular: Conceptual confusions in the way we speak about speech, *Texas Review of Law and Politics*, 22 (1), pp. 57–92, [Online], https://papers.ssrn.com/sol3/papers.cfm?abstract_id=3166234.

Smith, T. and Simpson, S. (2018) Common myths on free speech, *YouTube*, [Online], https://www.youtube.com/watch?v=zlkgVpj76Ms [7 Jul 2019].

Snow, D., Soule, S. and Kriesi, H. (2007) *The Blackwell Companion to Social Movements*, Malden, Oxford, and Victoria: Blackwell Publishing.

Soave, R. (2020) Yes, black NYU students demanded segregated housing. No, the university didn't agree to it, *Reason.com*, [Online], https://reason.com/2020/08/24/black-nyu-students-segregated-housing-race/ [26 Oct 2020].

Students for a Democratic Society (1964) The Port Huron statement, *The Progressive Fox*, [Online], http://www.progressivefox.com/misc_documents/PortHuronStatement.pdf [13 May 2019].

Soriano, D. (2019) White privilege lecture tells students white people 'dangerous' if they don't see race, *The College Fix*, [Online], https://www.thecollegefix.com/white-privilege-lecture-tells-students-white-people-dangerous-if-they-dont-see-race/ [26 Oct 2020].

Sotirakopoulos, N. (2016) *The Rise of Lifestyle Activism: From New Left to Occupy*, Basingstoke: Palgrave Macmillan, [Online], http://capitadiscovery.co.uk/yorksj/items/469630 [4 Apr 2019].

Sowell, T. (1984) *Civil Rights: Rhetoric or Reality?*, New York: Quill.

Sowell, T. (1994) *Race and Culture: A World View*, New York: Basic Books.

Sowell, T. (2013) *Intellectuals and Race*, New York: Basic Books.

Sparks, H. (2019) White people's diets are killing the environment: Study, *New York Post*, [Online], https://nypost.com/2019/03/28/white-peoples-diets-are-killing-the-environment-study/ [31 Jul 2019].

Spencer, R. (2015) Rachel Dolezal and the quest for identity, *Radix Journal*, [Online], https://radixjournal.com/2015/06/2015-6-18-rachel-dolezal-and-the-quest-for-identity/ [2 Aug 2019].

Spencer, R. (2017) What it means to be alt-right, *AltRight.com*, [Online], https://altright.com/2017/08/11/what-it-means-to-be-alt-right/ [3 Aug 2019].

Stanley, J. (2017) Civil rights movement is a reminder that free speech is there to protect the weak, *American Civil Liberties' Union*, [Online], https://www.aclu.org/blog/free-speech/civil-rights-movement-reminder-free-speech-there-protect-weak [17 Jun 2019].

Steigerwald, D. (1995) *The Sixties and the End of Modern America*, London and New York: Palgrave Macmillan.

Strauss, N. (nd) *The Game: Undercover in the Secret Society of Pickup Artists*, Edinburgh and London: Canongate.

Strings, S. and Bacon, L. (2020) The racist roots of fighting obesity, *Scientific American*, [Online], https://www.scientificamerican.com/article/the-racist-roots-of-fighting-obesity2/ [27 Oct 2020].

Tapper, J. (2018) Netflix boss apologises to staff after executive sacked over N-word, *The Guardian*, [Online], https://www.theguardian.com/media/2018/jun/22/netflix-chief-of-communications-leaving-after-reports-of-using-n-word [27 Jun 2019].

Taylor, J. (2018) Race realism and the alt right, in Johnson, G. (ed.) *The Alternative Right*, loc. 563–659, San Francisco, CA: Counter-Currents Publishing Ltd.

thecaller.gr (2019) Ντοκουμέντο: Το πρώτο διάγγελμα- παραλήρημα του δικτάτορα Παπαδόπουλου μετά το πραξικόπημα της 21ης Απριλίου [Document: The first speech/rant by dictator Papadopoulos after the 21st April coup], *thecaller.gr*, [Online], https://thecaller.gr/xronomixani/apriliou-diaggelma-paralirima-diktatoras-papadopoulos/ [25 Dec 2019].

Thucydides (1999) Pericles' Funeral Oration, *HistoryWiz*, [Online], https://www.historywiz.com/primarysources/funeraloration.htm [7 Jul 2019].

Tolhurst, A. (2017) 'GET A GRIP' Julia Hartley-Brewer posts pics of her knees and says they're 'still intact' after Michael Fallon touching, *The Sun*, [Online], https://www.thesun.co.uk/news/4807422/julia-hartley-brewer-jokes-her-knees-are-still-intact-after-michael-fallon-admits-touching-up-the-journalist/ [10 Aug 2019].

Tolle, E. (2001) *The Power of Now: A Guide to Spiritual Enlightenment*, London: Mobius.

Tomassi, R. (2013) *The Rational Male*, Reno, NV: Counterflow Media.

Tomassi, R. (2015) *The Rational Male: Preventive Medicine*, Reno, NV: Counterflow Media.

Tomassi, R. (2017) *The Rational Male: Positive Masculinity*, Reno, NV: Counterflow Media.

Travis, A. (2014) Julien Blanc barred from entering UK, *The Guardian*, [Online], https://www.theguardian.com/lifeandstyle/2014/nov/19/julien-blanc-barred-entering-uk-pick-up-artist [26 Dec 2019].

Trotsky, L. (1924) Literature and revolution, *Marxists.org*, [Online], https://www.marxists.org/archive/trotsky/1924/lit_revo/ [29 Apr 2019].

Trotsky, L. (1938) Their morals and ours, *Marxists.org*, [Online], https://www.marxists.org/archive/trotsky/1938/morals/morals.htm [29 Apr 2019].

Tsoref, H. (2018) Golda Meir's leadership in the Yom Kippur War, *Israel Studies*, 23 (1), pp. 50–72.

Tucker, J. (2017) *Right-Wing Collectivism: The Other Threat to Liberty*, Atlanta, GA: Foundation for Economic Education.

Tucker, J. (2020) Woodstock occurred in the middle of a pandemic, *American Institute for Economic Research*, [Online], https://www.aier. org/article/woodstock-occurred-in-the-middle-of-a-pandemic/ [12 Oct 2020].

Turner, R. (2011) *Neo-Liberal Ideology: History, Concepts and Policies*, Edinburgh: Edinburgh University Press.

UN Women (2020) Welcome to Equiterra, where gender equality is real, *UN Women*, [Online], https://www.unwomen.org/en/digital-library/multimedia/2020/2/illustration-equiterra-gender-equality-utopia [16 Oct 2020].

UTMSU (2016) Transphobic and racist lecture given by Professor Jordan Peterson, *University of Toronto Mississauga Students' Union*, [Online], https://utmsu.ca/wp-content/uploads/2016/10/ReTransphobicand RacistLectureGivenbyProfessorJordanPeterson.pdf [26 Jun 2019].

Vaneigem, R. (1983) *The Revolution of Everyday Life*, London: Rebel Press.

Varon, J. (2004) *Bringing the War Home: The Weather Underground, the Red Army Faction, and Revolutionary Violence in the Sixties and Seventies*, Berkeley and Los Angeles, CA: University of California Press.

Wall, D. (1999) *Earth First! and the Anti-Roads Movement: Radical Environ-mentalism and Comparative Social Movements*, London: Routledge.

Walters, J. and Durkin, E. (2018) 'I feel outraged, exhausted and betrayed': Kavanaugh nomination—the feminist response, *The Guardian*, [Online], https://www.theguardian.com/us-news/2018/oct/06/women-brett-kavanaugh-confirmation-feminist-response [14 Aug 2019].

Warren Davis, M. (2019) Taking off the 'What Would William F. Buckley Do?' wristband, *The American Conservative*, [Online], https://www.theamericanconservative.com/articles/taking-off-the-what-would-william-f-buckley-do-wristband/ [3 May 2019].

Watkins, D. and Brook, Y. (2016) *Equal is Unfair: America's Misguided Fight Against Income Inequality*, New York: St Martin's Press.

West, D. (2013) *Social Movements in Global Politics*, Cambridge and Malden: Polity.

Westerman, F. and Garrett, S. (2011) *Engineers of the Soul: In the Footsteps of Stalin's Writers*, London: Vintage.

Whitesides, J. (2017) From disputes to a breakup: wounds still raw after U.S. election, *Reuters*, [Online], https://www.reuters.com/article/us-usa-trump-relationships-insight-idUSKBN15M13L [3 Apr 2019].

Williams, J. (2017) *Women vs. Feminism: Why We All Need Liberating from the Gender Wars*, Bingley: Emerald, [Online], https://yorksj.idm.oclc.org/login?url=http://ebookcentral.proquest.com/lib/yorksj/detail.action?docID=4867400 [27 Mar 2019].

Willinger, M. (2013) *Generation Identity: a Declaration of War Against the '68ers*, London: Arktos.

Wise, T. (2011) *White Like Me: Reflections on Race from a Privileged Son*, Berkeley, CA: Soft Skull Press.

Wood, J. (2018) 'The wolf of racial bias': the admissions lawsuit rocking Harvard, *The Guardian*, [Online], https://www.theguardian.com/education/2018/oct/18/harvard-affirmative-action-trial-asian-american-students [31 Jul 2019].

Woods, T.E. (2009) *Meltdown: A Free-Market Look at Why the Stock Market Collapsed, the Economy Tanked, and Government Bailouts Will Make Things Worse*, Washington, DC: Regnery Publishing.

Wright, D. (2019a) The place of the non-initiation of force principle in Ayn Rand's philosophy, in Salmieri, G. and Mayhew, R. (eds.) *Foundations of a Free Society: Reflections on Ayn Rand's Political Philosophy*, pp. 15–44, Pittsburgh, PA: University of Pittsburgh Press.

Wright, D. (2019b) The scope and justification of Rand's non-initiation of force, in Salmieri, G. and Mayhew, R. (eds.) *Foundations of a Free Society: Reflections on Ayn Rand's Political Philosophy*, pp. 76–114, Pittsburgh, PA: University of Pittsburgh Press.

Xu, K. (2018) Asian-Americans' unrequited love of Harvard, *Quillette*, [Online], https://quillette.com/2018/10/13/asian-americans-unrequited-love-of-harvard/ [31 Jul 2019].

Young, C. (2015) The pecking disorder: Social justice warriors gone wild, *The Observer*, [Online], https://observer.com/2015/06/the-pecking-disorder-social-justice-warriors-gone-wild/ [23 Jun 2019].

Younge, G. (2017) Gary Younge interviews Richard Spencer: 'Africans have benefited from white supremacy', *The Guardian*, [Online], https://www.theguardian.com/world/video/2017/nov/06/gary-younge-interviews-richard-spencer-africans-have-benefited-from-white-supremacy [2 Aug 2019].

Zerofsky, E. (2019) Steve Bannon's roman holiday, *The New Yorker*, [Online], https://www.newyorker.com/news/dispatch/steve-bannons-roman-holiday [23 Dec 2019].

Zhang, E. (2020) California surfing has a serious diversity problem, *SF Weekly*, [Online], https://www.sfweekly.com/culture/california-surfing-has-a-serious-diversity-problem/ [27 Oct 2020].

Zimonjic, P. (2020) Stockwell Day exits CBC commentary role, corporate posts after comments about racism in Canada, *CBC Canada*, [Online], https://www.cbc.ca/news/politics/stockwell-day-systemic-racism-canada-1.5597550 [14 Oct 2020].

Zizek, S. (2008) *Violence*, London: Profile Books.

Zizek, S. (2009) *In Defense of Lost Causes*, London and New York: Verso.